Torah Li
Shemot: Defining a Nation

OHR TORAH STONE
תורה ותיקון עולם

מגיד

MAGGID

Shlomo Riskin

TORAH LIGHTS

SHEMOT: DEFINING A NATION

Maggid Books

Torah Lights
Shemot: Defining a Nation

Second Edition 2009

Maggid Books
An imprint of Koren Publishers Jerusalem Ltd.

POB 8531, New Milford, CT 06676-8531, USA
& POB 2455, London W1A 5WY, England
& POB 4044, Jerusalem 91040, Israel
www.korenpub.com

ISBN 978 159264 273 1, *hardcover*

A CIP catalogue record for this title is
available from the British Library

Typeset by KPS

Printed and bound in the United States

To our Beloved Children

Batya and Eddie
Yosef, Mevasseret, Naomi and Akiva

Elana and Menachem
Avishai, Amiel and Elai HaKohanim

Hillel and Limor
Eden Barkai and Yaal David HaKohanim

Yoni and Limor
Shalev Hod Harel and Maayan Ivri HaKohanim
Nehora Yafit and Shoham Ahava

In the hope that they receive from us
a fraction of what I received
from my parents and grandparents

In profound gratitude
to my beloved friend

BERNARD GOLDBERG

for having sponsored this edition
of Biblical Commentary
to honor his mother

ELSIE GOLDBERG

Who has graced the world
for well over a century of years

Contents

xi

Tribute

I want to thank my revered teachers, Rabbi Joseph B. Halevi Soloveitchik, ztz"l, Prof. Nehama Leibowitz, z"l and Rabbi Moshe Besdin, z"l, for their many insights into the words and commentaries of the Torah. Much of what is written here is based upon lectures and discussions I was privileged to have had with them – as well as with many great Torah scholars from whom I have learned throughout the years. Although I have attempted to give proper attribution so as to help bring redemption to the world, I am certain that there are insights I may have derived from others which I have come to think of as my own; suffice it to say that whatever may be worthy in this volume was derived from my teachers, but I assume complete responsibility for whatever may not be deemed worthy.

I am most appreciative to Sheldon Gewirtz, who originally urged me to begin writing a weekly commentary on the *parasha*, and to Jacob Lampert, who helped in the writing of the columns during the early years of this activity. The congregations I have been privileged to serve as rabbi and preacher, Lincoln Square Synagogue in Manhattan and the many synagogues of the City of Efrat, Israel, as well as my students at the Ohr Torah Stone Institutions served as the original sounding boards for these commentaries, which were then written and distributed in weekly columns for *The Jerusalem Post* and additionally in some thirty Anglo-Jewish newspapers worldwide. Hopefully each additional rendering helped improve my formulation and understanding.

My beloved family and extended family – and especially my cherished wife and life-partner, Vicky – have not only heard these ideas around the Shabbat table, but have also questioned them, argued with them and certainly refined them.

Most of all, I must give tribute to the Almighty, who has enabled me to labor in the vineyard of Torah during these last forty years as Rabbi and educator, a calling which has made the Five Books of Torah my constant guide and companion.

כִּי אִם בְּתוֹרַת ה׳ חֶפְצוֹ וּבְתוֹרָתוֹ יֶהְגֶּה יוֹמָם וָלָיְלָה

Introduction to Exodus

> *Were the Torah not my delight I would have*
> *perished in my affliction.*
>
> PSALMS 119:92

These immortal words of the Psalmist accompanied me to the nuptial canopy more than four decades ago, and remain the hallmark of my life. My profession required that the numerous study sessions I was called on to give each week – and especially each Sabbath – be linked to the biblical reading of that week. This demand increased dramatically when I began writing weekly columns on the biblical portions, syndicated in more than thirty newspapers throughout the world. Hence, the Bible has indeed been my steady companion – always within arm's reach and even at my bedside during the night.

I have constantly found that its eternal words provide crucial interpretation and direction both for events occurring in the world and for individual events – confrontations, decisions, successes and setbacks – in my own life. Ours is truly a timely and timeless Torah!

Conventional scholarly wisdom suggests that for the great

philosopher and legalist Maimonides, the most important biblical book was Genesis, with its universal and humanitarian message of the Lord as the creator of the universe and as having formed every human being in the divine image. In contrast, for Yehuda HaLevi, the passionate poet and lover of his people, the most important biblical book was Exodus, with its national story of the birth of Israel. What I hope you will find in the pages of this commentary is that the book of Exodus – with its ringing declaration of freedom and its insistence upon morality – is no less universal than the book of Genesis. More to the point, it extends the divine message of freedom and morality beyond the purview of a specific family – the family of Abraham – to address and encompass the entire family of nations!

On a more personal and historic note: For close to two thousand years of Jewish exile before the re-emergence of the State of Israel in 1948, traditional Jews attempted to live by the revelation of God the Creator of the Universe, *El Shaddai*. But it is only in our generation, after almost two millennia, that we are once again meeting *YHVH*, the historic God of redemption, the God of war and peace, of totalitarian and democratic regimes, of Israel the nation in a world of member nations having anatomies of leadership that succeed and anatomies of leadership that fail. In short, the book of Exodus speaks to us in a way in which it has not spoken for almost two thousand years. How vitally crucial it is for us to hear God's words and internalize the divine message.

Shemot

From Genesis to Exodus:
From Joseph the "Insider" to Moses the "Outsider"

> *Blessed art Thou, Lord our God, and God of our*
> *fathers, the God of Abraham, the God of Isaac,*
> *the God of Jacob…*
>
> THE OPENING BLESSING OF THE "AMIDA"

The opening of the Amida prayer stops with Jacob's name. But why should the patriarchal line be limited to three – why not four patriarchs: Abraham, Isaac, Jacob and Joseph? After all, Joseph's role in the Genesis narrative is unquestionably central to the entire book of Genesis. A case could be made for showing that he shares a similar fate to those of all three patriarchs. Like Abraham, he lives among idolaters and must maintain his faith and traditions within a hostile environment. Like Isaac, he suffers a personal *akedah*, about to be slain not by his father but by his brothers, saved not by a ram but by Midianite traders. And like

Jacob, who set the foundation for the twelve tribes of Israel, Joseph provided Jacob's descendants with life and sustenance as the Grand Vizier of Egypt. Moreover, in resisting the seductive perfumes of his master Potiphar's wife, Joseph merits the unique accolade *haTzadik* (literally, 'the righteous one') appended to his name. As a result, he has come to represent for all of his descendants the mastery of the spiritual over the physical. If indeed Joseph is known to us forever as Joseph the *Tzadik*, and being that he is the son of Jacob, why is he not considered the fourth patriarch? After all, there are four parallel matriarchs!

To understand why, we must compare and contrast him not with the patriarchs who precede him, but with the personality who, from the moment of his appearance in the book of Exodus, stands at center stage for the rest of the Torah and all of subsequent Jewish religious history: Moshe Rabbenu, Moses our Teacher.

The idea of linking Moses and Joseph comes from the Midrash. Moses, the giant liberator of Israel, never enters the Land of Israel himself, and is even buried on Mount Nevo at the outskirts of the Promised Land – exactly where, nobody knows. Joseph, on the other hand, is buried in the heartland of Samaria – Shechem – which lives as a national shrine to this very day. Why does Joseph merit such preferred treatment?

The midrashic explanation is based on two verses that highlight contrasting aspects of their respective biographies. When Joseph was imprisoned and he spoke to the wine steward for the sake of interpreting his dream, he asked to be remembered to Pharaoh: "For indeed I was stolen away from out of the land of the Hebrews" (Gen. 40:15). Joseph does not hesitate to reveal his Jewish background.

Moses, on the other hand, after having rescued the Midianite shepherdesses, hears the women reporting to their father how "…an Egyptian delivered us out of the hand of the shepherds, and drew water for us, and watered the flock" (Ex. 2:19). He does not correct them, saying "I am not an Egyptian but a Hebrew!" This silence, explains the Midrash, is why not even his bones may be brought back to the Land of Israel.*

In justifying the burial of Joseph's bones in Israel, testifying to

---

* See *Midrash Devarim Raba, 2:8.*

his unflinching recognition of his roots, the Midrash may be adding a notch of pride to Joseph's belt. But in truth, I believe that our sages are merely attempting to temper the indisputable fact that Moses is a far more "Jewish Jew" than Joseph in the most profound sense of the term.

In many ways, Joseph and Moses are contrasting personalities, mirror images of each other, with Moses rectifying the problematic steps taken by Joseph. Joseph was born in Israel, but became professionally successful in Egypt; Moses was born in Egypt, but established his place in history by taking the Jews on their way to Israel. Joseph was the insider who chose to move outside (he dreamt of Egyptian agriculture, as well as the cosmic universe). Moses was the outsider (Prince of Egypt), who insisted on coming inside (by slaying the Egyptian taskmaster). Joseph brought his family to Egypt, Moses took his people out of Egypt. Moses saw Egypt as a foreign country, and names his son Gershom "for he said I have been a stranger in a strange land" (Ex. 2:22). Joseph has at best ambiguous feelings about his early years in Canaan, naming his firstborn in Egypt Manasseh "since God has made me [allowed me to] forget completely my hardship and my parental home" (Gen. 41:51). Joseph, through his economic policies, enslaves the Egyptian farmers to Pharaoh; Moses frees the Jews from their enslavement to Pharaoh. And Joseph's dreams are realized, whereas Moses' dream – the vision of Israel's redemption in Israel – remained tragically unfulfilled at the end of his life.

The truth is that for the majority of Joseph's professional life he functions as an Egyptian, the Grand Vizier of Egypt. He may have grown up in the old home of the patriarch Jacob, heir to the traditions of Abraham and Isaac, but from the practical point of view, his time and energies are devoted to putting Exxon, Xerox and MGM on the map. Ultimately his professional activities enable him to preserve his people, the children of Israel; but day to day, hour to hour, he is involved in strengthening and aggrandizing Egypt.

A good case could easily be made in praise of Joseph. He never loses sight of God or morality, despite the blandishments of Egyptian society. And God would even testify that He had a special task for Joseph, personally chosen to save the descendants of Jacob and the world from a relentless famine. Nevertheless, he must pay a price for being Grand

Vizier of Egypt: The gold chain around his neck is Egyptian, his garments are Egyptian, his limousine is Egyptian, and even his language is Egyptian. Indeed, when his brothers come to ask for bread, an interpreter's presence is required for the interviews because his very language of discourse is Egyptian, with his countrymen totally unaware of his knowledge of Hebrew!

The difference between Moses and Joseph takes on its sharpest hue when seen against the shadow of Pharaoh. Joseph's life work consists of glorifying and exalting Pharaoh, in effect bestowing upon the Egyptian King-God the blessings of a prosperous and powerful kingdom, whose subjects are enslaved to him; Moses flees Pharaoh's court with a traitorous act against him, ultimately humiliating and degrading him by unleashing the ten plagues.

A shepherd and the son of shepherds, Joseph becomes the first Jewish prince in history, while Moses, a genuine prince of Egypt, begins his mature years as a shepherd on the run, risking his life for his commitment to free the Israelites. Jealousy and destiny force Joseph to live out his life away from his brothers, estranging himself from them. But Moses, despite his foreign, Egyptian background, nevertheless cares for his Hebrew brothers and identifies with them. As the Torah most poignantly records:

> And it happened in those days [after the baby Moses was taken to the home of Pharaoh's daughter] that Moses grew up and he went out to his brothers and he saw [attempting to alleviate] their sufferings.
>
> Exodus 2:11

Even though Joseph and Moses both change the world and preserve the Jewish people through the divine will that flows through them, their energies get channeled into different directions: Pharaoh and Egypt on the one hand, the Jewish people and Torah on the other.

This may be the significant factor in explaining why our sages stop short at calling Joseph a patriarch. He may be a *tzadik*, two of his sons may become the heads of tribes, and he may even deserve burial in Israel; but ultimately a hero who spends so much of his energies on behalf of Egypt cannot be called a patriarch of the Jewish nation.

It is recorded that the first chief rabbi of Israel, Rabbi Abraham Isaac Hakohen Kook, was tended to in his final years by an internationally known physician. His last words to the doctor were: "I yearn for the day when Jews who are great will also be great Jews." It was Moses who was undoubtedly the greatest Jew who ever lived.

Women and the Exodus

> *And these are the names of the children of Israel who came to Egypt with Jacob; each individual and his house came.*

EXODUS 1:1

The book of Exodus opens with a throwback to that which we already know from the last portions of the book of Genesis: the names of Jacob's children and the seventy Israelite souls – the Jewish households – who came to Egypt. Why the repetition? The great commentator Rashi attempts to explain that "even though Jacob's progeny were counted by name previously, the names are here repeated to show us how beloved they were..." (Rashi ad loc.). However, these first few verses of the book of Exodus are actually a prelude to the enslavement in Egypt, the tragedy of the first Jewish exile. I understand a loving recount when times are joyous but I find such mention superfluous when we are facing suffering and tragedy.

What is more, Pharaoh makes a striking distinction between males and females when he orders Jewish destruction:

> And Pharaoh commanded his entire nation saying, every male
> baby born must be thrown into the Nile and every female baby
> shall be allowed to live.
>
> Exodus 1:22

Pharaoh was apparently afraid to keep the Israelite men alive, lest they
wage a rebellion against him; he seems to be fairly certain that the women
will marry Egyptian men and assimilate into Egyptian society. However,
logic dictates a totally opposite plan. Fathers often love and leave without
having had any influence upon their progeny; indeed many individuals don't even know who their biological fathers are! Offspring are far
more deeply attached to the mother in whose womb they developed
and from whose milk they derive nourishment. Genocide might have
been much easier for Pharaoh had he killed off the women and allowed
the men to continue to live.

I would argue that although our Bible understands the critical
importance of women – we have already seen how Abraham is the first
Jew because he is the first individual who is introduced together with
his wife who has her own name and identity – Pharaoh is totally oblivious to the pivotal role women play in the development of a nation. The
Midrash on the first verse of Exodus – that we thought superfluous –
provides an original meaning to the words "individual and his house":

> When Israel descended to Egypt, Jacob stood up and said, "These
> Egyptians are steeped in debauchery." He rose up and immedi-
> ately married all of his sons to women.

The Midrash is intensifying an oft-quoted statement in the Talmud, "I
always call my wife 'my house'," since the real bulwark of the home is
the woman of the house. As the Jewish nation emerged from a family
and family units are the bedrock of every society, it is clearly the women
who are of extreme importance.

Pharaoh was blind to this. Apparently he had no tradition of
matriarchs like Sarah and Rebecca who directed the destiny of a national
mission. For him, women were the weaker sex who were there to be used
and taken advantage of. Hence Pharaoh attempts to utilize the Hebrew

midwives as his "kapos" to do his dirty work of actually murdering the male babies on the birthstools. To his surprise, the women rebelled: "And the midwives feared the Lord, so they did not do what the king of Egypt told them to do; they kept the male babies alive" (Ex. 1:17). It goes much further than that. The Midrash identifies the Hebrew midwives as Yocheved and Miriam, mother and sister of Moses and Aaron. The Midrash goes on to teach us that their husband and father Amram was the head of the Israelite court, and when he heard Pharaoh's decree to destroy all male babies, he ruled that Israelite couples refrain from bearing children. After all, why should men impregnate their wives only to have their baby sons killed!? Miriam chided her father:

> Pharaoh was better than you are, my father. He only made a decree against male babies and you are making a decree against female babies as well.

Amram was convinced by his daughters' words – and the result was the birth of Moses, savior of Israel from Egyptian bondage.

Perhaps the importance of women protectors of the household and guardians of the future of Israel is hinted at in the "anonymous" verse, "And a man from the house of Levi went and took a daughter of Levi" (Ex. 2:1). Why are the two individuals – Amram and Yocheved – not named? You will remember from the book of Genesis that it was Levi together with his brother Shimon who saved the honor of the family of Jacob by killing off the residents of Shechem, a gentile people who stood silently by while their leader raped and held captive Dina, daughter of Jacob. When Jacob criticizes them on tactical grounds, they reply, "Can we allow them to make a harlot of our sister?" With these words Chapter 34 of the book of Genesis ends; Levi and Shimon have the last word.

Moreover, we know from Jacob and his family that it is the wife who gave names to the children. Even more than Amram and Yocheved, true credit must go to the mother of Amram and the mother of Yocheved. Each of these women gave birth to children in the midst of black bleak days of Jewish oppression. Despite the slavery and carnage all around one mother gives her son the name Amram, which means "exalted nation"; the other mother gives her daughter the name Yocheved, which means "glory to God." These two women were seemingly oblivious to the low estate to which Judaism had fallen in Egypt; their sights were held high, upon the stars of the heavens which God promised Abraham would symbolize his progeny and the Covenant of the Pieces which guaranteed the Hebrews a glorious future in the Land of Israel. These two proud grandmothers from the tribe of Levi merited grandchildren like Moses, Aaron and Miriam.

Pharaoh begins to learn his lesson when Moses asks for a three-day journey in the desert; Pharaoh wants to know who will go. Moses insists:

> Our youth and our old people will go, our sons and our daughters will go – our entire households will go, our women as well as our men.
>
> Exodus 10:8

A wiser Pharaoh will only allow the men to leave; he now understands that he has most to fear from the women. And so Judaism establishes Passover, the festival of our freedom, as being celebrated by "a lamb for each house," with the women included in the paschal sacrificial meal by name no less than the men. And so the women celebrate together with the men – the four cups, the matza and the haggada – the Passover *seder* of freedom.

The Smiter and the Smitten

*And it came to pass... when Moses was grown up,
and he went out unto his brethren, and looked on
their burdens, and he saw an Egyptian man [ish]
smiting a Hebrew man [ish], one of his brethren.
And he looked this way and that way, and when
he saw there was no man [ish], he smote the
Egyptian, and hid him in the sand. And he went
out the second day, and behold – two Hebrews
were fighting. "Why are you beating your brother?"
he demanded of the one in the wrong. And he said,
"Who made you a ruler and judge over us? Do you
mean to kill us as you killed the Egyptian?"*

EXODUS 2:11–14

Moses, the redeemer of the Hebrews, enters the stage of
history like a man stumbling into a nightmare. The world, in contrast
to the delights inside the palace, is filled with violence and hatred; the
delicate prince is witness to the murder of a kinsman, a brother. He must

take some kind of action, but in which direction and for what price? And how does this incident foreshadow his life's destiny? Indeed, only if we understand what Moses did and why, will we understand why the Almighty chose him as the supreme leader of his people.

First of all, we see from the above citation that a prerequisite for becoming the great prophet of the Exodus is renunciation of injustice and the courage to remove its perpetrator, even if as a result the prince will become the outcast, and his life will be placed at risk.

In fact, the great biblical scholar-teacher Prof. Nechama Leibowitz points out that in his own apprenticeship towards achieving his divine vocation, Moses will face three variations on the theme of unjust action: Egyptian striking Hebrew, Hebrew striking Hebrew, and Midianites taking advantage of Midianite – the Midianite shepherds chasing the Midianite shepherdesses, Tziporah and her sisters. In each instance, Moses acts on behalf of the oppressed. This is apparently the primary qualification of a leader-redeemer of Israel.

But the above-quoted verses, especially the one dealing with the conflicts between Egyptian and Hebrew, raise several questions. First of all, upon examining the text we find that the Egyptian and the Hebrew are not simply identified by their nationality, but also by the extra Hebrew appellation "*ish*" (man):

> He [Moses] saw an Egyptian man [*ish mitzri*] smiting a Hebrew man [*ish ivri*].
>
> Exodus 2:11

After Moses turns "this way and that way," the text again uses the word "*ish*" in describing how he saw that there was no person around, no *ish*, presumably to view the incident and report Moses to the Egyptian authorities. However, having used "*ish*" three times in rapid succession, when the Torah comes to Moses' slaying of the oppressor, the text merely reads "he smote the Egyptian" without the additional *ish* – and the absence of that word "*ish*" requires our attention.

A second problem arises from an apparent discrepancy in Moses' two encounters. After morally castigating the two Hebrews, he finds himself being counter-attacked. And the line that puts dread into Moses' heart, forcing him to flee for his life, is: "Do you mean to kill us as you killed the Egyptian?" (Ex. 2:14). But haven't we just been told that Moses looked in all directions before going ahead and killing the Egyptian murderer? Obviously he had been on the lookout for witnesses. So how is it possible that the next day, what was presumably done in secret is known to all?

Rashi, apparently disturbed by this issue, comments (on Gen. 2:12) that when Moses, prior to killing the Egyptian, looked all around, he didn't merely cast his eyes to his immediate right and left; rather, he looked into the future, to make sure that he wasn't about to kill someone from whom a convert to monotheism would eventually emerge. Apparently, Moses was more concerned with this Egyptian's future progeny than with the actual proximity of potential prosecution witnesses.

An additional answer to our problem of Moses' faulty "look-out" may be derived from a mishna in Ethics of the Fathers:

> In a place where there are no men, strive to be a man...
> *Avot* 2:6

Moses witnesses a terrible event, the murder of a Hebrew, and he wants to make sure the Egyptian doesn't go unpunished. But Moses is a prince of Egypt. If he takes action and is found out, he will be placing in jeopardy his exalted status in Pharaoh's palace – and even possibly his very life. Certainly, he has much more to lose than any typical Hebrew slave. Therefore "he turns this way and that way" to see if there is anyone else who will come to the defense of the innocent Hebrew; someone else who will become the "man." But unfortunately, "there is no man" and so he himself must act and be that man. Thus, the next day when two Hebrews ask if he plans to kill them as he killed the Egyptian, he isn't surprised that he's been discovered; he was looking out for someone else with the fortitude to confront this moral challenge rather than for an eyewitness to his own slaying of the Egyptian.

But the first question still remains: Why the repetition of the word "*ish*" three times, and then the strange absence of the word at the end of the verse?

The Netziv explains that the Hebrew language possesses four

basic terms for the human being: *adam, gever, enosh, ish*. Each one is a grade in the scale of human potential, and the highest achievement is reserved for the term *"ish"*, the category of man who reflects most closely the image of God. In fact, our sages tell us that whenever there is an unidentified *ish* in the Torah, we should know it is speaking about an angel. (For example, when Joseph is sent by his father to locate his brothers, the text reads, "And a certain man [*ish*] found him" (Gen. 37:15), and Rashi points out that this *ish* is none other than the angel Gabriel.)

Keeping the Netziv's concept in mind, the text now takes on added resonance. In the first verse, Moses sees two men – a Hebrew and an Egyptian – locked in unequal and unfair combat. But they are not mere random representatives of their respective nations. They are both men, extraordinary, accomplished and respected individuals, personages, each one worthy of being called *ish*. But as a result of their shared fate, they each lose their special status. When Moses looks "this way and that way" at each of them, "he sees that they are no longer 'personages.'"(Ex. 2:2) This implies that both the Egyptian and the Hebrew have lost their *ishiyut*, their special quality, the one because he was doing the smiting and the other one because he was being smitten.

No one would argue that the Egyptian killer loses his *ish* quality, so that when Moses slays him he slays an Egyptian, not an Egyptian personage, *ish*. But even the Jewish victim's *ish* level is shattered. After all, the victim didn't fight back; he was devoid of the most minimal self-respect, which demands self-defense. When a person is beaten, contrary to popular notions, one's *ishiyut* is not increased, but diminished. The hard reality is that being beaten reduces a person to wounds and pain. And someone who is unable to protect his integrity as a person cannot live as an *ish*. James Baldwin once said that he can forgive the whites for persecuting the blacks, but he can never forgive the whites for making the blacks feel that they were worthy of persecution. Similarly, the real tragedy of abused wives and children is that they feel guilty and deserving of their pain.

Obviously, this use of the word *"ish"* also explains our second question, as to why in the subsequent verses we read that the men wanted to know if Moses planned to kill them too. Again, the Torah is telling us that once a person becomes either an oppressor or one of the oppressed, he ipso facto loses the unique human quality within him (although with no fault attached to the one oppressed).

During the Holocaust, many Jewish victims uprooted heaven and earth to retain their dignity, never to lose their *ishiyut*, their human quality, despite their oppression. And since 1948, the great moral challenge of the nation of Israel has been how to deal with acts of violence and terror perpetrated by the Arab population without losing our *ishiyut* in the process, how to vanquish our enemies and still retain our humanity.

The challenge in Israel today is to be strong enough never again to suffer as the smitten and sensitive enough never to abuse our strength. The challenge is to belong neither to the smiters nor to those who are smitten; the challenge is to insist upon our rights with strength and compassion, with courage and sensitivity.

God and the Thorn Bush

> *And the angel of the Lord appeared unto him*
> *(Moses) in a flame of fire out of the midst of a*
> *thorn bush; and he looked, and, behold, the bush*
> *burned with fire, and the bush was not consumed.*
>
> EXODUS 3:3

The revelation of God to Moses that "I will be what I will be" [*Ehyeh asher Ehyeh*] (Ex. 3:14) provides one of the most profound statements in the Torah concerning the nature of God. We must not forget that the manner in which this revelation takes place – the context of the burning bush that is not consumed – conveys an equally profound truth about the nature of God.

Turning to the *Midrash Raba*, we read how a gentile once approached R. Yehoshua ben Korha and asked why God chose to appear from the midst of a thorn bush. After all, is it not unseemly that the Almighty chose such an ugly, thorny, prickly, stunted form of vegetation in which to make His Presence manifest?

R. Yehoshua ben Korha's answer turns the question on its head:

since, as the holy *Zohar* teaches, "there is no place in the world empty of God," the best way to teach us this profound truth is through God's appearance in a thorn bush! In effect, the Almighty is teaching: Don't think that the awesome nature of God can be apprehended only in the majestic mountains of the Himalayas or in spectacular views of blue oceans, soft beaches and lofty palm trees. No, God is to be found even (and perhaps, especially) in the thorn bush, with the scorned and the rejected and the lowly. This idea continues to resonate in the words of the prophet Isaiah, who depicts Israel the nation as a suffering, wounded servant (Is. 53), in the talmudic picture of the Messiah standing together with all the wretched beggars (*Sanhedrin* 88), and in the midrashic comment on the divine name: "I will be what I will be, I shall always be with those who suffer" (Rashi ad loc.).

Many centuries later, the harsh theological wars between the Hassidim and the Mitnagdim often expressed themselves in the divergent understanding of this midrashic interpretation of the burning bush. The Hassidim – or, more specifically, Rabbi Shneur Zalman of Liadi – understood the Midrash literally, that the Divine Presence informs every object and even the meanest of objects, literally and in actuality. To the Gaon of Vilna, this Hassidic conception of God bordered on heresy, a form of pantheism in the guise of Judaism, with links to the worst aberrations in Jewish history from Spinoza to Shabbetai Tzvi. From his vantage point, all that the Midrash wishes to convey is that God's awareness and concern extend to every object, but not that an aspect of His very essence is to be found in every object. So adamant was the Gaon that he refused to meet with Rabbi Shneur Zalman himself, who only pleaded for an opportunity to explain the movement's theological basis. Although the tragedy of World War II dimmed the intensity of the battle, to this day remnants of that war still exist, and in certain parts of the community threaten to surface again.

I would like to suggest an interpretation of the Midrash which sidesteps the theological difference of opinion between these two intellectual giants of Jewish history. When we examine the biblical account, we dare not forget that fire is an intrinsic element of this revelation: the thorn bush is burning, but is not consumed by the flames.

On the one hand, fire is a universal symbol for the mystery of

God's presence. In the Covenant of the Pieces between God and Abraham we read the Torah's description of a flaming torch passing between the pieces of the sacrifice. As to the nature of this fire, Rashi writes:

> ... so here, too, the smoking furnace and the flaming torch which passed between the pieces (v. 17) were representative of the Divine Shechinah, which is fire.
>
> Rashi on Genesis 15:10

Fire is also how the prophets describe divine prophecy, "like a fire locked up in his bones," and in the book of Psalms we read:

> [God is] He who makes winds His messengers, flaming fire His servants.
>
> Psalms 104:4

For the purposes of our interpretation, the most revealing aspect of fire is that it was created *in potential*; it was not an initial creation like earth or water. Fire must be ignited; it must be sparked and extracted. Perhaps more than any other aspect of physical being, fire has no neutral quality. It can either bring warmth or devastation; it can temper ovens or forge weapons. Fire is the very essence of potential.

It seems to me that this is the main teaching of the midrash. We dare never despair of any situation, no matter how hopeless or hapless it may seem. The potential always exists that "from the bitter will emerge the sweet": from the depths of despair can emerge the design of the divine. Out of the ugly, incestuous relationship between Lot and his daughter – which brought forth a son Moab (literally, "born from father") – eventually emerged Ruth the Moabite, grandmother of David, progenitor and model for the Messiah. From the shameful Egyptian servitude emerged an Israelite nation sanctified at Sinai and committed to being sensitive to the slave and to loving the stranger. The unseemly and hated (Heb. *sanu*) *s'neh* (thorn bush) ultimately led to the sacred Sinai. Potential godliness is to be found in every place and event, no matter how submerged or wretched.

Often being forced to confront difficult and even tragic situations enables individuals to realize potential powers and strengths they never knew existed within themselves, the Godly gifts rooted in the divine spark which informs each of us. It was that divine spark which cried out to Moses at the burning bush, and which gave him the courage to reject Egyptian palatial grandeur and risk his life to save his Hebrew brother.

The burning thorn bush is the paradigm for Natan Sharansky, who created his own idealistic and ideal world of heroism for the sake of freedom from within the filthy and cruel confinement of the Communist Gulag. In Efrat, Dassy Rabinowitz z"l sanctified God's name when, from the depths of her own debilitating disease of cancer of the lymph nodes, which had turned her body into a private torture chamber, she became consumed with the mission to bring warmth and love to others who were suffering in the ward where she herself was confined. Few places in the world are as emotionally crippling as a children's cancer ward. But Dassy turned recesses of living hell into a haven of hope, faith and joy because she was able to bring God even into that harrowing place.

God says, "I will be what I will be." Every situation can produce God, every human being can represent God. There is no prickly thorn bush. There is only the fire of divine potential, which can never be consumed and which will ultimately redeem us and the world, no matter how difficult our straits may appear to be.

The Reluctant Leader

> *And Moses said to God, "Who am I, that I should go unto Pharaoh, that I should bring forth the children of Israel out of Egypt?"*
>
> EXODUS 3:11

There is a striking dialogue between God and Moses in which the Almighty tries to convince the shepherd to assume leadership of the Israelites. Moses is clearly the best choice, from the divine perspective. Did he not sacrifice a life as prince of Egypt in order to avenge the life of a Hebrew slave? Moses himself extracted the very opposite message from that same incident. When, shortly afterwards, he tries to stop two Hebrews from fighting, his previous involvement is scorned by the Hebrews themselves:

> Who made you a ruler and judge over us? Will you kill me as you killed the Egyptian?
>
> Exodus 2:14

Moses has understandably concluded that being the leader of the Jewish people will bring only criticism and heartache, and so he lets God know that he is not in the market – not even for a draft. If nominated, he will not run; if elected, he will not serve.

The entire dialogue covering Chapters 3 and 4 is a textbook case of finding more and more ways of saying "no" to God, concluding in the very extreme divine reaction: "…the anger of God was kindled against Moses…" (Ex. 4:14). The Midrash even deduces that the Almighty punishes Moses for his reluctance by removing the priesthood from his shoulders and transferring it to Aaron.

> Was it not Aaron your brother the Levite whom I chose to be your spokesman?
>
> Exodus 4:14

Aaron was initially slated to be the Levite and you, Moses, the *kohen*, but I God shall now switch the honors. I shall elevate Aaron to priest and demote Moses to Levite (Rashi ibid.). What gets the Almighty so angry? Cannot the hesitations of Moses be seen as an expression of humility?

We discern four distinct stages in God's attempt to get Moses to accept leadership. Moses initially declines by claiming that he is not the right person for the job.

> Who am I, that I should go unto Pharaoh, that I should bring forth the children of Israel…
>
> Exodus 3:11

Such initial reluctance can be understood; Moses needs reassurance. One burning bush does not a leader make.

God explains that it is not a problem: "I will be with you…" (Ex. 3:12). Presumably this tells us that true self-identity is linked with thinking of ourselves in terms of our relationship to God. As long as He is with us, then we need never say, "Who am I…?" To be alone with God is always to be with a majority of One.

Moses remains unconvinced. After all, he, Moses, has come to know God at least partially and is therefore impressed that God will be with him, but the Israelites don't really know this God. And a leader must be accepted first and foremost by his people. Hence, Moses asks that when the Israelites will ask for God's name (or definition), what may he tell them? (Ex. 3:13).

God informs Moses that there are two aspects to His name. First, "I will be what I will be" (Ex. 3:14), which fundamentally teaches that the divine is the God of future first and foremost, the God of becoming and not just of being, the God who must continually be sought in history rather than merely the God of a set catechism of definitions. The Almighty continues, "I am the God of your fathers, of Abraham, Isaac and Jacob" (3:15). This God has already introduced Himself to Abraham, Isaac and Jacob, has given them laws and commandments, and has revealed to them His ultimate plan to redeem the Hebrew slaves from Egypt in the Covenant of the Pieces. God is gently reminding Moses that the God of Israel was already apprehended in the book of Genesis.

At this point Moses should have raised the white flag of surrender, accepting the wisdom of God's choice. But no, Moses continues, there is the simple fact of credibility. The Israelites might well accept God, but they will not necessarily accept Moses as God's messenger (4:1).

The Almighty still does not lose patience. He gives Moses two signs or symbols. "What is that in your hand?" he asks, and Moses answers, "A staff." God then instructs Moses to throw the staff on the ground, and it miraculously turns into a snake. "Grasp onto it," orders God, and it miraculously becomes a staff again. The second sign or symbol: "Put your hand into your bosom…and when he [Moses] took it out, behold his hand was leprous, as white as snow." But when Moses again removes his hand from his bosom, the leprosy is gone, and the hand is healthy flesh once again. (4:6–7).

Let us look more closely at the nature of the two signs or symbols God demonstrates to Moses. I would like to suggest that in addition to their dramatic presence, they actually reflect what's at the heart of leadership. God is telling Moses: If you want the people to believe in you, the first criterion is that you must believe in yourself. Know that in your hand, Moses, is the staff of leadership, a mastery you earned when you smote the Egyptian taskmaster. Remove the staff of leadership from yourself and it will turn into the serpent, symbol of Egypt as well as of

Egyptian tyranny and hedonism. In this world you either lead or you will be led, you either administrate or you will be administrated. Now, grasp on to the tail of the serpent, and you will once again be grasping the staff of leadership. It depends on you!

The second sign is a continuation of the first. Placing one's hands in one's bosom is a symbol of inaction, of paralysis. When this is what you do, or more correctly do not do, and there are sins of omission as heinous as those sins of commission, your hand will become leprous.

Leprosy for the biblical mind is not merely an illness; it is a divine punishment for slander, as the Torah teaches regarding Moses' sister Miriam (Num. 12:10). What is the sin of Moses in this context? Allow me to recall a story about Rabbi Yisrael Meir Kagan, known as the Hafetz Haim. Although he was famous as a great halakhic scholar and pietist, at the turn of the century when photos of the famous were hardly as widespread as today, it was possible for a Jewish hero not to be recognized, even by his seatmate on a train.

This is how it happened that the great sage found himself on a train, not recognized by his seatmate, a simple Jew, who was dressed not that differently from the Hafetz Haim himself, who shunned rabbinic garb. As such things happen, conversation turned to the great holy Jews of the era, and the person began to praise the Hafetz Haim. In harmony with his humble nature, the sage would meet each adulation on the part of his seatmate with a simple line of denial. "The Hafetz Haim is not at all great," he would demur. At length the pious Jew became so fed up with the insolence of his neighbor that he boxed his face, and told him he did not want to hear another word from him.

When the train arrived in Radin, word had spread that the Hafetz Haim was arriving, and a crowd gathered to meet the sage. When the man on the train realized the identity of the person he had struck, he began to tremble. What had he done! He begged the great rabbi for forgiveness. "No, you must forgive me," remonstrated the sage. "You taught me a most valuable lesson. I always believed that it was merely forbidden for an individual to speak slander against others. You taught me that it is equally forbidden to speak slander against oneself."

God is telling Moses that he must accept the mantle of leadership.

He must be forceful and proactive, and he must believe in himself; then, as long as God remains with him, the people will believe in him as well.

Moses still is not convinced, and must suffer God's anger and punishment by forfeiting the priesthood. Perhaps one of the tragedies of this greatest of prophets was that his humility never permitted him to be the dominant leader of the nation that his times so desperately required.

Moses, the Prophet of Heavy Speech

> *I am not a man of words, not yesterday and not*
> *the day before, for I am heavy of mouth and*
> *heavy of tongue.*
>
> EXODUS 4:10

The first two portions of the book of Exodus contain at least three lengthy conversations between the Almighty and Moses. But what is especially strange is the kind of repetitious and even zig-zag nature of the dialogue. Three times Moses explains his reluctance on the basis of his "heaviness of speech." The first time: "I am not a man of words, not yesterday and not the day before, for I am heavy of mouth and heavy of tongue"" (Ex. 4:10); the second time, fully two chapters later: "And I have uncircumcised lips" (Ex. 6:12); and the third time, eighteen verses later: "Behold, I have uncircumcised lips, so how can Pharaoh listen to me" (Ex. 6:30).

But stranger still are the two divine responses of repair, the first of which seems to be inexplicably rejected out of hand by Moses, while the second seems to be alternatively offered, taken back and then offered again by God. When Moses initially explains that he is "heavy of tongue" and therefore limited in his powers of persuasion, the Almighty – logically – promises a cure for the speech impediment:

> And the Lord said to him, "Who places a mouth in a human body? Who makes a person mute or deaf or seeing or sightless? Is it not I, the Lord? And now go [assume the leadership role], and I shall be with your mouth."
>
> Exodus 4:11

What better guarantee could Moses have received? Nevertheless, Moses rejects God's guarantee, requesting that He find another agent for His mission (Ex. 4:13).

The Almighty understandably becomes angry with Moses, but offers an alternate possibility:

> Don't I know that Aaron your brother the Levite is a gifted speaker? … He will speak for you to the people and he will be for you as a mouthpiece; you will be for him as a judge.*
>
> Exodus 4:14, 16

Moses appears to be satisfied with this compromise. And indeed it is Aaron (and not Moses) who speaks to the elders and presents special signs to the people, which instills faith and confidence in the hearts of the nation and inspires them to bow down and prostrate themselves (Ex. 4:29).

However, this more public role of Aaron seems to be short-lived. The very next verse, which begins a new chapter, opens with Moses preceding Aaron:

> And afterwards Moses and Aaron came and spoke to Pharaoh.
>
> Exodus 5:1

The conversation initiated by Moses and Aaron with Pharaoh fails. Not

---

* Lit. *Elohim*, which may be referring to the symbol of the divine morality.

only are the Hebrews not allowed to spend three days in the desert, but their workload is increased.

The Almighty still guarantees the eventual exodus of the Israelites from Egypt cataloguing the four expressions of redemption, and Moses (this time only Moses) conveys this message to the Hebrews, who do not listen to him "because of impatience and hard service" (Ex. 6:9). It is at this juncture that Moses again complains about his inability to stand and speak at the forefront because of his "uncircumcised lips" (Ex. 6:12), to which God responds by "speaking to both Moses and Aaron" to command "the Children of Israel and Pharaoh to take the Children of Israel out of the land of Egypt" (Ex. 6:13). The genealogy of both is then presented: "they are Moses and Aaron" (Ex. 6:28), with Moses before Aaron. Moses, for the third time, complains to God about his uncircumcised lips which prevent Pharaoh from listening to him (6:30), and God then repeats His past offer which had obviously been taken back, because it was never put into effect that Moses would be as god (symbol of the divine ethic and morality) to Pharaoh, but Aaron would be the spokesman. How can we possibly understand this repetitive plaint of Moses, as well as the reluctance of the Divine to allow Aaron to truly be the public spokesman?

I believe the answer lies in our proper understanding of Moses' heaviness of speech and the implications this has for a definition of successful leadership. The Ralbag (Gersonides) suggests that in the verse "And the Israelites did not listen to Moses because of impatience and hard service" (Ex. 6:9), the Torah is referring not to the impatience and hard service of the Israelites, but rather to the impatience and hard service of Moses. Moses was on such an exalted and lofty spiritual level in terms of his close relationship with the divine – after all, only he spoke to God "mouth to mouth," *peh el peh* (Num. 12:8) – that he had no patience to deal with the complaining, cantankerous and often small-minded Jews; he was so immersed in and exhausted by his difficult divine service that he lacked the emotional energy to deal with the mundane dissatisfactions of the people.

I would suggest that one who regularly speaks to God is naturally heavy or serious of speech; he has no time for small talk, no patience for picayune perturbations. He who speaks to God *peh el peh* will of necessity be "heavy of speech" in his social dealings; he can't be expected to be an omnipotent pastor, a public relations expert, a super salesman, or a successful fundraiser. Moses' initial refusal, therefore, had nothing to do with false modesty; he was the "husband of God" (Deut. 33:1), and to a great extent that canceled out the possibility of his functioning as a populist leader. He was ready to convey to the people what they needed to know from God, but not necessarily what they wanted to hear. He was an uncompromising man of truth, who believed that

> the divine law must pierce the mountain, allowing the chips to fall where they may.
>
> *Sanhedrin* 6b

Not even for the sake of peace, not even in the interests of educational development, would he be constitutionally able to sell his product in a more palatable form or in stages.

Aaron was the man of peace, the beloved and popular "people person."* He was much "lighter of tongue," adept at the act of compromise. Moses (who certainly understood himself if he could so well understand the divine secrets of the Torah) is ready to accept the position of prophet of the divine if Aaron will serve as the public spokesman.

But the Almighty knows that this arrangement will never succeed. God knows it, tries to prevent it, endeavors to strengthen Moses to develop the necessary "lightness of speech", and encourages Moses to speak to Pharaoh and the Israelites even after He offers Aaron as a possibility, but God ultimately goes along with Moses' condition. God, after all, always leads us along the path we wish to follow.*

Despite all of the inherent difficulty, the prophet of God must still be the priest of the people. The person who speaks to God must find the way to convey the divine ideals to people, even if it has to be in measured doses over a long period of time. People need to eat, dance, laugh and cry together with their supreme teacher-prophet; no partner-substitute can effectuate the change needed for redemption. Reliance

---

*   *Sanhedrin* 6b.

on Aaron will lead not to a dance of Simhat Torah, but rather the dance of the golden calf.

And, tragically, Moses eventually dies with neither he nor his generation realizing their ideal and entering the Promised Land. That must wait for the next leader – Joshua, a man who Moses understands must be appointed by "the Lord God of the spirits of all flesh as a man of the congregation, who will go out before them and come in before them, who will take them out and who will bring them in, so that the congregation of the Lord will not be as sheep without a shepherd" (Num. 27:16, 17).

Va'era

What's in a Name? – God's Name

> *And God spoke to Moses and said unto him, I*
> *am the Lord, and I appeared unto Abraham,*
> *unto Isaac, and unto Jacob, as Almighty God* [El
> Shaddai], *but My name YHVH* [Four-letter
> Name of God] *I have not made known to them.*
>
> EXODUS 6:2–3

What is the secret of Jewish eternity? If medical opinion is beginning to maintain that one of the most important variables in achieving longevity is an optimistic outlook on life, one of the most unique and important messages that Judaism gave to the world is the optimistic notion of world redemption. Our Western culture is formed by the Greco-Roman civilization and by what is generally known as the "Judeo-Christian" tradition. The Greeks saw the world and life in a cyclical pattern of endless repetition without purpose or end-game: the myth of Sisyphus who is doomed to take the boulder up and down the mountain endlessly; the tragedy of Oedipus who suffers the sins of his parents and whose children are doomed to repeat the very crimes committed by their forbears; Shakespeare's "tomorrow and tomorrow and tomorrow beats on this petty pace to the last syllable of recorded time" and "life is a tale told by an idiot, full of sound and fury, signifying nothing." Judaism, on the other hand, teaches that world and history are linear rather than cyclical, progressing towards repair and redemption, the prophetic notion of eventual human perfection at a time when "nation will not lift up sword against nation and humanity will not learn war any more" (Is. 2:4). I would maintain that what has kept us going despite exile, persecution and pogrom is this fundamental belief that what we do counts and that eventually we will succeed in perfecting the world in the Kingship of God.

This revolutionary optimistic concept is built around the name of God revealed at the beginning of this Torah portion: "And God spoke to Moses, and said to him I am the Lord [*YHVH*]" (Ex. 6:2). The Bible goes on to say that our patriarchs only knew of the name "Almighty God" (*El Shaddai*), but this generation of Moses will be privileged to know the new name of God, the Lord (*YHVH*). And it is specifically within the context of this new revelation of the name that God confirms the establishment of the covenant, the entry of Israel the people into Israel the land, and the exodus from slavery and oppression to freedom and redemption.

What does this new revealed name have to do with redemption? In the previous Torah portion we read of the dialogue between God and Moses that is the beginning of the explanation. The Almighty reveals Himself to Moses in a burning bush, and bestows upon him the mission of taking the Jews out of Egypt (Ex. 3:10). Moses asks for God's name, which is another way of asking for a working definition of God which he could communicate to the Israelites. God said to Moses, "*Ehyeh asher ehyeh*" (Ex. 3:14), which is best translated, "I will be what I will be." What kind of name is this? It seems to be vague, not at all defined, and very much open-ended. Moreover, the verb form around which this phrase is built is identical to the verb form of the newly revealed name of God, both of them coming from the verb to be (*HYH*).

In order to complete the elements of our puzzle, we must invoke the very first commandment which God will give the newly formed Jewish people:

> This renewal of the moon shall be for you the beginning of the
> months...
>
> Exodus 12:1

The Israelites are commanded to search the darkened sky for the new
moon, the light which emerges each month from the blackened heavens
devoid of light. The *Zohar*, in explaining the importance of the moon
and our celebration of its renewal each month with Psalms of praise
(*Hallel*), explains:

> The Jewish nation is compared to the moon. Just as the moon
> wanes and seems to have completely disappeared into darkness
> only to be renewed and reborn, so will the Jewish people often
> appear to have been overwhelmed by the forces of darkness
> and evil only to reemerge as a nation reborn in a march towards
> redemption.

Thus did the Babylonian Talmud emerge from the destruction of the
Second Temple and the reborn State of Israel emerge from the tragedy
of the Holocaust. From this perspective, the message of the moon is a
message of ultimate optimism. The Almighty God Himself guarantees
not only survival but also salvation. The paradigm for the optimistic and
life-affirming pattern of exile and redemption is our experience of slavery
in and exodus out of Egypt – and the fundamental change in Egyptian
society and world mentality wrought by that exodus.

And let us pay special attention to the words of this first commandment: "This renewal of the moon shall be for you the beginning
of the months..." The Hebrew phrase "for you" seems superfluous. Its
meaning, however, as explained by the sages of the Talmud, makes it
central and pivotal to the world as the Bible sees it. Our God is not only
the God of creation, *El Shaddai*, the God who set limits on each element
as He set boundaries on the heavens and the earth, the sands and the
seas, mineral, vegetable, animal and human life and activity; He is also
the God of history, "who will be what He will be," and who has a built-
in plan for the world which includes its ultimate betterment and even
perfection. And if creation was an act of One, events in history are the

result of partnership between the divine and human beings, God, Israel and world. Hence in the marking of the renewal of the month, which is really the marking of historical time, the Lord clearly tells His people that time is in their hands to do with what they will. If indeed how many months we may have depends on many factors aside from ourselves, what we do with the time at our disposal depends mostly on us.

Hence, when God asks Moses to be His agent, the first divine name He reveals to him is "I will be what I will be"; since I am the God of history, and I am asking you to be My partner in history, My ultimate design for the world will depend not only on Me but also on you. Yes, it will be within the context of the promises of redemption made to the patriarchs (Ex. 3:15). But when that will happen depends on you as well as on Me. No wonder this name of God is indecisive.

And this is the meaning of the newly revealed name which God gives to the generation of the Exodus: *YHVH*, literally, "He will bring about." This name reflects optimism because the redemption is after all guaranteed by God. The light will definitely someday emerge from the darkness, but exactly when cannot be revealed. That depends upon us. And although the uncertainty contains an element of frustration and even despair, as evidenced in the question that we Jews so often ask each other, "So what will be?", it also contains the seed of our salvation. After all, if God didn't think that we were capable, He would never have made us His partner in the first place!

*   *   *

A Story Postscript

It was a few summers before my *aliya*, when my family and I were spending time at Kibbutz Ein Tzurim. The father of one of the kibbutzniks had died and his funeral was to take place in Kfar Hassidim near Haifa. A group from the kibbutz made the trip there and a large congregation assembled in front of the large yeshiva of Kfar Hassidim, from where the funeral was to begin.

In actuality, two distinct communities had formed, the men from the kibbutz in shorts and sandals, and the men from the yeshiva in white shirts and long black pants, shoes and socks. Then, the *rosh yeshiva* appeared, Reb Elya, a tall, bearded patriarchal figure in black hat and long black gabardine *capote*. He seemed to tower over the assemblage, and suddenly rested his eyes on Yehudah Neumann, my close friend from Kibbutz Ein Tzurim. "Yudke, Yudke, *ilui* [talmudic prodigy], can that be you?" he cried out in Yiddish. "Yes, that was the name by which I was called at the yeshiva, Reb Elya," responded my friend, turning red as a beet.

Apparently my friend and Reb Elya had studied together many decades before at the yeshiva in Petah Tikvah, which had then been under the tutelage of Rav Shach, who later went on to head the Ponovez Yeshiva in Bnei Brak. "But you left the yeshiva, Yudke," cried out Reb Elya, "and it must have been against the wishes of Rav Shach," he continued in Yiddish. "Yes, I have many of Rav Shach's letters urging me to stay," responded my friend in Hebrew. "And these letters will comprise a wall of prosecution against you when you stand before God's heavenly throne after one hundred and twenty years," thundered Reb Elya in Yiddish. Everyone was silent; all eyes were on my embarrassed and humble friend, who surprisingly cried out in Hebrew, "And the wars which I fought and the kibbutz which I helped build for the State of Israel will act as my defense attorney, and I will win my case!" The kibbutzniks all smiled, and even the yeshiva students seemed impressed with my friend's ardent comeback.

Reb Elya relaxed, and smiled. "You remained the same Yudke prodigy," he said. "*Kol hakavod* [all honor to you]." "No, Reb Elya, I didn't remain the same. I looked around at the changes in the world with the Holocaust and the emerging State of Israel, and attempted to respond to these changes. It is you who remained the same…"

The dialogue concluded, and the funeral began…

Passover: The Festival of Everyone's Right to be Free

> Therefore say to the children of Israel, "I am
> the Lord. I shall **take you out** from under the
> sufferings of Egypt, I shall **save you** from their
> toil, I shall **redeem you** with an outstretched arm,
> I shall **take you** to Me for a nation, and I shall
> bring you to the land..."
>
> EXODUS 6:4

With these "four expressions of redemption" (in bold above),
the book of Exodus emerges as the biblical book of redemption; indeed,
the very Hebrew meaning of the name Moshe (Moses) literally means
the one who draws forth, the one who takes out, the one who frees from
slavery within the context of Egyptian enslavement of the Hebrews. And
so when the Mishna begins to describe the order of the yearly Passover
seder, we find the imperative, "And no one may drink less than the prescribed four cups of wine, even if they must take from the community

charity kitchen," with Rashi explaining the source: "Corresponding to the four languages of redemption regarding the exile of Egypt...in the portion of *Va'era*" (*Pesahim*, Mishna 10, 1, 99b, Rashi ad loc.).

The famed halakhic authority and arbiter of the last century, Rabbi Moshe Feinstein, of blessed memory, even initially requires four cups of wine rather than grape juice. This is because wine actually makes the individual feel "free" physiologically – and the four cups of wine at the *seder* are not only for the sake of sanctity, memory and joy (as is the case with ordinary Kiddush on the Sabbath and usual festivals) but are also for the sake of freedom!

But what is the precise nature of the freedom that we are celebrating on Passover in general and at the *seder* in particular? Conventional traditional wisdom would maintain that it is the freedom of the Hebrews, the special relationship between God and Israel which caused the Almighty to step into history, as it were, and free the children of Israel from their servitude under Pharaoh. And it is from this perspective that the great universalist philosopher Maimonides is generally associated with the biblical book of Genesis – the book he most usually cites as his proof-texts for the views he offers in his *Guide for the Perplexed* – whereas the more nationalist philosopher Yehudah HaLevi is more closely identified with the biblical book of Exodus – the book most widely drawn upon in HaLevi's *Kuzari*.

However, I would insist that such a distinction does not do proper justice to the biblical message. Moses' mission, and God's miraculous freeing of the Hebrew slaves, was never meant for Israel alone. Indeed, if the Almighty had merely desired to redeem Israel because of His special relationship with them, He could have simply airlifted the Israelites from Egypt without having to upset all of nature with the ten cataclysmic and fantastic plagues, and then with the sensational splitting of the Reed Sea.* The Almighty was rather attempting to teach a crucial lesson to Pharaoh, and to all subsequent despotic and totalitarian rulers in world history: slavery is a rank evil. No human being has the power to lord it over another human being. Every human being is created in

---

* The Hebrew term *Yam Suf* literally translates as 'Reed' – not Red – Sea.

the divine image, and therefore every human being has the inalienable right to be free!

It is largely from this perspective that the book of Exodus emerges from, and is based upon, the book of Genesis. You will remember that the Sabbath day, the seventh day wherein all manner of physical work is forbidden and in which the human being has the ability to exercise his existential freedom under God, has two distinct but intertwined biblical significances: first, the Lord Creator because "in six days the Lord made the heavens and the earth, the seas and everything which is in them, and rested on the Sabbath day. Therefore, the Lord blessed the seventh day and sanctified it" (Ex. 20:11); and second, the Lord Redeemer: "You shall remember that you were slaves in the land of Egypt, and the Lord your God took you out from there with a strong hand and an outstretched arm; therefore did the Lord your God command you to make the Sabbath day," (Deut. 5:16). Clearly, the second reason emanates from the first: the God who created every individual in His own divine image decries and abhors the enslavement of one human image of the divine over another human image of the divine. Every human being has the right to be free. Hence the second Decalogue includes the additional message of the Sabbath: "In order that your [gentile] manservant and your [gentile] maidservant may rest like you" (Deut. 5:14).

A fascinating support to this universal message of the Exodus may be found in the Jerusalem Talmud (*Pesaḥim* 10, 1), where the source for the four cups of freedom wine is not traced to the four expressions of redemption in the Torah portion of *Va'era*, but rather to the four instances of the word "goblet" in the dream of the butler that was interpreted by Joseph:

> In my dream, behold a vine was before me…and the goblet of Pharaoh was in my hand, and I took the grapes, and I squeezed them into the goblet of Pharaoh, and I gave the goblet into the hand of Pharaoh…And Joseph said, "In three days Pharaoh will lift up your head and restore you to your office; and you shall place the goblet of Pharaoh into his hand as you did before when you were his butler…"
>
> Genesis 40:9, 11, 13

Now the butler is an Egyptian, who was arbitrarily and unfairly imprisoned by Pharaoh; his dream portends his freedom from enslavement by an unjust despot. I believe that the Jerusalem Talmud – in making this passage from the end of the book of Genesis the source for the four cups of freedom wine at the Passover Seder rather than the passage from *Va'era* – is emphasizing the universal message of freedom for all of humanity rather than merely parochial freedom for Israel. In the interdependent global village in which we now live, when the ideal of freedom and world peace is so cardinal, when life-preserving democracy is locked in battle against suicide-bombing fundamentalist terrorists for world hegemony, this interpretation of the Exodus has never been so vital!

What Is a Fitting Legacy for
My Children and Grandchildren?

> *And I will bring you unto the land concerning*
> *which I raised My hand to give it to Abraham, to*
> *Isaac, and to Jacob; and I will give it to you for a*
> *heritage (morasha): I am God.*
>
> EXODUS 6:8

Every parent would like to leave an inheritance to their children and grandchildren; some even work their entire lives, denying themselves vacations and little luxuries, in order to amass some sort of nest-egg as an inheritance. And others live in disappointed frustration because they fear they will not have the wherewithal to leave behind a sizeable "will and testament." What does our Torah have to say about a proper bequest for future generations?

The Bible has two cognate words which relate to bequest: *morasha* and *yerusha*. *Morasha* – which appears for the first time in the Torah in the portion of *Va'era* with regard to the Land of Israel and only once again, with regard to Torah itself, "Moses prescribed the Torah to us, an eternal heritage (*morasha*) for the congregation of Jacob" (Deut. 33:4) – is generally translated as "heritage"; *yerusha* is translated as "inheritance" and is the frequently found form for everything except Torah and Israel. It is interesting to note that in Webster's Dictionary, the words "heritage" and "inheritance" are virtually synonymous. The lead definition for heritage is "property that is or can be inherited." The Hebrew of the Bible, however, is precise and exact. The use of different words clearly suggests a difference in meaning. The different contexts in which the two words "*morasha*" and "*yerusha*" appear can be very revealing about different kinds of bequests – and even different kinds of relationships between parents and children, different priorities handed down from generation to generation, which these bequests engender. Let us explore four different possible distinctions in meaning between *yerusha* and *morasha*, inheritance and heritage, which should provide important instruction to parents in determining their bequests to their children.

First, the Jerusalem Talmud speaks of *yerusha* as something that comes easily. A person dies, leaving an inheritance, and the heir is not required to do anything except receive the gift. But just being there is not enough when it comes to *morasha* . The added *mem* in this term, suggests the Jerusalem Talmud, is a grammatical sign of intensity, the *pi'el* form in Hebrew grammar. In order for an individual to come into possession of a *morasha* they have to work for it. An inheritance is what you get from the previous generation, without your particular input; a heritage requires your active involvement and participation. A *yerusha* is a check your father left you; a *morasha* is a business which your parents may have started, but into which you must put much sweat, blood and tears.

This will certainly explain why *morasha* is used only with regard to Torah and the Land of Israel. The sages remark that there are three gifts which God gave the Jewish people that can only be acquired through commitment and suffering: "Torah, the Land of Israel and the World to Come."* We understand that neither Torah nor the Land of Israel is acquired easily, passively. The Babylonian Talmud, confirming our earlier citation from the Jerusalem Talmud, specifically teaches that "Torah is

---

* *Berakhot* 5a.

not an inheritance," a *yerusha,* which comes automatically to the child of the Torah scholar. All achievement in Torah depends on an individual's own efforts. A student of Torah must be willing to suffer privation. Maimonides writes that on the path of Torah acquisition a person must be willing to eat only bread and drink only water, even snatching momentary sleep on the ground rather than in a comfortable bed.* Indeed, no one can merit the crown of Torah unless they are willing to destroy their desire for material blandishments while in pursuit of Torah expertise (ibid. 12). Similarly, the Land of Israel cannot be acquired without sacrifice and suffering. The final test in the life of Abraham and the source of Jewish claim to Jerusalem is the binding of Isaac on Mount Moriah; the message conveyed by the Bible is that we can only acquire our Holy Land if we are willing to place the lives of our children on the line. Nothing is more apparent in modern Israel today. A heritage comes hard, not easily, and our national heritage is Torah and Israel.

The second distinction between the terms is not how the gift is acquired but rather how it may or must be dispersed. Even the largest amount of money inherited (*yerusha*) can be squandered, or legitimately lost. In contrast, a *morasha* must be given over intact to the next generation. Its grammatical form is *hif'il,* and it literally means "to hand over to someone else." Silver is an inheritance, and can be invested, lent out, or melted down or used in whatever way the heir desires; silver Shabbat candlesticks are a heritage, meant to be passed down from parent to child and used from generation to generation.

Third, one must have the physical and objective inheritance in one's possession in order to give it to one's heir; that is not necessarily the case with regard to a heritage, or *morasha.* Jewish parents bequeathed the ideals of Torah and Israel to their children for four thousand years, even when they were living in exile far from the Promised Land and even if poverty and oppression made it impossible for them to be Torah scholars. Jewish mothers in Poland and Morocco sang their children to sleep with lullabies about the beauty of the Land of Israel and the paramount importance of Torah scholarship, singing "Torah is the best merchandise"

---

*   Laws of Torah Study 3:6.

and Jerusalem the most beautiful city. Paradoxically, one can pass on a *morasha* (heritage) even if one doesn't have it oneself!

And finally, a *yerusha* is a substantive object whereas a *morasha* may be an abstract idea or ideal. There is a charming Yiddish folk song in which the singer "laments" that while his friends' wealthy parents gave them automobiles, his parents could only give him good wishes: "Go with God." While his friends' parents gave them cash, his parents gave him aphorisms: "*Zai a mentsch* – be a good person." However, whereas the automobiles and cash were quickly dissipated, the words remained – and were passed on to the next generation.

The truth is that an inheritance pales in comparison to a heritage. The real question must be: Will you only have a transitory inheritance to leave your children, or will you merit bequeathing an eternal heritage?

Yichus, Lineage, and the Forebears of Moses

> *These are Aaron and Moses, whom God has said
> are to take the children of Israel from the land of
> Egypt... they are Moses and Aaron.*
>
> EXODUS 6:26–27

Lineage, or its Hebrew-Yiddish equivalent, *yichus*, is one of the most overused words in our contemporary Jewish vocabulary, especially in more religiously observant circles. "What is his background, from what type of family does she come?" is a frequent first question asked by anyone interested in effectuating a match (*shidduch*). This fact of life makes the biblical textual order of *Va'era* strangely disjointed: the lineage of Moses, liberator of Israel and probably the most important Jew in Jewish history, is not fully presented to us with the account of his birth – when it certainly ought to have been documented, seeing that he was found in a small ark floating on the Nile River by the daughter of Pharaoh! Instead, the Bible waits for five and a half chapters of *Va'era*, well into his life and ministry and just before the plagues against Egypt are about to begin, before presenting a complete genealogy. At his birth we are merely told, "A man from the house of Levi went and took a daughter of Levi, and the woman conceived and bore a son…" (Ex. 2:1, 2), a virtually anonymous parentage! Now when the genealogical account is finally given, it is a very complete one, beginning with the tribe of Reuben, firstborn to Jacob, and culminating with the advent of Moses from the tribe of Levi:

> These are Aaron and Moses, whom God has said are to take the children of Israel from the land of Egypt…they are Moses and Aaron.
>
> Exodus 6:26–27

Why here, why in such a detailed manner? The account begins with the children of Reuben and Shimon before we even come to Levi and then goes on to present all the various cousins from the tribe of Levi alongside Moses. And why is the order of Moses and Aaron switched in the very same verse which we just cited ("These are Aaron and Moses… they are Moses and Aaron")?

Rabbi Samson Rafael Hirsch, in his remarkable and most contemporary interpretation of the Bible, addresses our first question by explaining that until this point Moses really had not succeeded. After all, as a result of his first encounter with Pharaoh, not only were the Jews not freed – not even for a three-day respite – but their work load was made even harder. From then on, the Israelites had to gather the straw in addition to making the bricks! It is only at this point that Moses will begin to succeed and even produce the miracles of the Ten Plagues and the splitting of the Red Sea. The prelude to the successful Moses is the description of his genealogy.

Rabbi Hirsch adds another most significant dimension. Specifically at the time of Moses' phenomenal success and even supernatural abilities – albeit the work of the divine but effectuated by the hand of Moses – it is critical for the biblical text to record the wholly natural and human biological birth of our greatest prophet.

> Our Moses was a human being, born to human beings, remains a human being and will never transcend his fundamental humanity.

Samson Rafael Hirsch, ad loc.

Every human being, not any single prophet or even redeemer, is a child of God as well as of his or her mortal parents, and every human being has the potential to reach the heights of a Moses.

I would take Rabbi Hirsch's explanation one step further, and at the same time attempt to answer the other questions we have posed. At the conclusion of the preceding Torah portion we read one of the most mysterious and problematic passages of the entire Bible. Moses is directed by God to say to Pharaoh,

> Thus says the Lord [YHVH, *Hashem*], "My first born son is Israel." And I say to you, send out my son so he may serve Me, and if you refuse to send him out, I shall kill your firstborn son.
>
> Exodus 4:22, 23

And then the text continues with an almost unfathomable incident:

> And it happened on the road to the inn, and God met him desiring to slay him. And Tziporah [Moses' wife] took a sharp stone and cut off the foreskin of her son, causing it to touch his feet. And she said, "You are a bridegroom of blood for me," and He released him; then she said, "A bridegroom of blood for circumcision."
>
> Exodus 4:24–26

What happened here? Who wanted to slay whom, and why? What causes Tziporah to become the first *mohelet* (female *mohel*) in Jewish history? The Midrash suggests that Moses had neglected to circumcise his son, either because he had promised his Midianite father-in-law Jethro that his firstborn would be raised for a life of idolatry (*Mekhilta, Yitro,* 1) or because he was too involved in the process of redeeming his nation to worry about his paternal religious obligations (Rashi ad loc.). In either case, Moses transgressed, and the Almighty sought to punish him. Tziporah saved the situation by circumcising her son just in time.

This story, when understood from this perspective, contains a dire message not only for Pharaoh, but especially for the Israelites. You will remember that its prelude was a warning to Pharaoh that if he refused to free God's firstborn son, Israel, then his (Pharaoh's) firstborn son, and the firstborn sons of all Egyptians, would be slain as a measure-for-measure punishment.

At the same time, the entire book of Genesis takes a very strong stand against primogeniture, the pre-eminence of the biological firstborn, and is in favor of meritocracy. After all, Abraham's firstborn Ishmael is overtaken by Isaac. Isaac's firstborn Esau is overtaken by Jacob, and Jacob's firstborn Reuben is overtaken by Joseph (or Judah by the end of Genesis). It is achievement in life rather than placement at birth, merit rather than biology, which prevails.

God's referral to Israel as His firstborn is both compliment and challenge, divine choice but also divine charge. Israel must be worthy of the premiership; otherwise it will be forfeited, as was the case with the other firstborn of the Bible. To make the point indubitably clear, if Moses – the chosen of God to lead His firstborn Israel – is lax in circumcising his son, a crucial religious obligation of initiating one's progeny into Jewish fate and destiny, an act which connotes sanctifying the physical and tempering the sexual, then Moses himself will be punished by God. Israel will only retain its elevated status if it deserves to retain it. Israel must be committed – even to the point of shedding blood – to its national and religious ideals. God is a loving but demanding bridegroom.

I believe that this is the true meaning of the placement of genealogy immediately prior to the miracles which will make Moses the great liberator. Moses was chosen by God not because of his birth placement, but because of his life's achievement; not because of his biology, but because of his morality. Indeed, Reuben was the eldest son; Levi was only third in line. Datan and Aviram, sons of Reuben, Zimri, the prince of the tribe of Shimon, and Korach the next-in-line cousin of Moses, will all rebel against Moses because they demand leadership based on genealogy. When the Bible delineates Moses' biological roots beginning with Reuben and culminating in Moses and Aaron, it is confirming the principle of meritocracy over primogeniture. Even the elder brother, Aaron, must play second fiddle to the younger and more worthy Moses.

Israel may be God's firstborn son, but in order to retain that distinction, we must behave in a manner which is worthy and distinctive.

The Plagues: A Lesson in Morality

> *And the Egyptians shall know that I am the Lord,*
> *when I stretch forth my hand upon Egypt and*
> *bring out the children of Israel...*
>
> EXODUS 7:5

With each plague there is an accompanying verse that spells out that God is God!

> Thus says the Lord, in this you shall know that I am the Lord – behold, I will smite with the rod that is in my hand upon the waters which are in the river, and they shall be turned to blood.
>
> Exodus 7:17

This theme is repeated again and again:

…the thunder shall cease, neither shall there be any more hail,
that you may know the earth is the Lord's.

Exodus 9:29

Certainly God in all His magnificent splendor could have pulled off a
quick exodus for the Jews of Egypt had He so desired! It would seem
that the proliferation of plagues only prolongs the redemption of the
Jews as well as the suffering of the Egyptians. Why stretch it out with ten
when one devastating plague right at the beginning could have wiped out
Pharaoh and his meddling magicians? If God chose ten plagues instead
of one, we must attempt to understand why.

The Torah is telling us that wiping out the Egyptians in one fell
swoop, as devastating as it may be, would not have gotten the divine
message across, neither to Pharaoh's Egypt nor to subsequent history.
Only after ten plagues, each carving another notch into the stubborn
skulls of Pharaoh and the Egyptians, will their consciousnesses finally
absorb God's critical lesson. Although this may explain the necessity for
an ongoing plague-by-plague process, we still have to understand why
it seems so important to God that the Egyptians know who is boss, as
it were. Does the knowledge of this fact make a difference in the world
and the way it is ordered? After all, we cannot attribute to the Almighty
God the all-too-human trait of those who demand recognition for their
achievements, recognizing credit where credit is due. Does it really matter to God that Pharaoh knows who the star of the universe is, and that
His name must be spelled correctly? This could hardly be the divine
motivation.

We can arrive at one possible answer by examining the midrashic
approach to the meaning of the first plague and deducing from that the
idea behind the other nine. In *Pirkei deRabbi Eliezer* we read:

> Why did God bring the plague of blood against Egypt? Since
> the Egyptians threw the children of Israel into the sea, as it says,
> "Every son that is born you shall cast into the river" (Ex. 1:22).
> God judged the water in the river, and the water turned to blood.
>
> *Pirkei deRabbi Eliezer*, Chap. 19

The Midrash *Lekaḥ Tov* puts it in a slightly different way:

> Because they [the Egyptians] spilled the blood of Israel like water,
> "their water, or, rivers, were turned into blood so that they could
> not drink."
>
> Psalms 78:44

The idea common to both of these explanations is the universal need
for evil to be punished, a "measure for measure" cosmic morality. This
also expresses the essence of the book of Genesis, that even the exalted
patriarchs must pay for whatever transgressions they may have committed. After Jacob deceives his father Isaac, he is deceived by Laban in
regard to Rachel, and his sons deceive him with the false report that
Joseph has been killed. When Joseph's economic policy to ensure the
survival of Pharaoh's empire causes the Grand Vizier to virtually enslave
the Egyptians to Pharaoh, Joseph's own children and grandchildren are
eventually enslaved to the Egyptians. Clearly, "measure for measure" is
the operative force in Genesis. In effect, then, the two midrashic reasons
stress the continuation of the Genesis world in which sin is punished in
kind, even if it may take a few generations.

Hence, the first three plagues made the Egyptians feel like strangers in their own homeland: the bloodied Nile preventing them from
drinking water (Egypt is the gift, or child, of the Nile), the outbreak of
frogs preventing them from sleeping or eating comfortably, the lice caus-
ing then to constantly scratch themselves. The next three – wild animals,
illness and boils – harmed their possessions and property, and the last
three – hail, locusts and darkness – wrought havoc upon the atmosphere
in which they lived, culminating in the killing of the firstborn. This was
just punishment for the fact that the Hebrews were made to feel like
despicable strangers in Egypt, were forced to physically suffer and even
die by cruel taskmasters, and were prevented from enjoying the free air,
open spaces, parks, theaters and marketplaces of Egypt – indeed, God's
"firstborn Israel" were coerced to endure alienation (*gerut*), affliction
(*inuy*) and enslavement (*avdut*).

Another midrashic source, however, introduces a new concept.

> Why was the water first smitten with blood? Because Pharaoh
> and the Egyptians worshipped the Nile River. God then said,
> "First I shall smite their god, and then [I shall smite] the nation."
> *Shemot Raba*, 9:8

According to this view, the motivating force behind turning the Nile
into blood was to prove to the Egyptians that the river which they worshiped is a false god, devoid of life-nurturing powers. As a river of blood
it cannot even sustain a blade of grass.

This last midrash is saying that the reason behind the plagues is
not only to demonstrate that there is justice and ultimate accountability
for one's deeds in this world, measure for measure, but also to demonstrate to the world the undeniable, incontestable idea that God is God,
and that God alone is God; He does not share his godliness with Pharaoh (the smiting of the firstborn since Pharaoh too is a firstborn) and
He does not share His godliness with the Nile River. As we go through
the plagues, this theme is constantly repeated. It is not enough to destroy
Egypt; their beliefs in many gods must be destroyed. They must learn
that there is only one force in the universe who can declare 'I am God.'

This message lays the foundation for the additional lesson of the
book of Exodus. The book of Genesis first introduced us to God the
Creator, *Elohim*, the omnipotent force who demands ethical and compassionate conduct. Violence, trickery and debauchery must ultimately
be punished; Abraham must convey to his progeny to observe the way
of God by doing righteousness and justice (Gen. 18–19). Exodus, however, opens with God telling Moses that He is revealing a manifestation
of Himself not known to the patriarchs, the Lord [*YHVH*, *Hashem*, the
four-letter name], author of history and redemption who insists that
humanity not only act justly but also live in freedom. The corollary
of God the sole creator is that a human being is a mere creature, and
therefore no human being has the right to enslave another. God, the sole
creator, takes no partner along with Him – not the indomitable Nile
River and not the powerful Pharaoh. Hence, no human being dare lord
it over other human beings, no one dare arrogate unto oneself the right
to enslave others. It is only within the Hebrew struggle to free the slaves

that the next great move forward in human history can take place. This theme of "God-recognition" is crucial to the "dialogue" between Moses and Pharaoh; once Pharaoh realizes that only God is the author of life and death, no earthly despot can claim that power for himself and the Israelites must be free to leave Egypt!

God, sole creator, our parent in heaven, ensures the fundamental equality of all human beings, who are equally siblings and children of the one and only God. That's the point of the plagues, the moral message of the book of Exodus, the fundamental truth that must brand itself on the consciousness of humanity. Once it is understood that there is a sole God above and no God below, it becomes impossible to enslave any human being. That's the radical message of the book of Exodus.

The Decalogue in Exodus presents as the reason for Shabbat rest "because God created heaven and earth" (Ex. 20:11). The Decalogue in Deuteronomy presents as the reason for Shabbat rest "because with a strong arm God took you out of Egypt..." (Deut. 5:14, 15). On Friday night the sanctification over the wine begins with acknowledging and remembering God as Creator of the world, and ends with remembering God who took us out of Egypt. The link between these two historic moments is now obvious and inevitable. The idea of slavery is inimical to the idea of God as God. If God is the creator, then the corollary of that idea is that we are all creatures. And if we are all creatures, then one creature dare not enslave another. Hence the God of Exodus commands that on the Shabbat day:

> Your gentile slave must rest *like you* so that you may remember that you were slaves in the Land of Egypt and the Lord your God freed you from there.
>
> Deuteronomy 5:14, 15

Bo

Who Hardened Pharaoh's Heart?

> *And God said unto Moses: "Go in unto Pharaoh,*
> *for I have hardened his heart, and the heart of his*
> *servants, that I might show these My signs in the*
> *midst of them."*
>
> EXODUS 10:1

Why does God declare that He has "hardened Pharaoh's heart" so that the despot will not change his mind and free the Israelites? Doesn't this collide head-on with our notion of free will? Is the Torah telling us that God interrupts the ordinary course of human events to introduce His will into the hearts of people, sometimes even preventing them from making the right decision? What about the idea that absolutely nothing must stand in the way of repentance, that no one, not even a righteous person, can stand where a penitent stands?

Rabbi Shlomo Goren gives a novel explanation which was apparently inspired by the miraculous events he experienced with the rise of the State of Israel. There are times, he maintains, when God must introduce His will into the hearts of people, but this is limited to monarchs, emperors, and Pharaohs. Rabbi Goren cites a verse from Proverbs:

> Like water courses is the king's heart in the hand of the Lord: He directs it wherever He wishes.
>
> Proverbs 21:1

Rabbi Goren suggests that this verse comes to teach that in regard to freedom of choice, we have to distinguish between an individual and the leader of a nation.

Individuals always have free choice. However, since God has a master plan with Israel as the catalyst, the Almighty may sometimes be moved to control the choices of leaders of key nations during critical and fateful historical periods. Such a situation occurred at the very dawn of history with the confrontation between Pharaoh and the Hebrew slaves, and the Almighty had to step in.

Another way of looking at the issue is provided by the Midrash. True, God hardens Pharaoh's heart, as He declared He would, but we must note that the divine intervention only emerges with the sixth plague. Examining the first five plagues, we find that Pharaoh himself is the one who exercises obstinacy. This formulation is repeated again and again. "Pharaoh became obstinate" (the first plague [Ex. 7:22]); "He [Pharaoh] hardened his heart" (the second plague [Ex. 8:11]); "Pharaoh remained obstinate" (the third plague [Ex. 8:15]); "Pharaoh made himself obstinate" (the fourth plague [Ex. 8:28]); and "Pharaoh remained obstinate" (the fifth plague [Ex. 9:8]). Only when we reach the sixth plague do we arrive at a new formulation: "Now it was God who made Pharaoh obstinate" [Ex. 9:12]. The contrast is so sharp and the division so perfect – five on one side and five on the other – that it is clear that the Torah wants to tell us something.

The obstinacy on the part of Pharaoh provides the Midrash with a means for solving the tension between the notion of free will and God's initial declaration regarding "hardening his heart." In the *Midrash Raba* we read:

> The Holy One, blessed be He, gives someone a chance to repent, and not only one opportunity but several chances: once, twice,

three times. But then, if the person still has not repented, God locks the person's heart altogether, cutting off the possibility of repentance in the future.

Shemot Raba 13:3

The Midrash goes on to explain that Pharaoh had already been given five opportunities to repent, five opportunities to hear the voice of God demanding that His people shall be released from slavery – each of the plagues a direct "fax" from God – and still refused. God is now effectively saying to Pharaoh: "You stiffened your neck, you hardened your heart, now I am going to add stubbornness to your own inner stubbornness."

A similar idea is expressed in Maimonides' "Laws of Repentance." The great twelfth-century sage and philosopher attacks our problem frontally, dedicating parts of chapter 5 to the question of free will and then coming to the apparent contradiction between the general idea of free will and the hardening of Pharaoh's heart by God. Maimonides writes:

> Since Pharaoh sinned *on his own impulse* and mistreated the Israelites who sojourned in his land … justice required that repentance should be withheld from him until retribution had been visited upon him … When the Almighty withholds repentance from the sinner, he cannot return, but will die in his wickedness – wickedness which he had originally committed of his own will.
>
> Laws of Repentance 5:3

I would like to take this basic idea of both Maimonides and the Midrash as to how God sometimes cuts off repentance as a punishment for a certain class of sinner, and attempt to understand it in human psychological terms. As both of these classical sources point out, external influence began only after Pharaoh's own refusal the first five times despite the first five plagues. The result of such obstinacy is that Pharaoh himself became frozen, locked into a conception of how to behave; once that happens, it becomes exceedingly difficult for anyone to change their mind.

We must also remember that Pharaoh was not alone. He was surrounded by advisers, ministers and a corps of publicizers. After a clear policy of continued enslavement despite the suffering endured by the

Egyptian populace as a result of the first five plagues, how could Pharaoh suddenly change his policy and still save face? Had he been wrong the other times, had his citizenry suffered needlessly? How could a despot who called himself a god admit that his earlier policy had been a mistaken one? It is almost as if Pharaoh no longer had the real possibility of change; his earlier decisions locked him in.

I would like to suggest a third approach, based on a discussion of repentance near the end of *Yoma* 86b. The sages alert us to a seeming contradiction in the words of Resh Lakish regarding repentance. The first quote attributed to the master is:

> Great is repentance because it results in prior premeditated sins being accounted as errors [*shgagot*].

Then the Talmud points out that Resh Lakish also said:

> Great is repentance because it results in prior premeditated sins being accounted as merits [*zekhuyot*].

The apparent contradiction is resolved by the Talmud by pointing out that the first citation – former sins accounted as errors – is the result of repentance based on fear, the latter citation – penitents' former sins accounted as merits – is the result of repentance from love.

It seems to me that had Pharaoh come to the conclusion that it was wrong to enslave the Hebrews based on his own new-found convictions about the true God of the universe who guarantees freedom to all, his repentance would have emanated "from love," and would have been accepted. Since, ironically enough, it would have been his former sinful acts and obstinacy which had led him to such a conclusion, even his prior transgressions could now be seen as merits, according to Resh Lakish. After all, had it not been for them, he would never have switched positions and arrived at his new awareness and religio-ethical consciousness.

This is clearly not the position in which we find Pharaoh. Were he to release the Jews after the fifth plague, it would have nothing to do with a transformed and ennobled moral sensitivity and everything to do with his having been bludgeoned over the head by the power of the plagues. Such repentance out of fear is hardly true repentance, and cannot be accepted by God to atone for previous sins. Since Pharaoh is not truly repenting in any shape or form, God "hardens his heart" to the suffering of the plagues and allows him to continue to do what he really believes in doing: enslaving the Hebrews, who must wait until the Almighty deems it the proper time for redemption.

The Message of the Moon

God said to Moses and Aaron in Egypt: This month shall be unto you the beginning of months. It shall be the first month of the year to you.

EXODUS 12:1–2

The sanctification of the new moon, the first commandment which the Jews receive as a people, should not be seen as a commandment which just happens to be the first. Nothing in the Torah just happens to be. The firstborn commandment of God's firstborn people inevitably reveals basic truths about the Jewish psyche. The more we examine the nature of this commandment, the more we understand who the Jews are as a people.

According to the Midrash, this commandment is so important that God himself guides Moses' gaze across the sky to familiarize him with the different phases of the moon so that he can recognize exactly what the moon should look like when it is to be sanctified.

Halakhically we can see the significance of this commandment because, prior to Hillel the Elder's fixing of the calendar for all subsequent generations in the third century of the Common Era, the new moon was established on the basis of witnesses' testimony in court. The halakha even allowed these witnesses to desecrate Shabbat if necessary in order to get to the Sanhedrin in Jerusalem without wasting one minute. When their testimony was finally accepted after rigorous examination, the Sanhedrin declared: "The month is sanctified, the month is sanctified."

Even today, when first-hand testimony of the sighting of the moon has not been required for many centuries, the Sabbath before a new month takes on a special character and is known as *Shabbat Mevarkhim*, the Sabbath of the blessing of the new moon. A special prayer requesting a month of life, peace and sundry blessings* is chanted by a respected member of the congregation, and the time of the moon's exact appearance to a fraction of a second is announced. The day before the new moon appears, when the sky is pitch black, is called "Yom Kippur Katan," and is maintained by the very pious as a fast day. The first day of the month (or the last day of the previous month and the first day of the new month, if the previous month has thirty days) is a minor festival called *Rosh Ḥodesh*. On this day (or these days), half of *Hallel* is chanted during the morning service and the special prayer *Ya'ale Ve-Yavo* is added during the Amida and in the Grace after Meals. There is an additional scriptural reading, just as on any festival, and we recite the additional Musaf prayer, a reminder of the extra sacrifice in the Temple. General custom dictates that women are freed from certain domestic tasks, and fasting and eulogizing are forbidden. During the first half of the new month, generally on Saturday night after Shabbat, and preferably between the third and eleventh day of the month, the congregation leaves the synagogue, stands outside gazing up at the new moon, and recites the Kiddush Levana (the prayer for the sanctification of the moon). If the clouds are thick, the special prayers to be recited are delayed until the first clear night on the closest Saturday night. One New York-based Hassidic group (Bobov) rents a helicopter for the rebbe and his most respected aides to make sure that they will actually see the moon and recite the appropriate prayers. In most cities in the Diaspora, neighbors

---

* Composed by the first-generation *amora* Rav and found in *Berakhot* 16b.

and passers-by are mystified by these Jews gathered together in prayer, singing and dancing as they look up at the moon.

Why this fascination with the moon?

In the portion of *Bo*, as in a number of adjacent portions, the Jews find themselves in Egypt, a land where the calendar followed the sun. The Maharal of Prague points out that when the Jews were given this first commandment, they were actually given more than just a law telling them to start counting months according to lunar cycles; they were given a whole new way of life that would stand in sharp contrast to that of the Egyptians.

The sun is symbolic of constancy and power – the very image of Egypt. Discounting dark clouds (not too many in Egypt), every day the sun's warmth and light reaches someone in the world – 365 days a year we trust the sun to rise and set. "There is nothing new under the sun," writes the author of Kohelet (Ecclesiastes), because the sun is a symbol of constancy. The sun sees and oversees everything in an unchanging fashion. Under the moon there is something new at least twelve times a year. The moon is forever changing, going through its phases, getting smaller and smaller and then, when it seems to have disappeared completely, there is a sudden turnaround and rebirth in the heavens. To the ancient imagination, the permutation of the moon in its twenty-eight day journey was a constant source of speculation, wonder and mystery – and a ray of optimistic faith that from the depths of darkness and disappearance will re-emerge light and rebirth.

The *Zohar* compares the Jewish people to the moon because both the moon and the people of Israel go through phases, disappearing little by little until it seems that it is the end, but nevertheless, stubbornly insisting upon being born again. After each Temple destruction, even after a centuries-long exile climaxing in Europe's death factories – a new moon is suddenly sighted and the messengers run to Jerusalem.

The repetition of a monthly cycle – this law of change and rebirth – firmly established within the Jewish psyche the constant quest for renewal. Our sanctity as a nation is tied to our potential for national renewal. Our history attests to the phenomenon that when a Jewish civilization in one part of the world finds itself facing destruction, almost simultaneously a new culture emerges to replace it. The year 1492, for example, signaled the destruction of Spanish Jewry as well as the birth of an American haven.

The commandment of sanctifying the new moon is given when it is clear that Pharaoh himself, master under the Egyptian sun, will not change. After nine terrifying plagues, we might expect him to have a change of heart, but the leader of Egypt does not – cannot – relent. Despite all that he has witnessed, he refuses to let the Jews go.

All of the nay-sayers were certain that the Egyptian social hierarchy would never change. The Israelites were doomed to remain slaves in Egypt forever.

The message of this first commandment is that in contrast to the Egyptians, the Jews can and do change, emerging again and again as survivors from the fangs of evil. World society, individual nations and specific people can and will change, often for the better. "*Ḥodesh*" is the Hebrew word for month, "*ḥadash*" is the Hebrew word for new, and "*ḥidush*" is the Hebrew word for a brilliant, novel insight or invention as well as the word for renewal. Our optimistic scanning of the black-blue skies for the first sliver of the new moon is our testimony to the possibility of growth, change and development, and we must learn to sanctify that change. In the immortal words of Rabbi A.Y. Kook, the old must experience renewal, and the new must be sanctified (*ha-yashan yitḥadesh, ve-haḥadash yitkadesh*).

There is yet another significance to our fascination with the moon. The most fundamental human sin – jealousy – is reflected in the phases ("imperfection") of the moon. Initially, records the Midrash, the moon and the sun were to have been equal in size, co-rulers over the hosts of heaven and earth. After all, the Bible records: "And the Lord made two great lights..." (Gen. 1:16). It is only in the continuation of the verse that we read: "the greater light to rule by day and the lesser light to rule by night" (ibid). What happened? Rashi explains:

> [The lights] were created equal in size, but the moon was lessened when it complained, saying that it was impossible for two rulers to share one crown.
>
> Rashi ad loc.

The moon expected God to remove some of the glory of the sun, but as punishment for greed and envy, it was the moon who had to suffer imperfection. It is this jealousy and greed, perhaps built into the very fabric of human nature, which caused Cain to kill Abel, the brothers to sell Joseph. Similarly, the Second Temple was destroyed due to baseless hatred (*sinat hinam*) The new moon, with its promise of wholeness and perfection, symbolizes our faith that we will overcome jealousy and envy, that humanity will redeem itself and that messianic peace is within reach. Our prayers during the ceremony of the sanctification of the new moon are for the moon to become free of her imperfection and for David – King of Israel, Messiah and redeemer. Our greeting to one another in the midst of these prayers is *Shalom Aleikhem* – peace and wholeness. Kiddush Levana closes with these words:

> May it be Your will...to readjust the deficiency of the moon so that it may no longer be reduced in size. May the light of the moon be again as the light of the sun, as it was during the first seven days of creation, before it was reduced...

This prayer brings us full circle. Ultimately, when redemption finally arrives, the moon will return to its former glory and jealousy will no longer exist – neither between the lights in the sky nor between the lights down on earth, the human lights. Redemption will only happen when we humans join God in helping to make it happen – by sanctifying the moon, by sanctifying life, by sanctifying ourselves. The sanctification of the new moon is the first commandment: Our dream of renewal and redemption is our highest priority.

* * *

Postscript

Maimonides brings his crowning proof for Jewish faithful optimism in a more glorious future of world peace and harmony in defining the commandment to mark the new moon at the beginning of each month (*Book of Commandments*, Positive Commandment 153). He reminds us that our calendar was established by Hillel and that we could not maintain it today were the rabbis of our generation not considered the agents of that generation in Israel, which initially intercalated the months.

In addition, if a time ever came when there would cease to be a Jewish community in the Land of Israel or a religious court there, the agency could not be effective, because Torah (and therefore the calendar) can only come forth from Zion! But God would never allow such a possibility, since the Almighty guaranteed that "the Jewish community in Israel will never be erased…" (ibid.). Maimonides is telling us that built into our Hebrew calendar is the unshakeable belief that there will eternally be a Jewish community and a Jewish religious court in the Land of Israel!

Remember that Maimonides expressed such an awesome and stirring faith despite the fact that he was chased from pillar to post in his lifetime by the marauding Moslem Almohads, and he lived at the time of the European Christian Crusades. It is especially significant that Maimonides expresses his eternal faith in the command to mark the new moon. And what more reason have we to be optimistic about the Jewish future, since our generation has witnessed the miraculous return to Jewish national sovereignty in Israel after almost two thousand years of exile! May the Merciful Lord lead us to our land and enable us to walk on our land proudly and uprightly.

The Wicked Child – What Do We Say and What Must We Do?

> When you come to the land that God will give
> you as He promised, you must also observe this
> service. And when your children will say to you,
> "What is this service to you?" You shall say, "It is
> the Passover service to God. He passed over the
> houses of the Israelites in Egypt when He plagued
> the Egyptians [by killing their firstborn], and He
> saved our homes."
>
> EXODUS 12:25–27

Who is to be considered a wicked child – and how are we, the parents of the community, to relate to such a child? The author of the Passover haggada, in the fascinating aspect of the Passover *seder* highlighting the four children, refers to the questioner in the above mentioned verses as "the wicked child." Why? What is there in the question which would make us think that this child is wicked?

The first reason, which the haggada itself emphasizes, lies in the questioner's exclusion of himself or herself from the family ritual: "What is this service to you?" And so the haggada explains: "Saying 'you,' he excludes himself, and because he excludes himself from the group, he denies a basic principle of our faith." From this perspective, wickedness as a Jew happens when one excludes oneself from Jewish ritual-familial experiences.

There are other more subtle giveaways that tell us the wicked nature of this questioner. The Torah often prefaces a question with a phrase like "when your child will ask you tomorrow, saying." In this instance, the child tells rather than asks his or her parents: "And it shall come to pass when your children shall say unto you" (Ex. 12:26). An honest question reveals a willingness to learn, but a statement implies a certain superiority. The wicked child, who feels above the tradition, is not really interested in answers – only statements.

To add another discordant note to the rebellious music behind the words of this child, the biblical response is *ve-amartem* (Ex. 12:27), "you shall say," without the expected continuation "to him," a pronoun which would identify who it is that is being addressed. The answer thereby becomes a general, open-ended statement – giving the impression that the questioner asked and ran, was interested in saying what she thought but not in hearing what the parent had to say. From all of this we could logically conclude that a wicked child excludes himself from family traditions and traditional explanations – it's not that he disagrees, he simply isn't interested.

What might be our response to such a child? It is fascinating that the Bible itself gives one response, "It is the Passover service to God. He passed over the houses of the Israelites in Egypt [when he slew the Egyptian firstborn] and He saved our homes" (Ex. 12:26, 27), while the author of the haggada gives another "You cause his teeth to be on edge, and say to him, 'Because of this has God done for me when I went out of Egypt'" (Ex. 13:8). Why the difference, and what is the specific message of each response? After all, it is critical that we know how to at least try to respond to this most difficult child!

Let us begin with the biblical response.

The Netziv teaches that the wicked child's statement reflects his belief that the Passover service is an anachronism, that it has no significance or relevance because we've left Egypt behind generations ago. After all, he argues, perhaps in Egypt there was a need for the paschal lamb in that it reflected the reality of the blood of the Jewish sacrifice being placed on the doorposts as a sign to save the Jewish firstborn. But now that we've arrived, sitting here at a *seder* so many hundreds (if not thousands) of years after the original events, is there any rational reason for retaining such an old-fashioned and outmoded service? The biblical answer in our Torah reading is that it is a Passover sacrifice to God who saved our homes and families.

We must remember that there are two central pillars in Judaism: family ties and togetherness as well as divine laws and directions. The covenant with Abraham emphasized our family-nation-homeland while the covenant at Sinai emphasized our God-laws-service. On Passover we achieved our national freedom, and the Jewish nation was developed from the matrix of the first Jewish family. A family as well as a nation has shared experiences which have been repeated over tables of celebration passed down from generation to generation, in order to weld the individuals together and provide fundamental continuity between past and future. The family has been an important Jewish value from the very beginning of our history, when Abraham is told that he is distinguished and loved by God "so that he command his children and his family after him that they do righteousness and justice" (Gen. 18:19). And when Pharaoh's servants agree to allow Moses to leave Egypt – but only with the males – Moses and Aaron respond, "We shall go with our young and with our old, with our sons and with our daughters" (Ex. 10:9). It's a family affair.

Hence, the Bible tells this wicked child that the Passover sacrifice is a reminder of a critical occurrence at a crossroads of Jewish history, a divine miracle which preserved the Jewish family. It is precisely the kind of family ritual which is crucial for familial continuity.

The author of the haggada goes one step further, citing another verse: "And it will be when the Lord brings you to the land which He swore to your fathers to give to you, you shall do this service on that month… And you shall tell your child on that day, saying, 'Because of this has God done for me when I went out of Egypt'" (Ex. 13:5, 8).

The Bible pictures a situation many generations after the Egyptian Exodus. Nevertheless, parents are commanded to tell their children: God took me out of Egypt, therefore I continue to perform these rituals. I am my past; my past formed and informed me. To deny my past is to deny my truest essence; to consciously forget my past is to will oneself into a state of Alzheimers.

The key words here are "done for me." The continuity of the generations requires the ability to transform past history into one's own existential and personal memory. The initial biblical answer emphasizes the importance of familial experiences for familial continuity; the author of the haggada adds that without incorporating past into present there can be neither meaningful present nor anticipated future! I am my past.

The author of the haggada has yet another message. Despite the fact that the wicked child has denied her roots (*kafar ba-ikar*), we dare not tear her out of the family. She may want to remove herself from historical continuity, but it's the family's job to bring her back, to welcome her into the *seder* celebration.

The haggada instructs us to set the teeth of the wicked child on edge. The phrase in Hebrew is *hakheih et shinav*. It doesn't say *hakeh* which means to strike, to slap him in the teeth, but rather *hak-heih*, (*heh, kuf, heh, heh*) from the language of the prophet Ezekiel, "The fathers eat the sour grapes, and the children's teeth are set on edge." (Ez. 18:2). The prophet is here expressing the fundamental unfairness of the fact that the parents have sinned, but their children must suffer the pain of exile. Indeed, children do suffer for the sins of their parents – always. Anyone who comes from a difficult or dysfunctional home will bear the burden.

Children need nurture; children deserve parental time and concern. The author of the haggada is therefore reminding each parent that just as the child has responsibility to his past, the parent has responsibility to the future. Are we certain that the wicked child's teeth are not set on edge because of the sour grapes we, the parents, have eaten?

Have we lovingly demonstrated the beauty and the glories of our traditions, have we been there to hear her questions when she was still ready to ask them and to listen to answers, have we been the appropriate models for her to desire continuity within our family? The author of the haggada – subtly, but forthrightly – reminds both parents and children of their obligations to each other, to past and to future.

The Chosenness of Israel Revisited and Redefined

*And it came to pass that at midnight the Lord
smote all the firstborn in the land of Egypt, from
the firstborn of Pharaoh that sat on his throne,
to the firstborn of the captive that was in the
dungeon, and all the firstborn of the cattle.*

EXODUS 12:29

Why is the killing of the firstborn the last, and consequently most significant, plague? True, it brought death into every household, rattling Egypt at its foundations, but certainly the plagues of hail, or fire in blocks of ice falling from the sky, or total, crippling darkness for three days and nights, could not be considered lightweight and inconsequential demonstrations of God's power. Easily any of these plagues could have dealt a knockout punch to the most cold-hearted of dictators. So what is it about the killing of the firstborn that proves to be the most effective of all the plagues? Perhaps the reason is that the final plague owes its importance to having dealt a death-blow to a certain institution of ancient culture which God found objectionable: primogeniture, the primacy and veneration of the firstborn. Turning to the earliest pages of Genesis, we find the theme of the firstborn right at the start of the Bible when sibling rivalry between Cain and Abel is translated into the rejection and acceptance of their respective sacrifices to God: the hypocritical gift of the firstborn Cain is rejected, while the more sincere offering of the younger Abel is accepted.

Part of Cain's vexation is due to the fact that he sees his firstborn status as having been overlooked – and so it was, since birth placement had to take a back seat to heart placement, to sincerity of devotion. A fundamental message of the Bible is that deed, not birth date, establishes status.

Thus Abraham's eldest son Ishmael must step aside for the younger Isaac because the former is a *metzahek* – a scorner and an adulterer, which renders him unfit for the birthright. Of Isaac's two sons, Esau must give way to Jacob, since the former scorned the birthright, both by selling it for a mess of pottage and by taking Hittite wives. Jacob also has a firstborn, Reuben, but having "moved" his father's bed* (either an attempt to determine with whom his father would sleep after the death of Rachel or a euphemism for illicit relations with his father's concubine) he is deemed unfit. In his place, leadership passes on to Judah and Joseph.

With the creation of the Jewish people in the book of Exodus, a revolutionary concept emerges on the world stage. The prevailing rule of the firstborn – which means that birth status is more important than merit – is rapidly coming to an end. Indeed, the essence of the Egyptian-Hebrew confrontation boils down to the idea that if you're born an Egyptian you have the right to enslave, and if you're born a Hebrew, you become a slave. Slavery was not exclusive to Egypt. The Greeks and the Romans believed that anyone born into a race other than theirs was barbaric, and that they had the moral right to enslave all barbarians.

Indeed, less than 150 years ago a bloody war was fought in the United States because nearly half the country chose secession rather than adhering to the law that condemned slavery as illegal. And little

---

* See Onkelos translation to Gen. 48:4.

more than five decades ago, the world was almost subjugated by a nation that believed in the Aryan right to dominate and exterminate. From the moment it began its ascent in the world, Judaism's message was that individual merit is more important than genes or genealogy. Therefore the killing of the firstborn of the Egyptians not only strikes terror in the heart of every household member, but it also tolls the death knell for the institution of the firstborn. People are to be judged by merit, by character, by deeds; people are not to be judged by birth.

Historically, the movement towards a meritocracy describes a fascinating evolution within the Jewish people. Despite the biblical rejection of firstborn sons, primogeniture continued to hold sway in the desert, with the leadership of the nation consisting of the firstborn sons of the various tribal families. The rule of the firstborn comes to a dramatic end when the nation – including the firstborn – worships the golden calf. Leadership is then transferred to the Levites because they alone restrained themselves from engaging in idolatry, paving the way for the birth of a priestly class. Nevertheless, we can still find traces of this firstborn institution in the *pidyon haben* ceremony when the father of every firstborn "redeems" his son from being dedicated to divine service by giving five shekels to a priest. (Since Judaism develops organically, the earlier firstborn system retains a place, if only in terms of a ritual, within Jewish life-cycle celebrations. And the firstborn son does receive a double inheritance because he must often assume the burden of caring for the family if the father is no longer able to – a widespread phenomenon when life expectancy was a good deal lower than it is today.)

Moreover, the priestly class also fell into disuse; after all, the *kohen* is a *kohen* because his father is a *kohen*. In an agricultural society, there may be the necessity of a priestly tribe of scholars who would be exempted from land and labor and so would be freed to learn, teach and tend to the Holy Temple. With the growth of industry, this system lost its force.

When the Hellenists threatened to destroy the Jewish character of the nation, the Hasmoneans fought off the Greeks, preserving the integrity of the Torah. Not long afterwards the Hasmoneans, although themselves of the priestly class, arrogated kingship for themselves. However, they became corrupt and strife-ridden. After their failure and the resultant civil wars, leadership passed to the sages, the institution which survives today as the most complete and democratic expression of Judaism. One becomes a rabbinic leader through study and devotion, and not as a result of genealogy and ancestry. Rabbi Akiva, the classic sage, was a boorish, uneducated shepherd from a boorish, uneducated family – until at the age of forty he began to dedicate himself to Torah. The world of the Sanhedrin was based on solid intellectual and ethical achievements. The ultimate expression of this change of attitude is to be found in a mishna:

> A *mamzer* [person born of adultery or incest] who is a sage takes precedence over a High Priest who is a boor.
>
> *Mishna Horayot 3:8*

The slaying of the Egyptian firstborn was a dramatic confirmation of the divine desire for meritocracy.

Keeping in mind the concept of the gradual dissolution of the institution of primogeniture, we are struck by a strange verse early in the book of Exodus. There we read how God instructs Moses to address Pharaoh: "Thus says the Lord: Israel is my son, my firstborn" (Ex. 4:22). Doesn't this expression of Israel as "firstborn" contradict everything we've been saying until now? Let's consider three possibilities. First, these words can be seen as a warning to the Egyptians. You Egyptians, who see yourselves as the firstborn of the world, the greatest civilization to which all mankind gives homage, must understand that if there is a firstborn in this world, then God, the father of all nations, will choose whom He wants – and it's not you, it's Israel! Second, these words can be seen as a warning to the Israelites. The Almighty may well be saying to Israel, "I have established a relationship with you first, but you have to prove yourselves to be worthy in deed as well; otherwise you too can be replaced." Third, these words may be a combination of the above.

There is an interesting difference of opinion between Rabbi Yehuda HaLevi and Maimonides regarding the essential character of the Jewish people. According to Rabbi Yehuda HaLevi, the Jewish people are inherently holy. The Jewish soul possesses a unique, mystical quality called *segulah* which makes the Jew spiritually special. Maimonides, on the other hand, argues that there is nothing unique about a Jew qua Jew; if a Jew keeps the Torah, they are worthy of their name, and if not, they become like a non-Jew. Torah is what makes a Jew special, unique, and holy. Only the Jew who lives a life grounded in ethics and morals can claim uniqueness. Judaism is a meritocracy. Rabbi A.Y. Kook* addresses this difference of opinion and provides an interesting resolution to the conflict. He cites a talmudic passage:

> "You shall therefore keep My statutes, and My ordinances, which if a man [*adam*] does, he shall live by them ..." (Lev. 18:5). R. Meir interprets that the Torah's choice of the word "human" [*adam*] means that even a non-Jew who keeps the Torah and *mitzvot* is as great as the High Priest.
>
> *Sanhedrin* 59a

Hence, insists Rabbi Kook, an individual – of Israel as well as of the other nations of the world – is to be judged only on the basis of their merit, completely discounting genealogy. However, the Torah does prophesy that ultimately it is the Jewish nation which will teach ethical monotheism to the world, and the Torah does guarantee the eternality of the Jewish nation.

Hence, when God instructs Moses to tell Pharaoh that he must free His people Israel, "My son, My firstborn...," these words don't contradict the dissolution of the primogeniture. Each Jew is an individual; Jews cannot rely on the firstborn status of the Jewish people. If a Jew doesn't keep Torah and *mitzvot*, R. Meir and Rabbi Kook are saying, then any committed gentile can be greater than a Jew who doesn't keep Torah and *mitzvot*. But the firstborn status of the nation must be kept sacred because its destiny and mission is to bring the message of God – ethics and morality – to the world. This is our unique national covenant which is inviolate.

---

*   *Letters*, Num. 64.

The Revolution and the Redemption

> *And it came to pass at the end of four hundred*
> *and thrty years, on that very day, all the hosts of*
> *the Lord went out from the Land of Egypt.*
>
> EXODUS 12:41

Most revolutions in history have failed dismally, with the architects of the rebellions – leaders of the new government regimes – acting far more cruelly and high-handedly than the despots against whom they rebelled; witness the French Revolution and the Communist Revolution, and remember the blood-battles and the terrorizing secret police which the rebels put into effect as soon as they assumed power. Generally, when former slaves begin to rule, they do so with a vengeance, zealously and vengefully expressing their new-found invincibility. The nation of Israel was born as the result of a revolution – the rebellion of the Israelite slaves against the despotic, totalitarian regime of the Pharaohs of Egypt. But this revolution did not fail; quite the opposite. Its message of the inalienable right of freedom for all and abhorrence of all forms of enslavement reverberate to the present day. It is important to attempt to understand – and learn from – this most uniquely successful revolution against oppression at the very dawn of history.

The Israelites were enabled to leave Egypt and to emerge from slavery to freedom, from light to darkness, as the result of ten plagues which descended upon the Egyptian populace and wreaked havoc on the most advanced civilization of that time. The Israelites celebrate – indeed, attempt to re-experience – their miraculous Exodus every year at a family-oriented *seder* dinner which is accompanied by the reading of the haggada and remembering the ten plagues. These plagues, declares Rabbi Yehuda, as cited in the haggada, are to be easily remembered and symbolically categorized by means of a linguistic mnemonic device that divides the plagues into three separate sections, DETZAK, (*dam, tzfardea, kinim*), ADASH (*arov, dever, shekhin*), and B'AHAB (*barad, arbeh, hoshekh, bekhorot*): blood, frogs and vermin; wild animals, animal illnesses and boils; hail, locusts, darkness and the slaying of the firstborn. Apparently, each grouping highlights the mastery of the Israelites – or rather the God of the Israelites – over another crucial aspect of Egyptian life: the first three, in which the Nile turned to blood, the waters spewed forth omnipresent frogs and the dust turned into vermin, demonstrate control over the waterways and the land; the second three, wild animals, animal illnesses and boils, demonstrate control over those who populate the land; and the last three, hail, locusts and darkness, demonstrate control over the heavens and what comes out of the heavens and affects the earth. The slaying of the firstborn expresses power over life and death.

Both the Maharal of Prague and Rabbi Samson Rafael Hirsch provide an even deeper insight into these three categories of plagues. These great scholars hark back to the prophecy included within God's initial covenant with Abraham, when the patriarch is awesomely and frightfully informed that "your seed will be strangers in a land which is not theirs, they shall be enslaved and they shall be afflicted" (Gen. 15:13), after which they will inherit the Promised Land of Israel. Since the Egyptian experience serves as a paradigm for all subsequent Jewish and human exiles and persecutions, this original prophecy delineates the three characteristics perpetrated by every totalitarian persecutor on any minority group: alienation (*gerut*), enslavement (*avdut*), and affliction (*inuy*). These are what Pharaoh did to the Hebrews, what Hitler did to all non-Aryans, and what Stalin did to any group he thought might be posing a threat to his omnipotent authority, be they liberal intellectuals or Yiddish writers. Certainly the Hebrews in Egypt (as well as the Jews in Germany three millennia later) were first delegitimized as aliens or strangers in a foreign country to which they did not belong (*gerut*), were then enslaved and forced to build the storehouses of Pitom and Ramses (*avdut*), and finally were mercilessly afflicted through the mass murder of the Hebrew male babies and the back-breaking labor under inhuman working conditions (*inuy*).

The Maharal and Rabbi Hirsch ingeniously suggest that the God of the Israelites and the world punished the Egyptians measure for measure by means of the plagues – and Rabbi Yehuda brings this allusion to the forefront in his tripartite division of the plagues. The first plague in each of the three categories – blood, wild animals and hail – would make the Egyptians feel like aliens in an Egypt taken over by some strange force totally foreign to their experience until this point: the familiar life-giving Nile turned to blood (remember, Herodotus called all of Egypt the "gift of the Nile"), wild animals running rampant and seemingly controlling human movement, and hail uncharacteristically raining – and reigning – down on a defenseless Egyptian populace. The second plague in each of the three categories – frogs, animal illnesses and locusts – would make the Egyptians feel enslaved, devoid of ownership of any property, which is the chief characteristic of a slave. The frogs took over their homes, the *dever* (animal illnesses) destroyed their livestock, and the locusts completely consumed their agricultural crop. And the last plague of each of the three categories – vermin, boils and darkness – afflicted every Egyptian with severe personal discomfort, making it impossible to continue living, working and socializing in any humanly endurable fashion. The Egyptians became subjected to the very alienation, enslavement and affliction to which they had subjected the Hebrews!

The most important point of all this, however, is that it is not the Hebrews who turn the table on the Egyptians – as is the general case with most revolutions – but rather it is the God of both the Hebrews and the Egyptians who teaches the world the lesson of the necessity of universal freedom under God, the God of all humanity. The Hebrews have no right to feel like invincible conquerors after their successful Exodus; they can only feel beholden to the God of their redemption, before whom every human is creature and not creator, servant and not master. The creator-hood and parenthood of God ultimately ensures the creature-hood and sibling-hood of humanity, and under such a God, no human creature has the right to enslave another human creature.

And indeed, this is the true message of our revolution against Egypt as well as of the four expressions of redemption which are the major source for our four cups of redemption-wine highlighting the Passover *seder*.

> I have taken you out from under the sufferances [*sivlot*] of Egypt [they "suffered" your alien presence in their Egypt], I have saved you from their work [enslavement], I have redeemed you with great miracles [from their affliction], and I have taken you for Me for a nation so that I may be your God.
>
> Exodus 6:6

We dare not exit from our revolution in order to lord it over any other minority; God freed us from Pharaoh's enslavement in order that we be able to serve God, the only and ultimate true Redeemer. God teaches us and the world that we must "love the stranger because you were strangers in the land of Egypt," and gave us a Sabbath day in order that our gentile servants "may rest like you" – for everyone must be free under God. And only a people committed to universal freedom for all humanity has the right to benefit from a revolution and create its own nation-state; the formation of yet another totalitarian regime would only increase human misery and prevent the advent of a world of peace.

Beshallaḥ

Joseph, the Teacher of Jewish Return and Universalism

> *And Moses brought the bones of Joseph with him,*
> *since [Joseph] had adjured the children of Israel*
> *to take an oath; [Joseph] had said, "God will*
> *surely remember you; bring up my bones with you*
> *from this [place]."*
>
> EXODUS 13:19

At the very opening of the Torah portion of *Beshallaḥ*, just as we've reached the climax of the ten plagues and the Israelites have been sent forth out of their Egyptian bondage, we find a fascinating throwback to a former heroic personality from the Book of Genesis: Joseph.

Why interrupt the drama of the Exodus with the detail of concern over Joseph's remains? From a certain narrative perspective, Joseph's name even evokes a jarring note at this moment of Israel's freedom. After all, Joseph may well be seen as the very antithesis of Moses: Joseph begins within the family of Jacob-Israel, and moves outside of it as he rises to great heights in Egypt, whereas Moses begins as a prince of Egypt and moves into the family of Israel when he smites the Egyptians. Joseph is the one who brings the children of Jacob into Egypt whereas Moses takes them out; Joseph gives all of his wisdom and energy to Egypt whereas Moses gives all of his wisdom and energy to the Israelites. It can even be argued that the very enslavement of the Israelites by the Egyptians was a punishment for Joseph's having enslaved the Egyptians to Pharaoh as part of his economic policy (Gen. 47:19–23). So why bring up the remains of Joseph at this point in the story?

The fact is that Joseph is a most complex and amazing personality, who very much stands at the crossroads of and makes a vital connection between the Books of Genesis and Exodus. We have previously pointed out that the jealous enmity of the brothers towards Joseph was in no small way rooted in the grandiose ambition expressed in his dreams: sheaves of grain evoke Egyptian agriculture rather than Israeli shepherdry, and the bowing sun, moon and stars smack of cosmic domination. While yet in the Land of Israel, Joseph had apparently set his sights on the then superpower, Egypt – and the second dream suggests that Egypt is only a stepping stone for universal majesty.

But then, does not the Torah picture the Almighty as the creator and master of the entire world, and is it not Israel's mission to be a kingdom of priest-teachers and a holy nation with the mandate of perfecting the world in the Kingship of the divine? And with his very last breaths, in the closing lines of the book of Genesis (Gen. 50:24–25), does not Joseph profess absolute faith in God's eventual return of the Israelites to their homeland, at which time he makes his brothers swear that his remains will be taken "home" to Israel as well? The full picture of Joseph seems to depict a great-grandson of Abraham, who fully grasps the importance of the Land of Israel for his nation, but who also recognizes the eventual necessity of their being a source of blessing for "all the families of the earth" (Gen. 12:3), their mission of peace not just for the family but for the world.

The Midrash describes a fascinating scene:

> At the exact time when all of the Jews were occupied in gathering the booty of Egypt, Moses was occupied in gathering the bones

of Joseph. Who informed Moses as to where Joseph was buried? Serah, the daughter of Asher, who was still living in that generation [of the Exodus]. She went and told Moses that Joseph had been buried in the River Nile. Moses then stood at the foot of the Nile River and cried out: "Joseph, Joseph, the time of redemption has come, but the Divine Presence is holding it back. If you will show yourself, good. If not, I shall be freed of the oath which you made me swear." Immediately the coffin of Joseph rose to the surface of the Nile River…

Hence, when the Israelites went forth from Egypt, two casks [*aronot*] accompanied them for forty years in the desert: the cask of the life of all worlds [the divine Torah which they had received as family tradition until that time] and the cask [casket] of Joseph. The nations of the world would ask, "What is the nature of these two casks? Is it necessary for the cask of the dead to go together with the cask of eternal life?" But in truth the one who is buried in this [cask] fulfilled whatever is written in that (cask).

Tanḥuma, Beshallaḥ, 2

Generally this midrash is understood to be saying that Joseph fulfilled the moral commandments already expressed in the Torah from the story of creation up until and including the Exodus. After all, Joseph was moral and upright, even to the extent of rebuffing the enticements of the beautiful "Mrs. Potiphar," thereby earning the appellation of "the righteous." However, I would suggest an alternate interpretation: The Torah of the book of Exodus encased in one cask fulfilled the dreams, expectations and prophecies of Joseph buried in the other cask. Joseph foresaw an eventual exodus from Egypt and return to Israel. Joseph also foresaw a cosmic obeisance of the sun, moon and stars to the universal God of justice and peace whom he represented. This too was fulfilled when the world was paralyzed by the force of the plagues, when the nations trembled at the destruction of Egypt and victory of the Israelites when the Reed Sea split apart:

Nations heard and shuddered; terror gripped the inhabitants of Philistia. Edom's chiefs then panicked, Moab's heroes were seized

> with trembling, Canaan's residents melted away… God will reign
> supreme forever and ever.
>
> Exodus 15:14–15, 18

Yes, at the supreme triumphant moment of the Exodus, Moses stops to fulfil a vow and take the bones of Joseph, the essence of Joseph,* out of Egypt and into Israel with the Israelites. Moses wanted the faith of Joseph, the universality of Joseph, the majesty of Joseph, the grandeur of Joseph, to accompany the Israelites throughout their sojourn in the desert. After all, the casket of Joseph imparted a crucial lesson: God's rule of justice, compassion and peace must capture the entire world, all despots must be seized with fear and trembling, and all human beings must be free. May Joseph's eternal gravesite in Shechem be salvaged and re-sanctified as a beacon to Jewish faith in a world redeemed.

---

* The Hebrew word "*etzem*" translates both as "bone" and as "essence."

When Do We Pray and When Do We Act?

> And the Lord said to Moses, "Why do you cry out
> in prayer to Me? Speak to the children of Israel
> and let them start moving."
>
> EXODUS 14:15

How does Judaism orchestrate action and prayer, which are actually two contradictory directives? It has often been said that when we act, we must act as if everything depends on us, and when we pray, we must pray as if everything depends on God. What does this mean in theological terms?

The portion of *Beshallah* presents a terrifying picture. After Pharaoh has supposedly freed the Israelite slaves, the Egyptian charioteers relentlessly pursue them. If the Israelites continue their flight, the Red Sea will drown them. If they stay put, the chariots will crush them. The Bible records: "*Vayitzaku*" – "they cried out in prayer" (Ex. 14:10). Rashi adds: "*Tafsu omanut avotam*" – "they grabbed onto the artistry of their ancestors," a poetic reference to the prayers established by Abraham, Isaac and Jacob whose "art" is apparently the "art of prayer."

Moses then confronts God, apparently entreating for the safety of his people. Answers God: "Why do you cry out in prayer to Me? Speak to the children of Israel and let them start moving" (Ex. 14:15). Here Rashi is even more explicit than in the previous verse. He comments:

> This teaches us that Moses too stood and prayed. God said to him, "It is not the time now, when Israel is in danger, for you to engage in lengthy prayers [*leha'arikh ba-tefila*]."
>
> Rashi 14:15

What else should Israel do when in danger but pray? Isn't prayer the most obvious and mandatory course for a religious society to take in time of trouble?

But perhaps Rashi is telling us that the Almighty is not chiding Moses and the Israelites for praying: He is rather chiding them for their overly lengthy prayer, for their prayer without action in a situation which calls for both prayer and action. Indeed, all of life requires a combination of prayer and action, a realization that history is the unfolding of a magnificent partnership between human action and divine intervention.

There is a fascinating talmudic passage which may well be the source for Rashi's condemnation of lengthy prayer devoid of action.

> R. Yosi said, Once I was traveling on the road and I entered one of the ruins of Jerusalem in order to pray. Elijah appeared, and after I finished my prayer, he said to me, "My son, why did you go into this ruin?" I said, "To pray." He said: "You ought to have prayed on the road." I answered, "I feared that a passerby would interrupt me." He said, "You ought to have prayed a short prayer." I learned three things from him. One must not go into a ruin, one must pray on the road, and when one recites a prayer on the road, one recites a short prayer.
>
> Berakhot 3a

In effect, Elijah, the herald of Israel's ultimate redemption, is teaching R. Yosi, a talmudic sage who is suffering the aftermath of the destruction of the Second Temple, the true act of Jewish prayer. Do not merely pray in the place of destruction and wallow in misery. Start out on the road, on the path towards redemption. There will be attempts by pass-ersby to stop you; they may even shout at you and make war with you, and you must certainly pray. But pray while you are in the process of achieving your goal. Pray while you are rebuilding your state. Of necessity, make it a short prayer so that there is adequate time and energy for human initiative.

The talmudic passage continues, illuminating one of the most popular and poignant of our prayers, the Kaddish.

> I heard in the ruins a divine voice mourning like a dove and say-ing, "Woe to My children, because of whose sins I have destroyed My house." And Elijah said to me, "Not only that, but whenever Israel enters their synagogues and study houses, and responds 'May His great name be blessed' the Holy One blessed be He shakes His head in assent and declares 'Happy is the King who is praised in such a manner.'"

The reference is to the Kaddish prayer, a central feature of our synagogue liturgy and recited by mourners at the gravesites of their loved ones. "May [God's] name become great and holy," it begins, referring to the prophetic words of Ezekiel and Zekhariah, who teach that as long as the world is not yet redeemed, as long as tragic suffering and death remain an integral part of the world's landscape, and as long as God's name and essence are diminished, God is not yet manifest in the fullness of His greatness and sanctity. God's name is yet to become great and holy, and the achievement of redemption depends in no small measure upon our actions and repentance. As long as Israel merely weeps in the ruins, God weeps as well and continues to mourn for the destruction of the Temple. When does God describe Himself as a happy king? When the Jews leave the ruins, when they set out on the path of rebuilding, when they enter their re-established synagogues and study houses in Israel and declare that it is His great name which is to be blessed. His name will be one and manifest to all only at the time of a more perfect soci-ety. Since the Jews recognize this truth, they also recognize their role in helping to bring it about. God rejoices when He realizes that He has partners in His great task of redemption, when He sees that Israel has started out on the road to renewal.

The road is also the road to the Land of Israel and the city of Jerusalem. Let us explore the link between prayer, action and the settlement of Israel as it appears in the words of two giants of Jewish law and theology, Maimonides and Nahmanides. In his opening halakha in his section on prayer, Maimonides sets down the biblical necessity of praying each day.

> To pray is a positive commandment, as it says, "And you shall serve the Lord your God" (Ex. 23:15).
>
> Laws of Prayer, 1:1

Examining the section in the Torah cited by Maimonides, we discover that the verse appears in a sequence dealing with God's guarantee to Moses when Israel was on the path towards conquering Israel, the land of the Amorites, the Hittites, the Perizites the Canaanites, the Hivites and the Jebusites:

> Behold I send an angel before you, to guard over you on the road [*baderekh*] and to bring you into the place I have prepared [the Land of Israel]...Do not bow down to their gods...but you shall utterly overthrow them and break into pieces their pillars. And you shall serve the Lord, your God.
>
> Exodus 23:20–25

In effect, Maimonides is teaching us that prayer must be linked to the very concrete action of settling Israel and combating the evil of idolatry in the world.

Nahmanides* disagrees with Maimonides, insisting that the Bible commands prayer only when an individual feels endangered. His proof-text:

---

* See Nahmanides 'Strictures on Maimonides' *Book of Commandments*, Positive Commandment 5.

> And when you go to war in your land against the nation that is
> oppressing, then shall you sound the alarm with the trumpets
> and you shall be remembered before the Lord your God, and
> you shall be saved from your enemies.
>
> Numbers 10:9

Clearly, prayer is seen as an adjunct to an obligatory war, which is legitimate only for self-defense. We can see a striking example of this tension
between prayer and action in the following vignette. In the beginning
of the twentieth century, the city of St. Petersburg was blessed with a
chief rabbi who was a saintly scholar named Isaac Blazer, affectionately
called Reb Itzele Petersburger. He became an avid religious Zionist, and
in response the community announced that he was to be fired for heresy. After all, the community leaders argued, do not our prayers recited
thrice daily entreat the Almighty to return to Jerusalem, and do they
not conclude "Blessed art Thou, O God, the builder of Jerusalem"? This
declares quite explicitly that any return to Zion must depend solely on
God! How dare Reb Itzele attempt to build Jerusalem with his own
hands, and with the help of non-religious Jews at that!

Reb Itzele greeted his accusers with a smile, saying to them, "You
are right." He then said to the judge (*dayan*) of the city, "But then, what
about you, Reb Shmuel?" "Me?" the judge responded, aghast at the suggestion that he too was a heretic. "I am not a Zionist."

Countered Reb Itzele, "But when your daughter recently had an
asthma attack, did I not see you take her to a doctor, a non-religious Jew
at that! Yet we pray thrice daily, 'Heal us O God and we shall be healed…
Blessed are you O God, who heals the sick among your people Israel.'"
And then Reb Itzele turned to Reb Moshe, the president of the congregation. "You are also a heretic. Did I not see you keep your business
open until ten o'clock last night? And yet you also pray three times a
day: 'Blessed are you God who blesses the years with good sustenance.'"

Apparently, as in health and sustenance, prayer can only begin
after we have done whatever it is possible for humans to do. And that
must be the rule for all challenges of life!

A Practical Postscript

What is faith from the biblical perspective? Conventional wisdom would suggest that it means total and unremitting trust in God. Indeed, the Talmud records in the name of R. Aha:

> One who goes to a doctor for a blood-letting procedure is to say, "May it be Thy will, Lord our God, that this enterprise heal me and that I be healed, because You God are a faithful healer and Your healing is true. It is not the way of human beings to heal; they merely play-act."
>
> *Berakhot* 60a

Rashi interprets these words to mean that human beings ought not be involved in medicine, but should merely seek divine mercy. Nahmanides, who was himself a doctor, also taught that people on the highest level of faith in God should never seek human medical help, but should rather place their exclusive trust in God.

However, a strange dialogue between Moses and the Almighty in this Torah portion would seem to contravene this commonly accepted definition of faith. Pharaoh decides to go after the Israelites, whom he now believes never should have been allowed to leave Egypt. The Israelites, smitten with fear at the advent of the marching Egyptian armies, cry out to God and rail at Moses: "It would be better to be slaves in Egypt than to die in the desert" (Ex. 14:12). Moses then comforts the people, urging them on to what we would imagine to be genuine faith: "Don't be afraid; stand firm … God will wage battle for you, and you can remain silent" (Ex. 14:13–14).

But God is not satisfied with Moses' lesson in faith. The biblical narrative continues: "And the Lord said to Moses, 'Why do you cry out in prayer to Me? Speak to the children of Israel and let them start moving'" (Ex. 14:15). Rashi has God say, in effect: "This is not the time for prolonged prayer." It is rather the time for action!

I would submit that the Bible is imparting a critical lesson to the Israelites in this passage, providing a dramatic transformation of the pagan concept of faith. It is not by accident that the entire account of this dialogue opens:

> God spoke to Moses, saying: "Speak to the Israelites and tell them to turn back and camp before *Pi Hahirot* * facing the god of the North** near the sea."
>
> Exodus 14:1–3

The pagan gods demanded fealty, even to the point of child sacrifices; they expected absolute faith in their ultimate power. The only important act of human beings was to propitiate the gods through offerings and sacrifices. World events however were effectuated by the gods, and not by humans.

The first important message of the drama of the Egyptian experience was to demonstrate the supreme power of the one true God of Israel – the universal God – and not Pharaoh or the Nile. And the Israelites believed in God and in His promises with every fiber of their being. This was the faith of a Joseph, who made his brothers swear to bring his bones out of Egypt "for God will surely remember, yes, remember you" and bring you back to Israel. This was the faith of those parents from the tribe of Levi, who despite the unspeakably cruel Egyptian slavery and persecution of the children of Joseph, gave their baby boy the name Amram, Exalted Nation, and their baby girl the name Yocheved, Glory to God. They were nourished by the Abrahamic vision of the Covenant of the Pieces; they had perfect faith in ultimate redemption by God.

But they had yet to understand that Jewish faith expects not only faith in God but faith in self, faith in our ability to act meaningfully, in our power to begin the process of redemption, in our responsibilities to repair ourselves and our society. This is the fullness of the message of Torah and its recipe of commandments; this is the divine expectation

---

* *Pi Hahirot* may be translated either as "Freedom Valley" – where the Israelites are to learn the message of true freedom – or as "the mouth of (the pagan god) Horus."

** Lit., *Ba'al Tzefon* – a huge idol, the only one who survived the ravages of the plagues. See Rashi ad loc.

that we function not as God's chattel but rather as His partners in perfecting the world under the kingship of God.

So stuck were the Israelites in their former primitive concept of faith that they were not even capable of responding to Pharaoh's armies. The Egyptians had suffered a severe physical and traumatic defeat as a result of the plagues. Yes, Pharaoh was advancing against them with an army, but he commanded only 600 chariots with chosen crews. Josephus suggests that there were an additional 50,000 horsemen and 200,000 foot soldiers (Antiquities 2:15, 3). Ramses 11 is said to have had a force of 2,400 cavalry (Hertz, Pentateuch ad loc.). But there were 600,000 Israelite men! Why did they not think of organizing an army and fighting back?

And so, when Moses confirms the Israelite concept by saying that they ought to be silent and watch God do battle, the Almighty must correct him. If indeed the Israelites are to be His partners, they dare not stand silently by and wait. Much to the contrary, they must begin the process and act. Biblical faith means to do what has to be done in the physical, spiritual and ethical realms. Only after we have done whatever we can do have we the right and duty to faithfully rely on God:

Those who begin by purifying will be aided from on high.
Shabbat 104a

Hence, the Code of Jewish Law (*Yoreh De'ah* 336:1) does not accept the prayers suggested by R. Aha* when one enters a medical office. Rather, it agrees with Abaye, who stated:

Permission is granted by God to the doctors to do the healing.
Berakhot 60a

God works through human actions in the process of redemption. We must believe in God, but we must also believe in ourselves. And the most meaningful prayer is one in which we ask the Almighty to help us garner our own inner strength, courage and wisdom so that we may be able to help ourselves.

* See p. 104.

How to Praise God

> *This is my God* ve-anveihu, *my father's God, and I will exalt Him.*
>
> EXODUS 15:2

What is the best way to give thanks to God? As the walls of the sea come crashing down on the elite Egyptian chariots, and the Israelites realize that the Egyptians will never be able to attack or subjugate them again, a spontaneous song of gratitude and praise bursts forth. The *Shira* is Israel's magnificent cry of religious awe, an acknowledgment of God's "great hand" (Ex. 14:31) and direct involvement with their destiny.

To say that the Israelites were grateful would be a gross understatement. The accepted custom in most synagogues throughout the world, and for virtually all of Jewish history, is for everyone to rise when the *Shira* (Song of Praise at the Reed Sea) is read from the Bible. That Shabbat is known as *Shabbat Shira*. Every single day observant Jews recite the *Shira*, because it is included in the "Verses of Song" with which the morning prayer liturgy begins. The language of the *Shira* is highly charged and intense. The climactic exclamation of Israelite adoration and commitment is obscured by one word which is difficult to translate: "This is my God *ve-anveihu*, my father's God, and I will exalt Him" (Ex. 15:2). What does *ve-anveihu* mean?

Targum Onkelos translates the phrase as "This is my God, and I shall build a Temple for Him," "*naveh*" (from *ve-anveihu*) being the Hebrew word for home. Rashi prefers "This is my God, and I shall declare His beauty and praises [in prayer]," "*na'eh*" or "*noy*" (from *ve-anveihu*) being the Hebrew word for beauty and goodness. An anonymous talmudic sage builds on the same verb root as Rashi, but gives it a somewhat different twist:

> This is my God, and I shall beautify [His commandments before]
> Him by serving Him with a beautiful sukka, a beautiful shofar
> *Shabbat* 133b

The opposing talmudic view, in the name of Abba Shaul, divides the Hebrew into two words: I and Thou, *ani ve-hu*, turning the verse into a ringing endorsement of proper ethical conduct.

> This is my God, and I shall be like Him: Just as He is compassionate and loving, so must I be compassionate and loving...
> *ibid.*

These four views may be seen as an ascending order of commitment. The first opinion has the Israelites commit to building a temple for God. The second view, sensitive to the fact that an external structure says nothing about the nature of the spirituality within it, insists that the Jews declare their intent "to declare God's beauty and praise to all of those who enter the world" (Rashi, ad loc.), in other words, to publicly pray to Him. The third level is not satisfied with prayers alone, but prefers a whole panoply of adorned rituals. The final position maintains that the most important issue is not what we build, what we pray, or even what we do; it is rather who we are – the personality and character which make up our essential being – that really counts.

Perhaps there is an even deeper level to this difference of opinion. The *Midrash Mekhilta* (chapter 3), cited by Rashi (ad loc.), mystifyingly declares that a lowly maidservant at the moment of the splitting of the Red Sea had a deeper vision of the divine than even the great mystical prophet of the supernal chariot (*ma'aseh merkavah*), Ezekiel the son of Buzi. The sages of the Talmud make another comparison involving Ezekiel, when they declare:

> To whom may Ezekiel be compared? To a town dweller. To whom may Isaiah be compared? To a city dweller.
>
> *Hagiga* 13b

I heard a fascinating interpretation of this statement in the name of Rabbi Isaac Bernstein. When a city dweller from London, for example, has an appointment in New York, they go straight to the agreed-upon point of rendezvous. They are oblivious to the tall buildings and impressive plazas they are used to seeing at home anyway. Not so the unsophisticated town dweller. They are liable to become so distracted by the novelty of big-city architecture that they can miss their meeting altogether.

Isaiah and Ezekiel both have uplifting visions of divine splendor. Isaiah, the prophet of the Land of Israel, is likened to the city dweller who, used to living with spirituality all the time, goes straight to the heart of his vision:

> Holy, holy, holy is the Lord of Hosts; the whole earth is filled with His glory.
>
> Isaiah 6:3

Ezekiel, on the other hand, lives in Babylon, and is therefore compared to the town dweller. He is so wonder-struck by his exalted picture of the divine that he seems to gets lost in the myriad of details. Verse after verse describes the angels, the *merkavah* (mystical chariot), the accoutrements, with no mention of the Divine Presence itself, as it were.

From this perspective, the miraculous experience of the maidservant at the Red Sea enabled her, Isaiah-like, to have an even deeper perception than Ezekiel; she got straight to the central core of the issue when she declared "This is my God." She did not get distracted by the details surrounding the divine.

How are we to serve God in order to come closer to His essence, and to benefit from the divine sparks themselves? What can we learn from the vision and understanding of the Israelites at the Red Sea to help us in our quest for the divine? How can we offer thanks, and get close to God? If indeed the key word is *"ve-anveihu,"* then the Targum says that we ought to build a Temple for Him. But many individuals get so caught up in the engineering and aesthetic facets of the external structure that they lose sight of the spiritual raison d'etre. Look at any synagogue building committee and you know what I mean! Rashi says that we get close to God by praying to Him and singing His praises. How many synagogue attendees truly take prayer seriously, considering that they are in a house of God and not a social center? I generally define a proper synagogue as one in which the Almighty Himself would feel comfortable praying. With the exception of specific prayers at special moments, I am not sure I have ever *davened* in such a place!

The anonymous sage suggests that we must beautify the rituals we use in our divine service. Sadly enough, many people devote a great deal of energy to punctiliously observing every jot and tittle of Jewish law and custom, but neglect the God and Godliness which is supposed to be the purpose behind all their rituals. They simply miss the forest for the trees.

The Hafetz Haim makes the following analogy. A man sees his house burning. He rushes into the flames, emerging with pajamas, a woolen bathrobe and toys to comfort his baby daughter during the cold night outdoors. "But where is your child?'" cry out the anxious onlookers. The father was so obsessed with the paraphernalia that he forgot his daughter. So it is with many Jews, adept at every detail in their observance of the rituals, while they seemingly forget the God of love and compassion in Whose name they perform the commandments in the first place.

To this end, along comes Abba Shaul: "This is my God and I shall be like Him." If I am to truly serve Him, I dare never lose sight of His compassion and loving-kindness, and must adopt those traits as the infrastructure of my character and everyday activities. Only in such a way do I succeed at uncovering the divine essence.

From this perspective, Rabbi Samson Rafael Hirsch gives the

most meaningful and all-inclusive interpretation to the word "*ve-anveihu*" when he translates the verse as "This is my God, and I shall become His house": My body and my very being must become His dwelling place, the physical receptacle which expresses His will. Hirsch is saying that from the moment an individual wakes up in the morning to the last second before they go to sleep at night, their entire being, their total consciousness, must become a dwelling place for God and a living expression of the divine essential qualities. A person's very self and being, their every word and action, become the vehicle, or *merkava*, of the divine.

Birth and Rebirth

The nations heard and were seized with trembling... all the inhabitants of Canaan melted... The Lord will reign universally and eternally.

EXODUS 15:14–15, 18

If the Egyptian experience was the most seminal in the development of the nation of Israel, then the splitting of the Reed Sea was the zenith of that major historical event. The Song of the Sea has been memorized by Jewish children in day schools from time immemorial, and we even recite it as part and parcel of our daily, Sabbath and festival morning prayer service. And what emerges with exquisite clarity from this magnificent paean of praise to God is that our message of freedom is meant not for Israel alone but also for the entire world; Pharaohs, despots and so, even more localized communal rulers, must understand that only one Lord rules the world and all of His children must be free! That is the point of the verses quoted above.

And if the Jewish people was born – albeit in miniature but

certainly in potential – with the Covenant of the Pieces (Gen. 15) when Abraham, the founder of our faith-family-nation, was promised progeny and a land with borders, then it would be correct to say that the Israelite people was reborn as a nation with a mission to the world when we emerged from the Reed Sea freed from slavery, unscathed, and inspired with a message for the world. (Birth or rebirth is always associated with water: the fetus is surrounded by amniotic fluid, the mother's "water breaks" as a sign of imminent birth. Therefore conversion as well as baptism features immersion in water.)* Indeed, the Song of the Sea concludes with a vision of our building a dwelling for the divine, a Temple to the Lord, on the mountain of our inheritance (Ex. 15:17, 18), the very Temple towards which our prophets tell us that the gentile nations will rush, and will learn from our Torah the message of God's design of universal peace, freedom and tranquility (Is. 2, Mic. 4).

Paralleling our national birth and rebirth is the birth and rebirth of Moshe Rabbenu, the greatest prophet of our people, the one individual who understood and communicated God's eternal Torah to Israel and the world. If we carefully study Moses' emergence onto the stage of history, the parallels to the miracle and message of the splitting of the sea become inspiringly apparent.

The birth of Moses is described in the first four verses of the second chapter of the book of Exodus: A man from the house of Levi takes a wife from the house of Levi; she conceives and gives birth to a son, whom she hides (from the Egyptian police) for three months. When he cannot be hidden any longer, he is placed in an ark smeared with clay and pitch, and the ark is set afloat "in the reeds" (*ba-suf*) of the Nile River; his sister Miriam is stationed nearby to see what will happen.

The rebirth of Moses begins when Pharaoh's daughter goes down to bathe in the Nile, her maidens walk along the river, and she sees a basket among the reeds (*ha-suf*). She sends her maidservant, takes the Hebrew baby, has compassion for him, and allows Miriam to find a Hebrew wet-nurse for him. Pharaoh's daughter does not give birth to Moses, but she does save his life.

---

* See also my commentary on p. 134 for a fuller discussion on the issue of ritual immersion.

And in saving his life, she endangers her own life. After all, her father Pharaoh has ordered all Hebrew baby boys to be cast into the Nile; in rescuing this Hebrew infant, she is defying her father's decree. History confirms that totalitarian despots never hesitate to execute their closest family members who dare rebel against them. Indeed, the Netziv, in his biblical commentary *Ha'amek Davar*, suggests that once Pharaoh's daughter saw the floating ark, and suspected the existence of a Hebrew baby within it, she *sent away* her closest maidservant (Ex. 2:5) so that when she – Pharaoh's daughter – would rescue him, no one would witness the event to inform her father of her crime (the verse states that her other maidservants had left her to walk along the edge of the Nile). Pharaoh's daughter emerges as the courageous heroine of the moment! This fortunate rebirth concludes with the giving of a name:

> And the lad grew, and she [the wet-nurse, Yocheved, his biological mother] took him to Pharaoh's daughter; he became for [Pharaoh's daughter] a son and she called his name Moshe. And she said, "It is because I drew him out from the water."
>
> Exodus 2:10

The most commonly accepted interpretation of the name "Moshe" is that he was drawn forth from the river – but then proper Hebrew grammar would insist that his name be *Mashui*, in the passive form. Therefore, I believe that the Netziv provides the truest interpretation of this verse. The Egyptian word "*moshe*" means "son" (Hebrew "*ben*"); Pharaoh's daughter names him "son," her son, because she earned her motherhood by risking her life for him. Since she drew him forth from the Nile River in defiance of her father's orders, she could claim him as her son.

At this point in the narrative, there is no verbal connection whatsoever between the name "Moshe" and the Hebrew verb *meshitihu*, to draw out; after all, the name is Egyptian and the verb is Hebrew. However, the Bible is clearly making reference to the double-entendre inherent in the name: Moshe the son (in Egyptian) will draw forth (*Moshe*, in Hebrew) his people, the Israelites, from Egyptian servitude as well as from the Reed Sea. Just as the daughter of Pharaoh drew forth (and saved) the Hebrew child from the reeds of the Nile River, so will the adult Moshe draw forth and save his nation from the Reed Sea. He who learned the courage to rebel against evil totalitarian laws of servitude from an Egyptian princess will communicate a Torah which will eventually teach the entire world to have the courage to be free – even if it means putting your life on the line!

The Message of Marah, Forerunner to Moriah

> *And Moses cried out to the Lord, and the Lord*
> *instructed him regarding a tree. He [Moses]*
> *threw it in the waters, and the waters became*
> *sweet; there He made for them a statute and an*
> *ordinance and there he tested them.*
>
> EXODUS 15:25

Undoubtedly, the revelation of the Ten Commandments on Mount Sinai was the most momentous event in the history of the Jewish people; the "Dos and Don'ts" revealed by the Almighty Himself formed and informed the conscience of Israel and the world, and defined both our national identity as well as our universal mission.

But if the events at Mount Sinai loom so large in Jewish history, why does the Torah reading of *Beshallah*, right after the splitting of the Reed Sea – which took place one week after the Exodus and six weeks prior to the Sinai revelation – record how Moses leads the Israelites to

Marah where "…He [God] made for them a statute and an ordinance [*ḥok u-mishpat*]…" (Ex. 15:25). This obviously refers to some divine commandment of laws, which Rashi explains as "…several sections of the Torah: the Sabbath; the Red Heifer [or honoring one's parents, according to an alternate version]; and the civil laws of interpersonal relationships." Rashi's source is the Talmud (*Sanhedrin* 56b), where the sages maintain that not only were these three pillars of the law given at Marah, but also the seven Noahide laws of morality – for a total of ten. The sages seem to be drawing a fascinating parallel: ten commandments at Marah and the Ten Commandments at Sinai. Indeed the very name Marah certainly contains an echo of Moriah, the Temple Mount, the mountain from which Torah teaching (*mora'ah*) will emanate to Israel and the world. Why not wait another five and a-half weeks, and give all of the commandments at the same time? I believe that when studied in context, the commands at Marah serve as an excellent introduction to the revelation at Sinai and help us to understand its eternal significance.

Immediately after the splitting of the Reed Sea, the Israelites travel for three days in the desert without water. Then, when they finally do reach water, it turns out to be bitter, undrinkable. (Hence the name of the place, Marah, which means bitter). Despite the miracles of the plagues – which began with the waters of the Nile turning to blood – and the miracle of the splitting of the Reed Sea, which also involved water, the Israelites nevertheless complain at the lack of potable water.

> And the nation grumbled against Moses, saying, "what shall we drink?"
>
> Exodus 15:24

At this point, the text becomes almost inexplicable:

> And Moses cried out to the Lord, and the Lord instructed him [*vayoraihu*] regarding a tree. He [Moses] threw it in the waters, and the waters became sweet; there He made for them a statute and an ordinance and there he tested them.
>
> Exodus 15:25

What kind of magical objects and make-believe are being thrust upon us?

If we examine the word *"vayoraihu"* we discover that it has the same root as Torah, which means to instruct or direct. Hence, the translation of Targum Onkelos is *ve'alfai*, a word more connected to teaching or study. The Rashbam also looks at the root of *vayoraihu* and translates it to mean *yoru be-mishpatekha* – teaching or instructing (divine) laws. Thus God does not show Moses a tree as much as He teaches Moses the nature of this tree, or alternatively, God shows Moses a tree of teaching.

Clearly the tree of sweetening the waters is a symbolic reference to Torah as well as to perfection. Our Torah is biblically and liturgically referred to as a "tree of life":

> It is a tree of life for those who grasp it, and those who uphold it are content.
>
> Proverbs 3:18

And it is the "tree of life" in the Garden of Eden to which we yearn to return. The Torah is the formula by which the bitter waters of a transitory existence can be transformed into the sweet waters of eternal life. Torah will sweeten the waters of the world by returning us to Eden, peace and perfection, when

> knowledge of the Lord will fill the earth as the waters cover the seas.
>
> Isaiah 11:9

There is an even deeper message in this passage. After all, how could the Israelites have rallied against Moses only three days after they sang at the Sea, one of the most exalted moments in the history of our people?

> Then sang Moses and the Children of Israel this song unto God … I will sing unto God for He is gloriously sublime … God is my might and hymn, and He is become my salvation. He is my God and I will glorify Him, my father's God, and I will exalt Him …
>
> Exodus 15:1–19

Nothing in the Torah compares with the ecstatic emotions of faith expressed in these words – apparently totally forgotten in only three days of thirst! Our sages respond to the physical fact that human beings cannot live without water for three days by legislating that the community of Israel not live without the life-giving waters of Torah for three days as well (*Mekhilta, Beshallaḥ,* 2, *Bava Kama* 82a). Ezra therefore legislated that the Torah be publicly read Mondays, Thursdays and Sabbaths each week.

A well-known Midrash illustrates the enormous spiritual visions beheld at the splitting of the Reed Sea by pointing out that the lowliest maidservant at the Sea had a deeper prophetic insight than even the great visionary Ezekiel ben Buzi! That may be true, wryly and brilliantly pointed out the Kotzker Rebbe, but the day after the miracle at the sea, the servant still remained a servant and Ezekiel was still a prophet. In other words, the amazing effects of the miracles quickly evaporate and dissipate. Steven Spielberg productions, even if effectuated by God Himself, have little staying power. Momentous inspirations of the moment last but a moment; it is only painstaking, perspiration-soaked lessons and disciplines that ultimately and intimately bring about lasting personality changes.

This was the lesson that the Almighty taught Elijah after the prophet brought about a divine revelation at Mount Carmel during which 600,000 Israelites cried out: "The Lord He is God" – but nevertheless, the next day the false prophets of Baal continued to be worshiped. Elijah travels forty days and forty nights to arrive at Horeb – the place of the divine revelation, Mount Sinai – and receives a personal message from the Lord:

> … wind, but God is not in the wind; rushing noise, but God is not in the rushing noise; fire, but God is not in the fire. A still small voice…
>
> 1 Kings 19:11–12

In that still small voice – the voice of inner discipline, of outer kindness of law and love, of study and prayer – is God to be found. The daily prayer in which we speak to God, and the public Torah readings in which God speaks to us, are prime examples of this "still small voice."

The Torah describes how, only three days after the miracle at the Sea and the exalted singing of faith, the Jews bitterly complained against

Moses about the lack of proper drinking water. God teaches them that a yet-unredeemed world is filled with bitter waters. After all, water is both symbol of life – "The spirit of God hovered over the face of the waters" at the very dawn of creation (Gen. 1:2) – as well as a symbol of the destruction of life, as we see in the biblical story of the deluge at the time of Noah and the raging waters which inundated Jonah. These waters can be sweetened not by miraculous and momentous phenomena but rather by diligent and dedicated practice and study of divine law and love. It is the Torah, our tree of life, which has the capacity to sweeten and soothe life's waters and perfect society by restoring Eden's harmonious peace-perfect society to Eden regained.

At Marah, the place of bitter waters and ungrateful complaints, this lesson was learned. Therefore at Marah the initial three, or ten, statutes and ordinances were given to the Israelites. The Sabbath teaches reverence for all of life and denies any form of human enslavement and debasement. Honoring one's parents ensures continuity between generations and an extended family framework which provides firm support in the face of buffeting waves of adversity. The Red Heifer purifies from death and human mortality and the seven laws of morality are the only hope for society in the global village in which we live. And so, as the sequence at Marah draws to a close, Moses declares:

> If you will diligently hearken to the voice of God, your Lord, and will do that which is right in His eyes, and will give ear to His commandments and keep all His statutes, I will put none of the diseases upon you which I have put upon the Egyptians, for I am the Lord God who heals you.
>
> Exodus 15:26

In case there is any doubt about the deeper connection between the bitter waters and the "tree of Torah," the final words of the passage describe how

the Israelites came to Eilim* where there were twelve springs of

---

*   The word "*Eilim*," translated literally, means "strength" or "fortress."

water, and seventy date palm trees, and they encamped there by the waters.

Exodus 15:27

It is very difficult to encounter these numbers without eternal Jewish motifs springing to the mind: the pattern of the twelve tribes and the seventy Elders of Israel, as well as the seventy nations of the world. What the Torah is telling us is very simple: If we actively engage our lives with the Torah's teaching, we will see how bitterness may be transformed into the ultimate mission of redemption to the seventy nations of the world, via the twelve tribes of Israel and the seventy elders of the Sanhedrin; the Torah is our fortress and our tree of life.

What happened at Marah properly prepares us for the revelation at Sinai: the message that it is not amazing historical occurrences but rather commitment to divine law which transforms people and redeems society.

To Chastise with Love

> *Then said the Lord unto Moses, "Behold, I will*
> *cause it to rain bread from heaven for you, and*
> *the people shall go out and gather a day's portion*
> *every day, that I may test them, whether they will*
> *walk in My law or not. And it shall come to pass*
> *on the sixth day when they prepare that which*
> *they bring in, and it shall be twice as much as*
> *they gather daily."*
>
> EXODUS 16:4–5

In what way is the manna a test? After all, the very word "test" generally connotes a difficult challenge, a problematic obstacle – and here the Almighty is giving food on a heavenly platter. Rashi suggests that along with the manna comes individual self-discipline, since no one may retain leftovers or gather their portions on the Sabbath day. Nahmanides emphasizes the barrenness of the entire desert experience, the fact that the Jews had to follow God in a place devoid of natural sustenance, vegetation or animal life. Ibn Ezra maintains that the very fact that there were no leftovers, that after the meal was concluded the cupboards were bare and the refrigerator was empty, was the greatest test of faith in God that He would provide for the next day.

But the Seforno and the Ohr Haḥayim HaKadosh look at the fundamental miracle of the manna, the fact that the Jews didn't have to exert themselves to receive their food, and that their nourishment did not demand that they do any special cooking or preparation. Perhaps from this perspective the Hebrew word "*nisayon*," usually translated as test, ought be taken to mean "uplift," held aloft as a banner carried by God as a parent carries their beloved child. Perhaps what these commentaries – and indeed the literal Torah text – are trying to say is that God revealed to us through the manna His over-arching love and concern: He took us out of Egyptian bondage and provided us with all of our needs in the desert. Indeed, the manna is indelibly linked to the Sabbath laws: the prohibition of *muktzeh* (that a Jew may move an object on the Sabbath only if the object has been prepared for Sabbath use prior to the Sabbath), as well as the custom of the two *ḥallot* which adorn each of our Sabbath meals, are both derived from the verse about the manna cited earlier:

> And it shall come to pass on the sixth day when they prepare that which they bring in, and it shall be twice [*mishneh*] as much as they gather daily.
>
> Exodus 16:5

The manna, as the consummate expression of God's protective love and concern, must be the context from which we teach the Sabbath to the next generation. "Demonstrate a God of love," says the Torah, as it were, "and then I will truly know if the Jews will keep My commandments."

How can we, like God, attempt to teach Torah from the context of love?

Let me share two stories. The first takes place in the Volozhiner Yeshiva near the turn of the twentieth century. The *rosh yeshiva* was Rabbi Naftali Tzvi Yehuda Berlin, the famed Netziv, a central figure in the Lithuanian yeshiva movement.

When word reached him that one of his students had been caught smoking on the Sabbath, a flagrant violation which also smacked of inherent arrogance, for it had been done publicly, the Netziv called the student into his office. The student refused to apologize – and the Netziv was understandably upset. He instinctively slapped the student in frustration and disappointment. Apparently that slap burned through to the very core of the young man's being, and his honor badly shaken, the enraged student composed a letter forging the Netziv's name. The letter was a call to revolution, and such a document in Czarist Russia was tantamount to insurrection, a criminal act. The young man had expertly copied the Netziv's handwriting, and the venerable rabbi was immediately arrested. Presented with the evidence, the Netziv couldn't deny the authenticity of the handwriting, and his claim that he hadn't written the letter was rejected.

While examining his signature, the Netziv discovered the forger's one mistake. In Hebrew the name Tzvi ends with letter *yod*, and the name Yehuda begins with one. To write his name out completely would mean putting two *yod*s together, and since this constitutes one of God's names, the Netziv's custom was never to sign his complete name in such a fashion. Instead, he would use only one *yod* for both names, a fact the young man hadn't realized. That little *yod* saved the Netziv's life.

The young forger left Russia for America, and there he became a writer, editor, and active socialist. Not a friend of traditional Jewry, he saw his role in the new land as someone who must help the immigrant remove the taint of Europe, the taste of being a greenhorn, the remnants of a Jewish tradition. He was the main sponsor of the infamous "Yom Kippur dances," remaining an opponent of religious Jewry until he died.

The second tale is also about a cigarette, and another giant of the previous generation: the leader of world Jewry before World War II, the Hafetz Haim (Rabbi Yisrael Meir Kagan). The incident came to my attention while I gave a lecture in Miami, Florida in 1973. My subject was ethical exhortation, and I cited the talmudic statement by R. Tarfon that no one has the ability to chastise anymore: if one says to another "remove the flint from between your teeth," he will respond "remove the beam from between your eyes" (*Arakhin* 16b). Nevertheless, I concluded, apparently the Hafetz Haim was able to chastise.

The story is told that a student of the yeshiva in Radin was caught smoking on the Sabbath. He was about to be expelled, but the Hafetz Haim met with him in his house for two minutes. The student not only continued on in the yeshiva, but actually received rabbinic ordination from the Hafetz Haim himself. As I was recounting this incident, I noticed an elderly gentleman sitting in the fifth row trembling uncontrollably. When I stopped speaking he ran over to me, grabbed my sleeve, and asked me where I had heard the story. "It happened to me," he said, "fifty-five years ago." We were both very much moved, but I couldn't hold back from enquiring: "What did the sage tell you?" The retired rabbi had a far-away look in his eyes, and told me the following: "The Hafetz Haim was the greatest scholar in our generation, and we students were all in awe of him. When I had committed my transgression, and was all packed to leave, I was shocked to see the sage standing in front of me. He gently took my hand and asked – using the respectful term for 'you' in Yiddish (*ihr*) – 'Will you please come to my house?' We entered his tiny two-room house, devoid of a single piece of furniture which wasn't broken. He was still holding my hand. He looked up at me and said only one word: 'Shabbos.' He then began to weep, and if I live to be 120, I shall never stop feeling the burning heat of his tears as they dropped on my hand. Once again he whispered 'Shabbos,' embraced me, and saw me out the door."

How can we communicate Shabbat to the next generation? We can do it with Jewish leaders who communicate the love and significance of the day as well as of the God who gave it.

Yitro

The Prototypes of Very Different Gentiles

> *And Jethro the Priest of Midian, the father-in-law*
> *of Moses, heard all that God had done for Moses*
> *and his people; that He had taken Israel out of*
> *Egypt.*
>
> EXODUS 18:1

This Torah portion records how Jethro, Moses' Midianite father-in-law, heard of God's great wonders in redeeming the Israelites from Egypt and came to Moses amidst great praise to the Lord. Upon witnessing Moses' difficult workload in rendering judgments from dawn to night, Jethro gave sage advice in organizing and delegating a graduated judicial system, with only the most complex cases to come before Moses. One of the issues dealt with by the biblical commentaries is the exact time when Jethro arrived on the scene: Was it before or after the Sinaitic revelation?

In terms of the chronological sequence of the biblical account, it would appear that Jethro came to Moses immediately after the splitting of the Reed Sea and before the commandments were given at Sinai.

However, both Nahmanides and Ibn Ezra point out that since Moses could not have been occupied to the point of exhaustion with rendering biblical rulings before the Bible had been given, logic dictates that Jethro arrived and made his wise suggestion after the revelation at Sinai. But if so, why does the Torah record the advent and advice of Jethro before the account of the revelation, and why name the portion which includes the content of the divine words after a Midianite priest, especially since he came on the scene after that revelation took place!

Ibn Ezra explains:

> Since the Bible has just mentioned the evil which Amalek did to the Israelites [at the end of Exodus Chapter 17 as the conclusion of the previous portion of *Beshallah*], the Bible must [immediately thereafter] mention in contrast the good advice which Jethro gave to the Israelites [at the beginning of Chapter 18 in the opening of the portion of *Yitro*].

I would add that the Bible is contrasting two very opposite reactions to the miracle of the Exodus. In general, the nations of the world heard of the stunning rebellion of the Hebrews and became terrified:

> Nations heard and shuddered; terror gripped the inhabitants of Philistia ... Fear and dread fell upon them; at the greatness of Your Arm they fell silent as stone.
>
> Exodus 15:14–16

Two peoples, however, do not merely respond by panicking. Amalek, "first among the gentiles" (Num. 24:20), set out to make war against this emerging new star with the intent of heading them off at the pass. And Amalek played "dirty":

> Remember what Amalek did to you ... when they encountered you ... when you were tired and exhausted, and they cut off those who were lagging to your rear [the old, the young and the infirm].
>
> Deut. 25:17, 18

Jethro, on the other hand, is filled with admiration and praise: "And Jethro was overjoyed at all of the good which the Lord accomplished for the Israelites in saving them from the hand of Egypt. And Jethro said, 'Praised be the Lord who has saved you from the hand of Egypt and the hand of Pharaoh... Now I know that the Lord is the greatest of all of the gods...'" (Ex. 18:9–11). In effect, the biblical juxtaposition is teaching us that all gentiles should not be seen in the same light: there is the gentile who is jealous and aggressive (Amalek), but there is also the gentile who is admiring and willing to be of help (Jethro).

We are still left with the question as to why the biblical portion of the divine revelation should be referred to by the name of a Midianite priest – and I believe that herein lies one of the most profound truths of the Jewish faith. Undoubtedly the Torah was given to the Jewish people, as Maimonides teaches, "Moses our Teacher bequeathed the Torah and the commandments only to Israel, as it is written, 'a heritage to the congregation of Jacob,' as well as to anyone who may wish to convert [to Judaism]..."

But in the very same breath Maimonides continues to legislate:

> And similarly Moses was commanded by the Almighty to enforce upon the gentile world for everyone to accept the seven Noahide laws of morality.
>
> Laws of Governments 8:10

Maimonides concludes his religio-legal magnum opus *Mishneh Torah* with the "Laws of Governments,"* which climax in an optimistic description of the messianic age, a period of unusual peace and harmony when "nation will not lift up sword against nation and humanity will not learn war anymore" (Laws of Governments, Chapters 11, 12). Jewish redemption is seen within the context of world redemption; the God of justice, compassion and peace must rule the world, with Israel accepting the 613 commandments and every nation accepting His seven commandments of morality, especially "Thou shalt not murder."

---

*   Lit., *hilkhot melakhim*, Laws of Kings.

The paradigm for redemption, indeed the first example of Israel's liberation, was our exodus from Egypt. There are a number of lessons which must be extracted from this prototype. First of all, the Israelites must win the war against oppression; the God of Israel will only be respected if His people succeed. Second, the message of Israel must be a moral one: "I am the Lord thy God who took you out of the Land of Egypt, the house of bondage." Israel is entitled to live in freedom – and must be willing to wage battle against autocratic, Amalek-like governments which themselves utilize terrorism against innocent citizens and which harbor, aid and abet terrorists. And Israel must establish Jethro-like partnerships with those who – although they may still follow their individual religions – recognize the over-arching rule of the God of justice, compassion and peace.

The portion of the revelation at Sinai is called *Yitro* (Jethro); only if the Jethros of the nations of the world accept fealty to the God of peace will the ultimate vision of Torah become a reality for Israel and will the world as we know it be able to survive and prosper.

Who is a Jew

> *You have seen what I have done to Egypt... And now, if you will surely hearken to My voice and observe My covenant... then you will be for Me a kingdom of priest-teachers and a holy nation...*
>
> EXODUS 19:4–6

In effect, the drama of the Exodus and its aftermath have transformed Israel from a family to a nation-religion, from *Bet Yisrael* to *Am Yisrael*. But how do we define the *am*?* Are we a nation, are we a religion, or are we an amalgamation of both?

In truth, one of the most agonizing problems facing the Jewish people of Israel as well as the Diaspora, an issue which can potentially tear us asunder and make a mockery of the Jewish Federation slogan "We are one," is "Who is a Jew." From a technical, legal perspective, this question expresses itself in the requirements for conversion, the

---

* The Hebrew letters *ayin, mem* may form a word translated as "with," 'together,' or 'collective.'

ramifications of which impinge on who qualifies for automatic Israeli citizenship under the "Right of Return," an Israeli law that provides automatic citizenship for any "Jew" who desires to live there. This law was enacted as an obvious and proud reaction to the tragic situation in the 1930s and 1940s, when Jews were sent to the gas chambers because virtually no existing country would relax their immigration rules and allow the would-be refugees a haven from Nazi persecution. In a far broader way, however, the "Who is a Jew" controversy speaks volumes about "what is Judaism"; after all, the necessary criteria for entering our fellowship will pretty much define the cardinal principles of that fellowship.

The sages of the Talmud, as interpreted by Rabbi Yosef Karo's sixteenth-century code of Jewish Law, set down three criteria for male conversion, with the latter two forming the criteria for female conversion: circumcision, immersion in a *mikve* (ritualarium), and acceptance of the commandments (*Shulḥan Arukh*, Yoreh Deah, 268:3).

The casting off of the foreskin connotes the removal of gentiledom, the separation of the Jew from the licentious practices (especially in the sexual realm) which characterized the pagan world (interestingly enough, the sages saw women as "naturally circumcised.")

Ritual immersion symbolizes rebirth – after all, the fetus is encompassed in fluid and birth is presaged by the "breaking" of the mother's "waters" – into a new family-nation. (A similar ritual was adopted by Christianity in the form of baptism.)

The acceptance of the commandments signals the entry into a religion, a faith community bound together by common adherence to a system of ritual, moral and ethical laws. With this understanding it becomes clear that we are a nation as well as a religion, a nation with a separate language, culture and homeland and a religion with a unique code of law defining our prayer rituals, feasts and fasts, life-cycle celebrations, and ethical behavior.

Fascinatingly enough, the Bible records just such a process of development, a "national conversion," as it were, in the Torah portions in the middle of the book of Exodus. In the Exodus from Egypt, the Israelites separated themselves from the Egyptians, the Egyptian enslavement, the Egyptian concept of slavery as a societal norm, and the immoral Egyptian lifestyle. The Bible suggests that the Jews expressed this removal from

"Egyptiandom" with circumcision, since the Paschal lamb sacrifice could only be eaten by males who were circumcised (Ex. 12:48). The Midrash explains precisely when the circumcision took place. The Bible provides for the Israelite preparation for the Exodus, commanding each household to take a lamb on the tenth of Nisan, to guard the lamb until the fourteenth of Nisan, and then to sacrifice the lamb to God (their disavowal of Egyptian idolatry, since the lamb was one of the Egyptian gods) and place its blood on their doorposts. On the night of the fifteenth they were to eat the lamb – their first *seder* – and then exit from Egypt.

Asks the Midrash, why take the lamb on the tenth and wait until the fourteenth to sacrifice it? The Midrash answers that the male Israelites were to have themselves circumcised, and by merit of the twofold blood of the sacrifice and the circumcision they would be found worthy by God to be freed from Egypt (Ex. 12:6, *Mekhilta* and Rashi ad loc.). Indeed, in Temple times, a convert was expected not only to have himself circumcised, but to bring a sacrificial offering as well (Maimonides, Laws of Forbidden Relationships, 13:1).

The ritual immersion of the Israelites took place right before the revelation at Sinai, either when God commanded Moses to see that the people "be sanctified and their clothing be washed" (Ex. 19:10, see Maimonides, Laws of Forbidden Relationships, 13, 2–3), or when the Israelites jumped into the Reed Sea before it split ("and the children of Israel entered into the midst of the waters on the dry land..." [Ex. 14:22]). And of course the acceptance of the commandments came following the Decalogue and the subsequent legal code, but as a prerequisite to the confirmation of the eternal covenant between God and Israel: "... And the entire nation responded with one voice and declared.. 'All that the Lord has spoken, we shall do and we shall internalize'" [Ex. 24:3, 7]. Indeed, prior to the formula of acceptance, the Bible not only recorded the Ten Commandments as well as the major civil and ritual laws, but also outlined the eventual borders of the Land of Israel which the Jews would occupy (Ex. 23:20–25). In effect, therefore, the Israelites were accepting both Jewish nationality and Jewish religion. We came to be bound together (*am* contains the same letters as the word *im*, which means "together") by common genes, land and destiny as well as by a unifying system of laws, values and lifestyle.

Now, does this mean that a person can only convert to Judaism if he/she lives in our Jewish homeland and is observant of all of the commandments? Perhaps the book of Ruth suggests that this be the case, having Ruth say to Naomi, "Where you shall go [to your homeland Israel], there shall I go; your nation shall by my nation, your God [religion] shall be my God" (Ruth 1:16). However, since the Babylonian expulsion of the Jews from Israel (586 BCE), a majority of Jews have lived in the Diaspora – even during the Second Commonwealth. Hence the rabbis accepted even converts living in the Diaspora. And many religio-legal decisors have also ruled that although acceptance of commandments is a necessary prerequisite for conversion, there is no requirement to teach all of the 613 commandments with their respective rabbinic injunctions and enactments; indeed, the Talmud merely requires "several of the more stringent laws and several of the more lenient laws," specifically mentioning the laws of the Sabbath, kashrut and tithing (charity to the poor).* There is nevertheless a general consensus amongst the rabbinic authorities that circumcision for males, and ritual immersion and a general acceptance of commandments for both males and females, are clear and absolute requirements for conversion. After all, becoming Jewish is not merely an acquisition of a new garment; it is a commitment which connotes sacrifice, a willingness to share a national destiny of yearning for Zion and perfecting the world (*tikkun olam*) and participating in a tradition of faith and habitual norms which have united Jews from Ethiopia, Yemen, Jerusalem, New York and Melbourne for 4,000 years. And it was these very requirements which the Israelites fulfilled at the very dawn of their history.

---

* See *Yevamot* 45b–47a.

Religious Coercion vs. Religious Conviction

> *And the entire nation responded together and said,*
> *"Everything which the Lord has spoken, we shall*
> *do."*
>
> EXODUS 19:8

What would happen if one of the religious parties in Israel received a majority of the popular vote, or was at least in the position of leading a coalition government? Would they set up moral squads to separate amorous couples, open up prisons for those who mix meat and milk dishes, and mete out corporal punishment for Shabbat desecrators?

I truly believe that despite the fact that we believe in 613 commandments, not 613 options, or possibilities, secular Israel need not necessarily fear a fundamentalist religious state. In the words of Rabbi Joseph B. Soloveitchik, religious commitment and religious coercion are mutually exclusive terms.

A midrashic interpretation of a verse in *Yitro* seems to lead to the opposite conclusion of what has just been said.

> And Moses brought the people out of the camp to meet with God, and they stood at the foot of the mountain.
>
> Exodus 19:17

R. Abdimi bar Hama comments that the verse comes to teach us that God picked up the mountain and "held it over their heads like a barrel, threatening

> If you will accept the Torah – good; if not, there shall be your burial.
>
> *Shabbat* 88a

This is a difficult commentary at the very least. After all, the plain meaning of the biblical text portrays the Israelites as having accepted the Torah of their own free will. God enters into a covenant with the children of Abraham only after they declare, "We shall do and we shall obey [*na'aseh ve-nishma*]." R. Abdimi's midrashic reading contradicts this description at the conclusion of the Torah portion of *Mishpatim*.

Based upon our earlier citation, Rabbi Soloveitchik is obviously disturbed by the ramifications of this midrash. In a footnote to one of the passages in his novella *The Lonely Man of Faith*, the sage maintains that the biblical description of freely accepted obligation is dealing with the "in general" acquiescence of the Israelites to live by divine will. The talmudic addition of coercion refers to the details of the religio-legal structure, concerning which different individuals at different times must be forced to comply.

In order to understand this position in greater detail, it is important to study a passage in Maimonides' *Code of Jewish Law* pertaining to divorce. Maimonides writes that if a man is ordered by a Jewish court to grant his wife a divorce and he refuses to do so, he must be forced (through financial sanctions, the removal of professional and personal licenses such as a medical license or a driver's license, incarceration or even physical beatings) to comply

> until he says I want to divorce her. He then gives her a *get* [writ of divorce] and the *get* is valid [*kosher*].
>
> Laws of Divorce 2:20

Isn't this coercion? Doesn't Jewish law require that a *get* be given of one's own volition? How can a court coerce an individual into saying "I want to"?

Maimonides continues, explaining the logic of the Talmud:

> We do not consider anyone to be compelled unless he is forced to do something which the Torah does not obligate him to do...but someone whose evil desire encourages him to nullify a commandment or commit a transgression can be beaten until he does what he is obligated to do or until he stops doing what he is forbidden to do. This is not considered coercion because it is as if his own evil instincts compelled him to go against the Torah. Although this individual may not want to divorce his wife, since he does wish to be a member of the Jewish people, and he does desire to keep the commandments and keep away from transgression, except that in this instance, his evil instinct overpowered him, we therefore beat him until his evil instinct becomes weakened. He then says, "I want to give her a divorce."
>
> ibid.

Using terminology from the *Zohar*, Rabbi A.Y. Hakohen Kook would explain the dilemma of this recalcitrant husband in terms of two "wills" within the human personality, a "lower will" and a "higher will." Each person must somehow orchestrate these two inclinations. An individual who is on a diet, for example, and is offered chocolate cream pie, might well say, "My lower will wants it, but my higher will does not." Similarly in this case: the lower will of the husband might want to lash out at the woman, but the *Bet Din* knows that the individual's higher will truly wants to do what is right.

If this indeed is the correct interpretation of Maimonides' ruling, one might fear that when it comes to the question of keeping the Shabbat in a Torah majority government with the power to enact laws, the ruling party might very well argue that the higher will of the Israeli citizenry wants to go to synagogue and not the cinema on Friday night, wants to eat kugel and not cheeseburgers, and on this basis argue that religious legislation is the higher will of every Jew in Israel. In the final analysis it is rather paternalistic to tell the secular Jew "I know that what you really want is to *daven* rather than disco on Friday evening!"

Rabbi Meir Simcha of Dvinsk, a nineteenth-century commentator on the Bible and the *Mishneh Torah*, interprets Maimonides' law about the forcing of a divorce differently. Maintaining that the last two sentences in the previous citation regarding divorce seem superfluous, he interprets Maimonides to be saying that only a person who has announced that he is observant of religious law (*Torah u-mitzvot*) and that he wants to keep all the commandments may be compelled to listen to the sages. To return to our earlier example, if I am offered a piece of chocolate cream pie and my wife says "He does not want it," she is being paternalistic. But if I just joined Weight Watchers, she is being helpful.

Certainly, the interpretation of Rabbi Meir Simcha applies in the realm of purely religious actions, between the individual and God. In the area of interpersonal human relationships, a court of law can and must use coercion in order to establish a just society in which no one may be allowed to unjustly take advantage of the other. But in the area of religious law, of what value to God is a ritual act coerced by religious judges? Hence, only those who publicly identify themselves with the tradition may be considered to be exercising this higher will if they are coerced to perform a ritual act. The truth is that in the world at large this is exactly how we live. Assume for a moment that an individual is caught speeding and a policeman pulls him to the side. A natural tendency might be to try to get out of the ticket by coming up with all sorts of stories, explaining that he was driving to a special occasion to which one could not be late, or pleading a momentary lapse of awareness. But no one in their right mind would argue that they are opposed to the entire system of traffic laws, that it is everyone's democratic right to drive their car as quickly as (or in whichever direction) their fancy takes them. The assumption of whoever applies for a driver's license is their acceptance of the traffic laws. People understand that these laws merely help them to keep to the regulations which they know are for everyone's good, including their own!

We constantly see how laws intervene in the actions of people if such actions endanger others. This is the unspoken agreement between all members of society. When it comes to areas of ritual law between human and God, however, any enforced action will only empty the deed of any semblance of true religious significance or divine service. Only for those who privately and publicly accept the entire system of divine commandments and rabbinic interpretation, and who are desirous of a punitive structure to help keep them on the straight and narrow in terms of specific details, does any kind of external regulation begin to make sense. Everyone ought to be punished for traffic violations, but not necessarily for Shabbat desecration. Regarding the Shabbat, one must first be convinced, not coerced.

The Divine Marriage between God and Israel

> *The whole nation trembled... and they stood
> under the mountain. And Mount Sinai was
> completely enveloped in smoke because the
> Lord descended upon it in fire... and the whole
> mountain trembled exceedingly.*
>
> EXODUS 19:16–18

From Madonna to adult education classes from coast to coast, the Jewish (and even gentile) world has become enraptured with the heretofore esoteric study of the *kabbala* (literally, that which was "received" from earlier generations), which is largely based upon the mystical interpretation of the Bible found in the *Zohar* (literally, splendorous light) and its commentaries. In order to provide a glimpse into this kabbalistic approach to Bible study, let us examine the more mystical interpretation of the atmosphere surrounding the revelation at Sinai; you will immediately see that the mystical school of thought has transformed a *mysterium tremendum* of fear and trembling into a sacred marriage of love and commitment – with fascinating ramifications affecting our liturgy, our theology and our husband-wife relationships.

When the Bible reports that the "whole nation … stood under the mountain," Rashi cites the talmudic commentary:

> The Almighty held the mountain over them like a barrel [can also be translated as canopy], threatening them with death if they would not accept the commandments.
>
> *Shabbat* 88a

The *Zohar* accepts the interpretation that the mountain was held over them like a canopy; however, it was not a canopy of coercion, but rather a canopy of commitment, a nuptial canopy (*ḥuppa*) of love and marriage.

For the *Zohar*, there is only one great love in the Bible, the love-covenant between God and Israel. The revelation at Sinai formalized and legalized that love relationship, providing the marriage contract (*ketuba*) in the form of the Commandments, and the consent of the bride-Israel with the words, "We shall do [commit] and we shall obey [internalize], *na'aseh ve-nishma*" (Ex. 24:7).

Every human love relationship is merely a spark of that fiery passion at Sinai; hence, the bride and groom are walked to the nuptial canopy amidst the fire of candles, and the bride walks around her groom seven times, reminiscent of the seven expressions of betrothal enunciated by the prophet Hosea:

> I [God] shall betroth you [Israel] unto Me forever; I shall betroth you unto Me in righteousness, in justice, in lovingkindness and compassion; I shall betroth you unto Me in faithfulness and you shall know [love] the Lord.
>
> Hos. 2:21–22

You will notice that in this ritual of the seven expressions of divine betrothal of Israel, it is the woman who encompasses the man, the bride who seems to be the more dominant, representing the divine. You will also remember that in the kabbalistic-Hassidic tradition, the noun generally used for God is "*Shekhina*," literally the Divine Presence dwelling in the world, which is a feminine form.*

When we move into the realm of liturgy and Sabbath ritual, the kabbalistic imagery and all of its ramifications become magnificently clear. We recite three major and different Amidot (standing silent prayers) on the Sabbath: one in the evening, one the following morning, and the final one in the afternoon. The evening Amida evokes the Sabbath of creation, citing the biblical verses, "And the heavens and the earth and all of their hosts were completed. And the Lord completed on the seventh day His creativity which He had made…".

It is the woman (bride) who is endowed with the major spark of divine creativity, since it is she who nurtures the fetus in her womb and actually gives birth to the child. The *Kabbalat Shabbat* Friday evening prayer liturgy – introducing the evening service and created by the mystical interpreters of the *Zohar* in sixteenth century Safed – features the *Shekhina*, the feminine aspect of the divine: the Eshet Hayil (literally, Woman of Valor) Sabbath evening song actually refers to the *Shekhina* (so it is even to be recited or sung around the table if no woman is present), and in the "Lekha Dodi" chant we go out to greet the Sabbath – *Shekhina* – Queen-bride. Moreover, in this Sabbath evening Amida we ask that "All of Israel who sanctify Your name shall rest in her (*vah*)," a feminine pronoun, and the leader of the Sabbath table first slices the bottom *ḥalla* (of the two *ḥallot*), which likewise symbolizes the woman. No wonder the betrothal ceremony opens with the bride representing God and encompassing the groom! Indeed, the Hassidic sages note that the opening words of the Friday evening Amida are "*ata kidashta*," literally "You sanctified" or "You betrothed" (*kiddushin* can be translated as sanctification or betrothal); Friday evening likewise begins our sacred marriage with God.

The morning Amida evokes the Sabbath of revelation, describing the glory of Moses as he descended from Mount Sinai with the two tablets of stone in his hands, on which were written the laws of the Sabbath.

---

* The Hebrew feminine form consists of words ending in *ah* (*kamatz heh*), such as *yaldah*, a small girl, or *shifhah*, a maidservant.

In the act of revelation it was the masculine aspect of God which was dominant, the God-groom who chose His bride Israel and gave her His contract of marriage. Therefore, in the Sabbath morning Amida we ask that "all of Israel who sanctify Your Name shall rest in Him" (*vo*), a male pronoun, and the leader of the Sabbath morning table first slices the upper *halla* (of the two *hallot*), which symbolizes the male. And so it is traditionally the male who gives the ring – as well as the marriage contract – to his bride. Sabbath morning, explain the Hassidic sages, evokes the gifts and feasts (sacrificial meats of the *Musaf* Amida) of the betrothal meal.

The concluding Sabbath afternoon Amida pictures the Sabbath of Redemption, when You (God) are One and Your name is One, a God of peace accepted by the entire world. This can only come about when the masculine and feminine aspects of the divine, God and His bride Israel, act in concert together to bring about the perfection of the world in peace and tranquility. In this Amida we ask that "all of Israel who sanctify your name shall rest in them (*vam*)," a plural pronoun, and the leader of the Sabbath third meal table slices both *hallot* together.

The parallel to the wedding celebration is the *yihud*, or marital home, where bride and groom live together as one in harmony and equality, with neither dominating the other. And so the religious mystics transformed a biblical passage of awesome and even fearful dimensions into a song of love and mutuality which reverberates within our Sabbath liturgy and ritual as well as in the marriage ceremony and its message.

The Rationality of Revelation, the Song of Sinai

> *There was the sound of a ram's horn, increasing in volume to a great degree. Moses would speak, and God would respond with a voice.*
>
> EXODUS 19:19

The seminally defining moment for all of Jewish history – past, present and future – was undoubtedly the revelation at Sinai. This moment formed and informed the Israelites as God enthused and infused a nation destined to redeem the world with the ideal of ethical monotheism. It is clear even to the most secular-oriented historian that something unique must have transpired at Sinai to have transformed a bedraggled group of newly freed slaves into an inspired nation, centered upon God, united by a vision of "a holy people and a kingdom of priests" (Ex. 19:6). Exactly what happened – and how much was imparted to how many? Did God Himself, as it were, indeed transmit the commandments, or even the first two commandments, to the hundreds of thousands of

Israelites standing at the foot of the mountain? Did everyone actually hear the voice of the divine?

The terse biblical introduction to the event, described in *Yitro*, thrills even as it mystifies:

> Mount Sinai was all in smoke because of the Presence that had come down on it. God was in the fire, and its smoke went up like the smoke of a lime kiln. The entire mountain trembled violently. There was the sound of a ram's horn, increasing in volume to a great degree. Moses would speak, and God would respond with a voice.
>
> Exodus 19:15–19

This last verse is the most problematic. I heard in the name of the great and awesome Hassidic sage, Rabbi Menachem Mendel of Kotzk, the startling idea that perhaps the interpretation of the words "Moses spoke, and God responded with a voice" is that the special Sinaitic message was initiated by Moses, to which God responded with divine assent: God said Amen, as it were, to Moses' words. However, the Hebrew addition "with a voice (*be-kol*)" would then appear to be superfluous, and more to the point, such an interpretation is soon demolished by introductory words to the Decalogue:

> And God spoke all these words, saying "I am God your Lord, who brought you out of Egypt..."
>
> Ex. 20:2

And in the first person at that! At the very least, the Kotzker, a strong believer in the power of the individual, is saying that Moses was more than a mere "dictaphone" for God's words. This is borne out by many of our traditional commentaries. Both as the consummate student of the divine as well as the consummate communicator of the divine message, Moses certainly played a major role in the divine revelation, as we shall soon see in the words of our classical commentaries.

Rashi explains that the Israelites actually heard only the first two commandments from God Himself, and the rest from Moses, who acted as a mediator, imparting God's message in a less awesome and fear-inducing manner. Moses' voice was hardly strong enough to be heard by the multitude of Israelites (600,000 men, with the addition of a far greater number of women and children). Hence, "...the Holy One blessed be He helped to give him [Moses] the vocal strength so that his voice would be magnified and heard." The biblical text is therefore teaching that Moses spoke the last eight commandments, and the Almighty responded by increasing the volume of Moses' voice.

Rabbi Eliezer, in the *Midrash Mekhilta*, gives another interpretation: Moses had to give God the signal to speak, and to inform the Almighty that the Israelites were ready to accept His words; only after Moses said to God "Speak" was the Almighty ready to impart His message (*Mekhilta* ad loc).

Maimonides, perhaps building on these words of Rabbi Eliezer, provides a somewhat radical approach, which is at the same time eminently reasonable and rational. This great philosopher and legalist cannot accept the notion that all of the Israelites were at the peak of such prophetic power. For him this means the attainment of intellectual, spiritual and ethical excellence, that they could all hear the divine word, with everyone being on the same exalted level of spirituality and intellect. Maimonides maintains that, although the Israelites were all in the category of prophets:

> The people only heard the mighty sound, *kol,* not distinct words. It was only Moses [who had achieved the greatest distinction of prophecy] who heard the words, who was able to perceive the real message of the divine, and then reported them [that is, his unique perception and profound understandings] to the people.
> *Guide for the Perplexed,* Part 11, Chapter 23

The divine *kol* or voice takes on special meaning according to this interpretation of Maimonides. The Almighty responded with His voice to all of Israel, and it was Moses, and only Moses, who was able to speak distinct words to the Israelites in accordance with his prophetic understanding of that voice.

From this perspective of Maimonides, Moses was much more

than a dictaphone, transcribing a divine message. He was the greatest
of all prophets, whose high intellectual and spiritual elevation enabled
him to understand the divine message like no other person in the world.
Moses' active intellect had reached the highest level of prophecy and
joined, as it were, the divine active intellect.

The talmudic interpretation of the multi-faceted verse under discussion adds another dimension to Moses' greatness as well as to our
understanding of his ministry.

> R. Shimon ben Pazi says: "How do we know that the inter-
> preter [*metargem*] is not allowed to raise his voice louder than
> the reader?" Scripture teaches: Moses would speak, and God
> would respond with a voice. Scripture did not have to add "with
> a voice." What is the significance of "with a voice?" With the
> voice of Moses.
>
> *Berakhot* 45a

All of the commentaries understand the reader to be God, and the interpreter to be Moses. God made certain that His voice, as it were, and
Moses' voice were equal in volume when Moses transmitted the divine
message to the Israelites. Moses' major purpose and ministry lay in com-
municating the eternal words to the people of Israel. Since the Torah
was meant for the people of Israel and would serve no purpose on earth
had it not been accepted by them, there is a fascinating parallel between
the initiator of the word and the one who imparts it to the entire nation!

A return look at the *Midrash Mekhilta* will provide an even deeper
understanding of the very unique function of Moses, as well as of that
of every teacher of the divine word even today. We have seen how R.
Eliezer interpreted the verse in question as teaching that Moses had to
inform God of the Israelites' readiness to accept His commands before
He would present them.

> R. Akiva said to him: Certainly that is the case. So why does
> Scripture record: "Moses will speak"? It is in order to teach that
> the Holy One blessed be He gave strength and power to Moses...

and aided him with the voice and melody [*ne'imah*] which he
would enable Israel to internalize [*lehashmia*].

Mekhilta to Exodus 19:19

R. Akiva provides a fascinating addition not only to the words of R.
Eliezer, but to the words of Rashi as well. Rashi views God as techni-
cally magnifying Moses' voice, as increasing the volume of the sound.
R. Akiva views God as helping Moses discover the proper melody, the
music which would enable the divine words to take root in the hearts
and souls of each individual Israelite. Moses the interpreter, Moses the
educator, Moses the rebbe, must not only understand the divine message himself as a result of his exalted position as prophet par excellence,
he must additionally, and even more importantly, find the way to the
soul of every individual Jew. He must discover the open aorta within
each heart which would be receptive to a specific aspect of the eternal
message of God. The way to do this is by expressing not only the sense
of the Torah but also its song, not only the mentality of the word but
also its melody.

Words speak to the intellect; music affects the emotions. Ideas
enter the mind; melodies suffuse the soul. Torah is not only a system for
the brain; Torah is first and foremost the wisdom of the heart. A rebbe
must touch as well as teach. The teacher's task is to sensitize the soul as
well as to sharpen the thought processes. The sages of the Talmud teach:

> R. Yehuda says in the name of Shmuel: How do we know that
> the essence of song is from the Torah [because the Torah is
> referred to as a song]?...R. Yehoshua says: From here: "Moses
> would speak, and God would respond with a voice" – referring
> to music, which the voice is engaged in. Rashi interprets: [God]
> commanded Moses to sing, for Moses was a Levite [the tribe
> known for its cantorial abilities].

Arakhin 11a

This added understanding of the "mighty voice" or song (*kol*) of the
divine sheds new light on the very difficult phrase immediately following

the decalogue. "And the entire nation saw the voices [or the sounds, *kolot*]" (Ex. 20:16). Targum Yonatan ben Uziel writes:

> And the entire nation saw the voices, how they changed as they were internalized by every individual.
>
> Exodus 20:16

Perhaps they even saw the different notes which expressed the unique melodies specific to every soul.

There is a fascinating linguistic connection between the Hebrew word for shoots (as in planting) – "*zemorot*" – and the Hebrew word for songs, "*zemirot*." Jacob sent his sons with the gifts of fruits of the land for the Grand Vizier of Egypt, which he calls "*zimrat ha'aretz*," – "the song of the land" (Gen. 43:11). Just as shoots take root in the soil, so does a melody take root in the soul, and just as different shoots require different climatic conditions, different melodies will find their ways to different souls. It is no mere coincidence that both the Torah of Israel as well as the Land of Israel are biblically referred to as *morasha*, which our sages connect to *me'orasa*, or beloved fiancee. One must love the Torah as well as the land if one is to acquire both of them. The language of love is individual as well as collective, poetry as well as prose, music as well as words.

A story is told of Rabbi Shneur Zalman of Liadi, the founder of Habad Hassidut. During the third meal of the Shabbat, which he was sharing with his many disciples, he suddenly sent his *gabbai* outside to bring in a Lithuanian peasant. "I feel a connection to your soul," said the Rebbe. "Tell me your background." To the surprise of the assemblage, the peasant recounted that he was brought up as a Christian, but had been found on the doorstep by his adoptive parents. The Rebbe concluded that the peasant was Jewish, left at the door of a gentile when they fled from a pogrom, and indeed the stranger admitted to strong feelings of closeness to Jews and Judaism all of his life. The Rebbe sat him next to him, and gave a lengthy discourse on the Torah portion. "Do you understand?" he asked the guest. "Not at all, *nyet*," he replied in Russian. The Rebbe then recounted a parable. "Do you understand?" "*Nyet*," was the response. And then the Rebbe began to sing a melody, and his

Hassidim joined him. The Rebbe and the Hassidim clapped their hands and danced in a circle. The peasant sang and clapped and danced as well. "Now I understand," he cried out, tears coursing down his cheeks. "I've come home. I understand."

Moses used the same sounds of music to enable the truths of Torah to penetrate the soul of every single Israelite at Sinai. Moses continued his Song of the Sea with the Song of Sinai. God gave the words and Moses the Levite provided the melody (*nigun*), and so Torah is our greatest expression of *shira*.

The True Meaning of Holiness

Remember the Sabbath day to keep it holy.

EXODUS 20:8

What is holiness and how do we achieve it? The word for holy, *kadosh*, appears in its various grammatical forms more than two hundred times in the Bible, but a clear definition of the term itself is still difficult to formulate.

Generally, we associate holiness with a separation from mundane, materialistic pursuits, an isolation and insulation from the world and its temptations. But I'd like to suggest that the Jewish concept of holiness is almost the exact opposite of this idea of separation from the world; on the contrary, only by direct, vital and passionate involvement in the world will one achieve true sanctity.

The first time a form of the word "*kadosh*" appears in the Torah is at the very beginning of creation in the context of the first Sabbath:

... And God blessed the seventh day and sanctified [*va-yekadesh*] it, because on it He rested from all His work which God had created to perform.

Genesis 2:3

In the portion of *Yitro*, the fourth of the Ten Commandments is the mandate to keep the Sabbath, and, as we expect to find, holiness is at the heart of the ordinance: "Remember the Sabbath day to keep it holy. Six days shall you labor, and do all your creative activity. But the seventh day is a Sabbath unto God your Lord" (Ex. 20:8–9).

Interestingly enough, the Decalogue is repeated in the book of Deuteronomy, but with a slight word change in the introduction to the Sabbath commandment: "Observe the Sabbath day to keep it holy..." (Deut. 5:12). The opening stanza of the Friday evening prayer-song "Lekha Dodi," (Come My Beloved to Greet the Bride), "Observe [*shamor*] and remember [*zakhor*] in a single command, the one and only God made us hear," implies that the verbal imperatives are to be synthesized and taken together as one. Nahmanides suggests that "Remember" implies the positive commands relating to the Sabbath – such as Kiddush, the three festive meals and the joyous relaxation – whereas "Observe" implies the negative commands relating to the Sabbath, such as the prohibited acts of physical creativity. Hence, the sages and the Sabbath prayer book are enjoining us to take the positive and negative as two sides of the same coin, one reinforcing and enhancing the other.

I would like to suggest another interpretation and inter-relationship between these two versions of the Sabbath command in the two expressions of the Decalogue which will revolutionize our understanding of holiness. But first we must attempt to understand two seemingly contradictory rulings attributed to the great Mishnaic sage, R. Shimon bar Yochai.

In a well-known talmudic passage discussing professional pursuits, R. Yishmael teaches that the verse "You shall gather your grain" (Deut. 11:14) modifies the verse "You shall meditate [in Torah] by day and by night" (Joshua 1:8). He interprets the command to study Torah to mean for a period during the day and a period during the night, and advocates a lifestyle combining Torah study and an agricultural (or similar professional) pursuit. R. Shimon bar Yochai disagrees:

If a man plows in the plowing season, and sows in the sowing season, and reaps in the reaping season, and threshes in the threshing season... what is to become of the Torah? But as long as Israel performs the will of God, their manual labor will be performed by others, as it says, "And strangers shall stand and feed your flocks" (Is. 61:5). It is only when Israel does not perform the will of God that they must perform their work by themselves, as it says, "And you shall gather in your corn."

Berakhot 35b

However, in another talmudic text (*Menaḥot* 99b), the same R. Shimon b. Yochai surprisingly declares that merely by reciting the Shema (a Torah portion in its own right) for a few moments in the morning and for a few moments in the evening, one satisfactorily fulfills the command "to meditate [in Torah] by day and by night."

To resolve this contradiction, we turn to another fascinating talmudic text. Three sages of the Mishna are discussing Rome. The first praises Rome for building such fine bridges, bathhouses and marketplaces; the second sage is silent, and the third, R. Shimon bar Yohai, claims that Rome is only interested in Rome's material self-interest, building "...the marketplaces to put harlots in them, bath-houses to rejuvenate themselves and bridges to levy tolls..." The government of Rome apparently did not believe in freedom of speech, and a death warrant was issued for R. Shimon.

R. Shimon bar Yochai and his son flee to a cave in the hills of Peki'in, where they spend the next twelve years studying Torah in splendid isolation (one interpretation has it that they discovered the mystical secrets of the *Zohar*). They receive nourishment from a well and a carob tree which miraculously springs up for their sustenance. Elijah informs them that the Caesar has died and they may emerge from the cave.

The first thing they see, a Judean farmer plowing his land, fills them with dismay and shock: "How dare one forsake eternal life and engage in temporal life!" And whatever they cast their eyes upon is immediately burnt up. A *bat kol* (heavenly voice) rebukes them for their destructive gaze, asking, "Did you leave the cave to destroy My world?"

and they return to the cave. Twelve months pass before they leave, and this time the first thing that they see is

> ...an old man holding two bundles of myrtle and running during the pre-Sabbath twilight. "What are these for?" they asked him. "They are in honor of the Sabbath," he replied. "But one should be enough?" To which the old man answered that one branch is for "Remember" and the other branch is for "Observe." At this point, R. Shimon turned to his son and said, "See how precious are the commandments to Israel." And they were comforted.
>
> *Shabbat* 33b

R. Shimon bar Yochai's two contradictory responses to the world, initial contempt followed by eventual acceptance and affirmation, are reflected in the two contradictory passages that we cited earlier: In his denigration of gathering grain, where he disagrees with R. Yishmael's idea of combining Torah study with work and insists on total devotion to Torah, R. Shimon is expressing his position before emerging from the cave for the second time; the talmudic statement in R. Shimon's name maintaining that one need not dedicate all day and all night to Torah study and holding open the door to combining Torah and profession is an outgrowth of the lesson R. Shimon learned from the old man with the myrtle branches.

And what was that lesson? The Sabbath is a taste of a world of perfection and peace, truth and tranquility, the World to Come. But that vision is not yet our reality. We still live in a world of darkness as well as light, of chaos as well as order, of sin as well as merit, of persecution as well as joy. We must observe the Sabbath every seventh day in order to keep alive the vision and promise of a more perfect world which is to come, but we must remember the Sabbath day ideal and actively work towards bringing about that redemption during the other six days of the week. Our task is to change the world from what it is now, to plow and reap myrtle branches, to enhance our meal of Sabbath peace and taste of Eden during the days of preparation. And if we properly remember the goal of the Sabbath during the six days of labor, if our anticipation turns into preparation, then our means will contain the sparks of sanctity so crucial to our achieving the end. Hence our Torah contains laws of plowing and reaping: prohibitions against plowing with an ox and donkey together in concern for the welfare of the brute beast, leaving behind portions of our land and produce for the poor in consideration for the less fortunate, specific rules of conduct determining how we do business, how we conduct our most intimate family life, and what kinds of food we eat.

We must remember the sanctity of the Sabbath, when we prepare for redemption during the six days of the week by working in this world to achieve the goal of perfection, and we must observe the sanctity of the Sabbath in order to keep alive our vision of ultimate peace and harmony while we still live in an imperfect world. The old man with the myrtle branches taught R. Shimon the true message of sanctity:

> And God blessed the seventh day and sanctified it, because on it He rested from all the work which God had created [human beings] to perform.
>
> Genesis 2:3

It is a divine command for us to work six days to bring about the ultimate perfection; remember and observe are truly one commandment! And we achieve true sanctity not by separating ourselves from the world, but rather by our engaging the world and sanctifying every aspect of it.

The Decalogue: Morality for the World

> *Six days shall you labor, and do all your creative*
> *activity. But the seventh day is a Sabbath unto*
> *God your Lord.*
>
> EXODUS 20:9

As we have mentioned, the most stirring, supernatural and significant event in the entire Bible is the divine revelation at Sinai, the "Ten Commandments," which provided Israel and the world with a quintessential message of morality necessary for the transformation – and salvation – of humanity. When we attempt to analyze the content of these Ten Commandments, the first three speak of God (the Lord who took the Israelites out of Egyptian bondage, who shall have no other gods before Him, and whose name shall not be taken in vain), the fourth commands us to remember the Sabbath to sanctify it, the fifth enjoins honoring our parents, and the next five deal with universally accepted ethical principles: Thou shall not murder, thou shall not commit adultery, and thou shall not steal, thou shalt not bear false witness, thou shalt not covet (Ex. 20:1–4). One could not imagine a more finely crafted and relevant moral code for our postmodern, ethically perplexed, nuclear-empowered era – and we can only stand back in amazement to think that these words were uttered approximately four thousand years ago!

If we understand that the God in whom we are enjoined to believe – to the exclusion of false idols idealizing materialistic and even bestial end goals – is a God of love, compassion, graciousness, patient tolerance, loving-kindness and truth, then nine of these commandments deal with ethics and morality. After all, our religion is not only monotheism; it is ethical monotheism, believing in a God who demands justice, mercy and peace! Judaism has no respect for a monotheism which is not an ethical monotheism, the two words forming an inseparable compound noun. But then the one commandment of the ten which stands out as being different is the fourth one, "Remember the Sabbath day to keep it holy"; the Sabbath is a day dedicated to ritual, prayer and Torah study. It seems to be an exclusively Jewish religious expression, devoid of universalistic or even moralistic messages. How does the Sabbath fit into the universal design of the Decalogue?

I would like to even compound the question. The Decalogue was given barely six weeks after the splitting of the Reed Sea following the Exodus from Egypt. When the Torah tells us that God gave the Israelites at Marah a foretaste of the divine commandments, our sages teach that this "biblical introduction" consisted of the Sabbath laws, parental respect, and civil laws of business and neighborliness (Ex. 15:25, *Sanhedrin* 56b and Rashi to the Bible, ad loc.). Moreover, the Bible then records how the Israelites complain about the lack of food in the desert, and receive the special heavenly supply of manna: one sufficient portion each day for every family member, with a double portion for each on Friday in order that no one would have to gather the manna on the Sabbath. As the Bible expresses it:

> See that the Lord has given to you the Sabbath; therefore He gives to you on Friday a sufficient portion for two days. Let every

person dwell under himself.* Let no individual go out [or take out] from his place on the seventh day.

Exodus 16:29

Why this emphasis on the Sabbath only weeks before the central commandment will be given to the Israelites at Sinai as the fourth commandment? And what is the literal meaning of the rather difficult phrase just cited, "dwell under himself"?

I would argue that the single most revolutionary concept in the entire Torah is the concept of the Sabbath. After all, every totalitarian ruler, every slaveholder, insists that they control – nay, own – their citizenry or their slaves. As a result, it is the ruler or slaveowner who determines the hours and output of his servants. As a result, the Israelites worked in the slave-labor camps of Pharaoh building Pitom and Raamses for 210 years – and could not even get three days off for a religious celebration in the desert. Comes the Almighty and demands that every Israelite refrain from any kind of servile work on the Sabbath. In effect, God is insisting that He, and not Pharaoh, is the employer! Indeed, God is teaching that He is the ultimate employer because He – and not Pharaoh – owns the Israelites. He owns us because He created us, as the fourth commandment in the Decalogue teaches:

The seventh day is the day of rest before the Lord your God... For in six days God created the heavens and the earth... And He rested on the seventh day.

Exodus 20:9–10

And since God created all of humanity, He owns everyone. Hence, no human being dare enslave any other human being; we are, all of us, owned only by God, and therefore only He can determine when, and how, we are to work! The God of the Sabbath is the God of human freedom.

---

* According to Rashi, "under himself" means "within his own four cubits." Ibn Ezra interprets it as "within his own tent."

Therefore, immediately following the exodus from Egypt, we are already commanded at Marah the laws of the Sabbath, the consummate expression of the lesson of human freedom from enslavement which the Almighty taught in Egypt. Even Pharaoh himself learned this costly lesson at long last. When he summons his charioteers to overtake the fleeing Israelites, the text reads, "And he [Pharaoh] harnessed his chariot, and he took his nation with him" (Ex. 14:6). Rashi explains the "sea-change" in Pharaoh's mentality: he, himself, harnesses his own chariot. He is willing to lead his soldiers in the charge, endangering his own life first, and he even agrees to share the spoils of victory evenly with them (Rashi ad loc.).

The manna continues to emphasize this important lesson. Sustenance ultimately comes from God; no self-appointed patron has the right to demand enslavement in return for providing food. Since God is the ultimate employer (as well as benefactor), no human being – even if they are under orders from another human being – may leave his four cubits to gather food on the Sabbath day. The sacred *Zohar* even understands the phrase "Let every person dwell under him," to mean "Let every person dwell under Him," that is, only in fealty to the Divine Presence. Then a person will not go out to work on the Sabbath day. One will not even carry an object from place to place on the Sabbath day. After all, such transporting of objects connotes transference of ownership according to talmudic law – and the Sabbath teaches that the only true owner of the entire universe is the Almighty God.

The Decalogue opens:

> I am the Lord your God who took you out of the Land of Egypt, the house of bondage.
>
> Exodus 20:2

No law in any book of statutes expresses this revolutionary and universal truth with greater clarity than does the Sabbath, the fourth commandment of the Decalogue.

Observance without Religion, Orthopraxism without Spirituality

> *You shall not make with Me gods of gold or gods of silver...*
>
> EXODUS 20:20

Everyone knows that God gave ten commandments to Israel on Mount Sinai. But how many know that there were an additional three? Even as the sounds of thunder fade into the background and the smoke from Mount Sinai settles, the Torah adds three more commandments to the ten just given. What adds to the strangeness is that the portion of *Mishpatim*, which follows *Yitro*, is exclusively devoted to civil and criminal law. Thus it turns out that the three commandments after the Decalogue are uniquely centered between the cardinal Ten Commandments and the more day-to-day laws of *Mishpatim*, forcing us to consider what it is the Torah may be trying to teach us.

Let's look at these additional commandments themselves. God declares to Moses:

> ... You shall not make with Me gods of gold or gods of silver.
>
> Exodus 20:20

Next we read:

> When you eventually build a stone altar for Me, do not build it out of hewn stone, for if you lift up your sword against it, you have profaned it ...
>
> Exodus 20:21–22

And finally,

> You shall not climb up My altar with steps, so that your nakedness will not be revealed on it.
>
> Exodus 20:23

The first commandment against silver and gold gods directly prohibits idolatry; the second commandment, forbidding the creation of an altar from cut stone, suggests the sin of murder because the same instrument used to cut stone – iron – is also the substance from which armaments are fashioned. And walking up the altar in a way that reveals one's nakedness is an allusion to sexual immorality.

Rabbi Samson Rafael Hirsch points out that these three commandments are thematically unified by the fact that they allude to the three central pillars in Jewish law, prohibitions which are even held to be more important than an individual life: idolatry, murder and incest (or adultery). And so Rabbi Hirsch explains that after the Ten Commandments (which according to many commentators, especially Rabbenu Sa'adia Gaon, include all 613 commandments), the Torah gives us the three commandments that encapsulate the entire Torah – the most cardinal and stringent of our principles.

I'd like to suggest that these three commandments embrace three additional essentials in the Torah. If indeed the Ten Commandments are the seed for all 613 commandments, it turns out that after Moses gives the Torah to the people of Israel, he in effect is saying to them, "You think that now you have the whole Torah, and that if you do everything exactly the way it should be done, you'll be able to call yourself religious. But I want to remind you that after all is said and done, there are three issues that are absolutely vital and express underlying Torah ideology." Even the religiously observant may transgress these three. And if they do, they are behaving as scoundrels within the confines of the law. These three are guiding ideals which will prevent observance devoid of spirituality, orthopraxism empty of true ethical commitment.

"You shall not make *with Me* gods of gold or silver…" not only prohibits bowing down to images made of silver and gold, but also forbids living a materialistic way of life together with observance of Torah; it forbids turning the gold and silver itself into gods – the sin of worshiping a bank account. God, who must be worshiped exclusively, forbids you to combine commitment to Him with commitment to materialism and hedonism. This warning is precisely for those people who keep the Sabbath, eat strictly kosher and remember all the festivals, but who have the kind of monetary and lifestyle goals whereby they have in effect established a temple of gold alongside their synagogue or study hall. If the goal of Torah is to perfect the world under the kingship of God, one cannot devote oneself to the goal of physical acquisitions; the two are mutually exclusive.

The second prohibition alerts us to the moral contradiction inherent in creating an altar fashioned from the very instrument that kills. If God goes so far as to command that on His altar we cannot have stones carved by iron, even though the actual tool in the stonemason's hand may have never shed blood, then how much more are we forbidden to kill in the name of our beliefs. Thus, utterly alien to Judaism is the idea of jihad, a holy war that imposes our will on others.

Third, when the Torah forbids using steps to go up the altar, it is saying that worship of God and sexual immorality are incompatible. When the Torah was given, the religions of that age were intimately connected with sexuality, temple prostitutes, and orgiastic rites. Judaism was revolutionary when it taught that even the possibility of revealing nakedness underneath a robe was prohibited. Even today, innocent and naïve faith in a religious leader on the part of congregants and students can often be used by charismatic religious figures to wield their influence in any direction they choose – and not "for the sake of heaven." All too often respected religious "icons" take advantage of their special position, especially with young religious adherents. Don't get to the point when you, the teacher of the law, begin to think that you control the law and that you are above the law.

The significance of steps or a ramp leading up to the altar can also be understood in another way. Rabbi Moshe Besdin once explained to me that with a ramp you either go up or go down, progress or regress. However, with steps you can rest. The Torah may well be teaching us that when you are interested in ascending God's altar, you cannot stop to rest; you dare not fall into the trap of self-satisfaction and complacency. Judaism asks for constant examination, self-criticism and growth. The Tzemach Tzedek, one of the great Habad rabbis, once asked his students: Who stands higher on the ladder, the individual on the third rung or the individual on the tenth rung? The individual on the tenth rung, they all responded. Not necessarily, he qualified. If the individual on the tenth rung is going down or standing still, and the individual on the third rung is going up, the individual on the third rung stands higher than the individual on the tenth rung!

This last prohibition may also be understood in a third way. The Torah uses the word "*ma'alot*," which is usually translated as steps, but which can also be translated as "good qualities." So now the verse reads, "Do not climb up to My altar with your good qualities; so that your nakedness will not be revealed on it."

In this reading, God warns us that if we ascend to the altar of God flashing our good qualities, proud of our achievements and self-satisfied about all that we know, then the danger is that our nakedness – our weaknesses, our vulnerabilities, our fatal flaws – will soon be revealed. The altar cannot be a center for self-aggrandizement, a stage of religious worship from which we let others know how great we are; if we fall into this trap, God tells us that ultimately our nakedness – and not our greatness – will be revealed. The altar of God must be approached with a fundamental humility in the face of a true sense of our inadequacies; it dare not become a center of self-satisfaction, religious one-upmanship, and arrogance.

The following Hassidic tale illustrates this last point. In a certain town in Europe, there lived two Jews: One was Reb Haim, a great scholar, and the other was also called Haim, but he was an indigent porter who could barely read the Hebrew letters. The scholar married well, because the richest man in town came looking for the most brilliant mind in the yeshiva as his son-in-law, and gladly supported him in style. He eventually gained the respect and admiration of the entire town because for several hours a day his study was open to everyone who needed help or advice.

These very different people confronted each other daily. It happened that the porter would pray early in the morning so that he could start working as soon as possible in order to earn his meager living. Rushing out after the service, he would run into the great Reb Haim who arrived a little early for his ("late") *minyan*, since he stayed up until the early hours of the morning, learning Torah. In this way they "met" almost every day.

Reb Haim the scholar would always look at Haim the porter superciliously, with a whisper of thanks on his upturned lips, grateful that he could spend the day with the Torah and not work as a porter. Haim the porter, on the other hand, would look upon the scholar with yearning, feeling sad and unworthy that he couldn't spend his life studying the holy words too.

They both died on the same day and were judged by the heavenly court. First Haim the scholar was judged. All of his good deeds, years of long study, and righteous acts were placed on one side of the scale, and on the other side his daily sneer of self-satisfaction. The sneer outweighed all the good deeds. Then Haim the porter was judged. On one side of the scale were placed all his sins, and on the other side of the scale his daily sigh of yearning. When the scales finally settled, the sigh outweighed the sins and the sneer outweighed the merits. Only the humble Jew went straight to heaven.

Mishpatim

What Constitutes a Jewish Court?

> *These are the statutes which you must place before them.*
>
> EXODUS 21:1

I f two religiously observant Jews are engaged in a disagreement which has financial ramifications, are they permitted to go to a secular court to arbitrate their dispute or must they go to a religious court or *bet din*? Is the law different in Israel, which has a religious as well as a secular court system, but where even the secular court judges are Jewish? And if indeed Jews are religiously ordained to go to religious courts exclusively, why is this the case? After all, secular courts in America are certainly fair and equitable!

The Torah portion of *Mishpatim* provides interesting responses to all three questions. It opens with the command: "These are the statutes which you [the Israelites] shall place before them [the religious judges]" (Ex. 21:1). Rashi immediately cites the talmudic limitation (*Gittin* 88b):

> Before the religious judges and not before gentile judges. And
> even if you know that regarding a particular case, they [the gen-
> tile judges] would rule in the exact same way as the religious
> judges, you dare not bring a judgment before the secular courts.
> Israelites who appear before gentile judges desecrate the name
> of God and cause idols to be honored and praised.
>
> *Tanḥuma Mishpatim* 3

According to this passage, it would seem that the primary prohibition
is to appear before gentile judges who are likely to dedicate their legal
decision to a specific idol or god; it is the religion of the judge rather
than the content of the judgment which is paramount. From this perspective, one might legitimately conclude that Israeli secular courts –
where the judges are all Jewish – would not be prohibited.* Moreover,
secular courts in America – where there is a clear separation between
religion and state in the judiciary – may very well likewise be permitted.

However, the great legalist and philosopher Maimonides would
seem to support another opinion. Although he begins his ruling, "Anyone who brings a judgment before gentile judges and their judicial sys-
tems … is a wicked individual" – emphasizing the religious or national
status of the judge rather than the character of the judgment – he then
concludes,

> … and it is as though he cursed and blasphemed [God], and lifted
> his hand against the laws of Moses.
>
> Laws of the Sanhedrin 26:7

Apparently, Maimonides takes umbrage at a Jew going outside the system
of Torah law, thereby disparaging the unique assumptions and directions
of the just and righteous laws of God.

In order for us to understand exactly what is unique about the
Jewish legal system, permit me to give an example of the distinctive

---

* This is the conclusion reached by Jerusalem Magistrate Court Judge Jacob
  Bazak, in 'Courts of Law in the State of Israel – Are They Indeed Secular?',
  Tehumin 11 (5741) pp. 523–528.

axioms of Torah law from another passage in this Torah portion, the prohibition against charging or accepting interest on a loan.

> If you will lend money to my nation, to the poor person with you, you may not be to him as a creditor, you may not place upon him an interest rate [*neshekh*]; and if you accept from him your friend's cloak as security for the loan you must return the cloak to him before sunset. Because, after all, it may be his only cloak and [without it], with what [cover] will he lie down?
> And if he cries out to Me, I shall hear because I am gracious.
> Exodus 22:24–26

In addition to noting the touching poignancy of the latter portion of the passage, I would like to ask four questions, one on each of the four earlier phrases of the commandment. First of all, the prohibition against interest begins, "If you will lend money to my nation." Although Rashi cites the teaching of Rabbi Yishmael that this is one of the three biblical instances where the usage of the Hebrew *im* is not to be understood as being volitional – if – but is rather to be taken as an imperative – "When you lend money to my nation," as you should do – nevertheless, one might legitimately query why the Bible chooses to use such an ambiguous term for an act of lending, when it is clearly God's desire that we perform this act!

Second, the Bible seems repetitious: "...to my nation, to the poor person with you." One or the other of these two phrases would have been sufficient to teach the point! Third, "You may not be to him as a creditor," says the Torah. This is interpreted by our sages to mean that not only is it forbidden for the creditor to remind the debtor of the loan, but the creditor must go out of his way not to cause the debtor embarrassment; if the creditor sees the debtor walking towards him it is incumbent upon the creditor to change direction. Why? After all, the debtor took money from the creditor, didn't he? Why not remind the debtor that the loan must be repaid?

Fourth and finally, the specific prohibition against interest itself seems problematic. The Hebrew word used in the Bible for interest – "*neshekh*" – also means the bite of a snake, which our sages compare to interest since the serpent initially injects his venom painlessly but it ultimately consumes the entire individual and takes his very life! Maimonides goes so far as to codify:

> Anyone who writes a contract with an interest charge is writing and causing witnesses to testify that he denies the Lord God of Israel…and is denying the exodus from Egypt.
>
> Laws of Lenders and Borrowers, 4:7

What is the logical reason for the prohibition against interest – and why the hyperbolic comparisons? After all, there is no prohibition against charging rent for the use of my house! Why should there be a prohibition against charging rent for the use of my excess funds?

Rabbi Haim ibn Attar, in a most brilliant illumination, beautifully explains this passage in his commentary Ohr Haḥayim. In an ideal world, he maintains, there ought to be no rich and no poor, no lenders and no borrowers; everyone should receive from the Almighty exactly what they require to live. But, in His infinite wisdom, this is not the manner in which the Lord created the world. He provides certain individuals with excess funds, expecting them to help those who have insufficient funds, appointing them His "cashiers" or "ATMs." Hence you must read the verse as "If you have [excess] money to lend to my nation, [understand] that what ought have gone to the poor individual is with you." You were merely given the poor person's money in trust, your extra funds actually belong to him!

If you understand this fundamental axiom – that the rich person is actually holding the poor person's money in trust as an agent of the divine – then everything becomes clear. Of course, the lender may not act as a creditor, because she is only giving the poor man what is in actuality his. And of course one dare not charge interest, because the money you lent out was never yours in the first place. This is the message of the exodus from Egypt, the seminal historic event which formed and hopefully still informs us as a nation: no individual ought ever be owned by or even indebted to another individual. We are all owned by and must be indebted only to God. This fundamental truth is the foundation of our traditional legal system which is uniquely just and equitable: it is especially considerate of the needs of the downtrodden and enslaved, the poor and the infirm, the orphan and the widow, the stranger and the convert, the "chained wife" and the indigent forced to sell their land. From this perspective, not only must we submit to Jewish law, but it is crucial that our judges be certain that Jewish law remains true to its ethical foundations.

What Takes Precedence – My Obligation to God or My Obligation to People?

> *Now these are the laws which you shall set before*
> *them. If you buy a Hebrew servant, six years shall*
> *he serve and in the seventh he shall go out free, for*
> *nothing.*
>
> EXODUS 21:1–2

Arriving as it does immediately after the Ten Commandments, it is not surprising that *Mishpatim* begins with legal requirements of a society dedicated to morality and ethics, specifically, the relationship between employers and employees. Actually, these first laws of servitude coming after the Decalogue seem to be a natural expatiation of the first of the Ten Commandments, "I am the Lord thy God who took you out of the land of Egypt, the house of bondage." It is as though the Bible is saying that from now on there are to be no more slaves among the Hebrews; in a brilliant silent revolution, the Bible utilizes the term *"eved"* (Hebrew for slave), but totally changes its definition, turning the *eved* into a hard worker for a limited portion of time, who does not act in a servile fashion and must be granted the same living conditions – in terms of lodging and food – as are enjoyed by his employer. One may even cite the primacy of the placement of these laws as proof of the importance of the commandments between human beings. However, a careful examination of the text reveals that *Mishpatim* is not exclusively dedicated to civil and criminal law.

We also find reference to laws between human and God:

> You shall not curse God, nor curse a ruler of your people. You shall not delay offering the fullness of your harvest, and the outflow of your presses.
>
> Exodus 22:27–28

Then after more ritual laws, the text returns to the laws within human society only to be followed once more with the ritual laws of Shabbat and festivals. Why this to and fro movement?

A strong argument can be made that although Torah law includes both the ritual and ethical, the Torah places priority not on the laws between human and God, but rather on the laws between human beings. We read in Vayera (Gen. 18:1) that after Abraham's circumcision he is graced by a vision of God. But then upon seeing three tired strangers in the distance, he abandons the Almighty, so to speak, to attend to the needs of his guests. The Talmud* points to this incident as an underlying principle that it is of greater importance to be involved with hospitality – sensitivity in interpersonal relationships – than to greet the Divine Presence.

In his work *Hegyonot el Ami*, the former chief rabbi of Tel Aviv, Rabbi Moshe Avigdor Amiel, argues that this principle is not just an aggadic hyperbole, but is a fundamental insight into the ideology of halakha. In ritual law there exists the notion of neutralization or nullification (*bitul*). Should a cupful of non-kosher chicken soup fall into a pot of kosher hot soup, one need not throw out the soup if the ratio of kosher to non-kosher is more than 60 to 1. The forbidden portion

---

* See *Shabbat* 127a.

becomes nullified in the larger vat. When it comes to laws between human beings, however, there are no such leniencies. If, for example, the ten shekels which I pilfered become mixed into an account where I have six hundred legitimately gained shekels, I cannot invoke the 60:1 nullification concept as I do regarding pots on the stove.

Similarly, when it comes to questions of ritual in the Torah, we have the principle that a positive commandment can push aside a negative prohibition. For example, although it is forbidden to wear clothes woven from a mixture of linen and wool (Lev. 19:19), the Torah nevertheless commands that the ritual fringes required on all four cornered linen garments should include a string of sky-blue wool (Num. 15:38). Here the positive commandment to wear *tzitzit* overrides the commandment forbidding a garment woven from wool and linen.

When it comes to laws between human beings and God, however, the same principle does not apply. Building a sukka is a positive commandment, but if one steals the necessary wood for construction, we call this a mitzva achieved through sin and the sukka is rendered invalid; no one suggests that the positive command to build a sukka overrides the negative prohibition against stealing.

Finally, emotional intent and devotion (*kavana*) are an important part of ritual law. Without proper intent, ritual becomes a mechanical act, its value diminished. According to many authorities, such performance of a ritual is of no account whatsoever. Hence, Maimonides rules that if one recites the Shema, expressing each syllable aloud and emphasizing each of the necessary consonants, but does not have the internal commitment to accept the kingship of the divine, the entire recitation is of no religious significance whatsoever. It is as if the Shema had never been recited. However, proper intent is not required in laws between human beings because the deed itself is so important that any lack of inner intent cannot undermine the accomplishment of the act. Therefore, if one gives money to a poor person, even if one only did it in order to make an impression on one's companion, the mitzva is nevertheless valid.

The court system in ancient Israel likewise reflects the seriousness with which we deal with interpersonal relationships. Property litigations require three judges, and questions of life and death require twenty-three judges. To rule on ritual law, however, kosher or *traif,* all we need is a solitary judge. From this perspective, we may readily under-stand the mishna regarding Yom Kippur, the Day of Atonement. Yom Kipper (automatically, or at least, when accompanied by repentance) forgives all transgressions between humans and God. But as far as the transgressions between people are concerned, only the wronged party has the right to grant forgiveness (*Mishna Yoma* 8:9).

The sages were less worried about the realm of divine rituals than about the realm of human relationships. The strongest statement I know on this subject is boldly declared by our sages:

> Does God really care if you slaughter an animal from the back or the front? The whole purpose of the commandments is to purify and to unite humanity.
>
> *Tanḥuma Shemini* 65

Our midrash is not questioning the necessity of the detailed laws of slaughtering animals, which it certainly accepts; it is, however, making the rhetorical point as to who benefits from ritual commandments. God is not in need of purification or unity, but we human beings certainly are. That this is the purpose of the commandments, all of them, is one of the subtle messages of *Mishpatim*. On the surface some command-ments may seem to be directed toward societal betterment and some directed toward divine connection, but common to all the command-ments is their unifying and purifying principle. In the laws between human beings, whose objective nature is about bringing people closer together, this unifying principle is self-evident. Multiplied enough times, love thy neighbor as thyself translates into a golden age of peace for all mankind. But as we shall endeavor to show, the same message is to be found within the ritual laws as well.

The Shabbat, a ritual which takes over our lives every seventh day, and is the climactic event for which we prepare the other six days, is biblically ordained as both a reminder of God's creation of the world as well as His redeeming us from Egypt. I have already explained the connection between these two events in my commentary on *Va'era* (page 58–60). If God is the creator of the world and we are all His creatures, no human has the right to enslave another. On this day of reverence for life, we cannot even pluck a blade of grass or pick fruit from a tree. Every creature of God has a right to be. We must recognize and respect every creature as a unique, separate and inviolate entity. Hence, the Shabbat, which seemingly comes to intensify our relationship to God, in reality strengthens our reverence for all life and our sensitivity towards all of existence, towards the whole of the universe. As Martin Buber magnificently taught, anyone who is incapable of saying Shabbat Shalom to a tree or to a dog simply doesn't understand the deepest meaning of the Shabbat. Similarly, the laws of kashrut. After all, the Torah itself expresses the prohibition of mixing meat and milk with the compassionate command "Thou shalt not seethe a kid in its mother's milk" (Ex. 34:26) and the necessity of salting and soaking meat to remove most of the blood because "the blood is the life" (Deut 12:23).

Hence the to and fro movement throughout the portion of *Mishpatim* between the ethical and the ritual: They are intertwined, with the bottom line being compassion and sensitivity for all of God's creatures.

And this is precisely as it should and must be. When Moses made of God the request of requests, "Reveal to me your glory" [the secret of your ways] (Ex. 33:18), God responds:

> The Lord, the Lord is a God of compassion and beneficence, long suffering, replete with loving-kindness and truth...
>
> Exodus 34:6

Our sages teach us, "Just as God is compassionate, so must we humans be compassionate – because we are created in His image and we are commanded: 'You shall walk in His ways.' "*

Indeed, the very term *"halakha"* ** is most probably derived from the command of walking in God's ways. Hence every ritual, such as prayers and blessings, which brings me close to God must, at the same time, bring me closer to an emulation of His ways, make me become more compassionate and loving, more sensitive in my human relationships. Conversely, if my behavior towards my fellow human helps me

---

*   See Maimonides, *Mishneh Torah*, Laws of Knowledge, 1:10.
** This is the Hebrew word for "Jewish Law," from the root *halakh* (to walk).

understand the part of God within every human being, then it is clear that the laws between humans will likewise bring me closer to God. Ultimately, these two dimensions are spokes on the same wheel, creating a magnificent human and cosmic unity. The commandments are there to help me see that godliness exists in every aspect of existence, and the goal of all the mitzvot is to create a more compassionate and sensitive human being to help bring about a world of peace and harmony. Hear O Israel the Lord our God the Lord is One. Just as God is One, so the purpose of His Torah and His commandments are one: to make all of humanity – indeed all of creation – one, the one in the One.

Judaism and Abortion

> *And if two men strive together, and hurt a woman,*
> *causing her to miscarry, and there is no fatal*
> *harm, he shall surely be fined… But if fatal injury*
> *[to the mother] follows, then you shall give life for*
> *life.*
>
> EXODUS 21:22–23

*M*ishpatim contains the first commandment in the Torah which brings up the personal status of a fetus. A woman who miscarries as result of being accidentally injured by two men fighting amongst themselves is awarded a monetary compensation for the unborn child, but if the injury proves fatal to the woman, the death penalty is to be invoked.

The rabbis gleaned from these two cases that a fetus was not considered a life. The basis for this interpretation is found in a Mishnaic ruling on the question of a life-threatening pregnancy:

> If a woman suffers a difficult childbirth, we are allowed to destroy
> the fetus in the woman, removing the fetus limb by limb, because

the mother's life takes precedence over the child's. But if the head [or major portion of the body] of the child has emerged, the newborn cannot be harmed because one life cannot push aside another life.

Mishna Ohalot 7:6

From the Mishnaic perspective, life or ensoulment takes place at birth – not from conception, for example, as the Catholics believe.

This view, however, which seems to look upon the fetus as less than life, is not the only one we find among the sages. In the Talmud (*Arakhin* 7a–b), R. Nachman reports in the name of Shmuel that if a pregnant woman dies on Shabbat before giving birth, we do everything necessary to save the fetus, even if it means desecrating Shabbat.

Keeping in mind the overriding principle that Shabbat may only be desecrated to save a life, it is clear that the life at stake cannot be the mother's because she has already died. Therefore, R. Nachman's ruling means that Shabbat may be desecrated for the life of a fetus.

With our aforementioned verse from Exodus and the mishna in *Ohalot*, is it appropriate to call a fetus a full-fledged life, with the protective rights entitled to all human beings?

One of Maimonides' rulings sheds light on the nature of the fetus and can orchestrate between the various sources already cited. We must take note that this abortion law appears in a section of the *Mishneh Torah* entitled Laws of Murder (1:9). In codifying the law that the mother's life takes precedence over the fetus as long as the fetus is inside the womb – although once the head has emerged, one life is not pushed aside for another life – Maimonides adds an explanation. We are obligated to destroy the fetus when the mother's life is threatened because the fetus is considered a *rodef*, a pursuer, in effect, a murderer. The fetus is threatening the life of the mother.

Earlier in this chapter of the Laws of Murder, Maimonides rules that if we come upon a *rodef* (a potential murderer clutching a knife in hot pursuit of someone in desperate flight), we are obligated to do whatever it takes to stop the pursuer, even if it means killing them. Halakha 9, dealing with abortion, continues the question of the *rodef*, this time extending the concept to include the fetus.

Maimonides, having placed the laws of abortion within the category of the laws of murder, and then having offered the analogy of the fetus to a legal position of *rodef* requiring destruction, provides a fascinating approach towards understanding the complex laws of the fetus. A number of commentaries, including Rabbi Haim Soleveitchik of Brisk in his commentary on Maimonides' *Mishneh Torah*, reasoned that if the fetus would be merely considered part of the mother's body, more like an extension, a limb or an organ, there would be a question as to the permissibility of amputating a "limb" to save the mother's life, and therefore we would not have to come up with the description of the fetus as a "pursuer."

Maimonides' *rodef* analogy, it is argued, renders unto the fetus an existence of its own which goes beyond the idea of its simply being part of the mother. The fetus may not be life (in accordance with the biblical account in *Mishpatim* and the mishna in *Ohalot*), but it assuredly is potential life, and potential life dare not be snuffed out capriciously. Shabbat can be desecrated to preserve potential life, and the mother's life must be endangered before we can destroy the fetus.

The laws concerning suicide may illuminate the question of the mother's individual freedom and "right" when it comes to determining the fate of what she is carrying inside her womb. The sages (*Bava Kama* 91b) consider suicide a major crime, indeed an act of homicide, based on a verse in the portion of *Noaḥ*:

> But the blood of your own lives will I demand an account … He who spills human blood shall have his own blood spilled by man …
> Genesis 9:5–6.

Suicide, in the Torah's view, is murder, and one doing the killing cannot use the argument that one has the right to do with one's life as one sees fit, even if it means ending it. We do not own our lives; we are simply the keepers of these bodies, a task to be performed as best we can, with the expiration date being God's choice, not ours. Similarly, though the fetus may be part of the mother during the period of its origin, that does not mean she owns the potential life developing within her womb, and that she is free to dispose of it whenever whim, will or fancy strike her.

Treating a human life seriously means that we have to treat potential human life seriously as well. If the mother is forbidden to destroy her "own" life, then how can she destroy "life" that is not her own?

In Judaism, what determines the future of the fetus is its potential for being dangerous. If it "pursues" the mother, threatening her life, then the fetus must be destroyed, for actual life does take precedence over potential life. To be sure, there may be a legitimate difference of opinion as to what falls into the category of life-threatening. According to many religio-legal authorities, the halakha recognizes not only physical danger to the mother's body, but also psychological danger to the mother's state of mind, each case to be judged on its own merits by rabbinic and medical counseling. Furthermore, there are also authorities who distinguish the first forty days, or consider the first trimester versus the last six months in the life of the embryo, or distinguish between an embryo with potential life and one with only potential limited life, such as one carrying Tay-Sachs disease. In all such instances, a competent religio-legal authority must be consulted. However, when no mitigating circumstances exist, and the proposed abortion proves to be only a desire to get rid of a financial or emotional inconvenience, Jewish law questions such decisions and clearly forbids the taking of potential life.

One of the most moving experiences I ever had in the rabbinate involved a couple who had been married for years without being blessed with children. Finally the woman did give birth, but the baby was born with a devastating disease, and died soon afterwards.

During the week of *shiva*, a congregant asked me to speak to a relative of his – all of 15 years old – who had gotten pregnant by her boyfriend and was about to go through an abortion. The young mother-to-be agreed to meet, and during the course of our talk, she became convinced that it was a mistake to abort the fetus, and that it would be better to give the baby up for adoption once it was born, specifically to this family that had just suffered the tragic loss of their own baby.

It is not very difficult to imagine how we all felt at the bat-mitzva celebration of this young woman who had been snatched from the abortionist's knife and is today an outstanding Torah student at one of the finest religious girls' high schools in Israel. According to Jewish tradition, a life saved is a world saved; therefore, it stands to reason that every potential life is nothing less than a potential world.

The Extent of Human Responsibility

> *If an ox gores a man or woman, and that person
> dies, the ox must be stoned to death, and its flesh
> may not be eaten. The owner of the ox, however,
> shall be guiltless.*
>
> EXODUS 21:28

What are the parameters of human responsibility? Am I responsible for a deed only when I do it with my own hands, only when I pull the trigger with my own finger? If the above-cited verse were the only source in the Torah dealing with the damages caused by one's property, then all those munition firms who, over the decades, have developed and sold chemical and biological warheads without regard to the murderous goals of the buyer could theoretically plead total innocence. Let the ox-perpetrator carry the burden of guilt, while the manufacturer-supplier can sleep and have pleasant dreams, with a clear conscience and an unsullied soul.

The facts are that the Talmud has a complex and multiple-guilt attitude regarding the extent of human responsibility. On the one hand, there is a famous talmudic dictum* which emphasizes ultimate individual human responsibility: "There is no agency for an act of transgression." If Bob urges Sam, who is of sound mind, to rob a bank or murder an innocent victim, only Sam can be held culpable in a mortal court. Nevertheless, Bob is not absolved of moral accountability before God if he gave immoral advice and especially if he derived, or paid out, material benefit as a result of that immoral advice.

On the other hand, the Talmud holds one responsible for probable results of one's actions in addition to the actions themselves.

> A human being is always considered forewarned, responsible and culpable [for any damage that one causes], whether it is done on purpose or by accident, whether one is asleep or awake.
>
> *Mishna Bava Kama* 2:6

A person is not only responsible for the results of their own actions, if, for example, they go to sleep next to a breakable vase which belongs to someone else, despite the probability that they will thrash about in a sleeping state, and indeed they break the vase while asleep, but one is also responsible for the damage caused by anything that one owns, a small child, a goring ox, a wild dog – as long as these "possessions" have no mind of their own and one guarded them insufficiently in light of their expected proclivity to cause harm.

The various talmudic commentaries, in trying to understand the nature of this responsibility, probe the following issue relevant to the damage perpetrated by a person, possession or minor. What is the basis for this culpability? Is the owner culpable because someone's property has been damaged and, being that an ox or a minor cannot be forced to pay, the next likely to pay the bill is the adult owner of the damager? If this is the logic, then the payment must be seen as a kind of fine paid by the owner of this property in order to right the wrong perpetrated by his property. The commentaries suggest another possibility: one's property is considered an extension of oneself, human responsibility extends even to one's inanimate possessions and minor charges, and so the payment

---

* See, for example, *Bava Kama* 79a.

made in such a case must be viewed as restitution that one must make for damage committed by an extension of oneself. If one's goring ox or restless child does damage, and they were not properly guarded, it is as if one had done the damage oneself!

Evidence for the second possibility in that talmudic query can be found in the Torah portion of *Mishpatim*. *Mishpatim* is the major source for criminal law in Jewish life. The verse immediately after the one quoted above states:

> If the ox was in the habit of goring on previous occasions and the owner was warned but did not take the necessary precaution of proper guarding, then if the ox kills a man or woman, the ox must be stoned, and its owner shall also be made to die.
>
> Exodus 21:29

"Made to die?" Must the owner of the ox actually pay for his ox's action with his or her life? The next verse provides a clarification. "An atonement fine must be imposed on him, and he must pay whatever is imposed on him as a redemption for his life" (Rashi, Ex. 21:30). The Torah provides redemption of the owner's soul by having the owner pay his or her worth as a slave on the open market.

The very first verse, in which the owner of the ox is "guiltless," is apparently dealing with a domesticated ox who could not have been suspected of a proclivity for goring. The second verse is dealing with a problematic or "goring" ox, with a previous history of goring. In such a case, the Torah goes out of its way to establish the grave consequences for the owner of a goring ox who gores and had not been sufficiently guarded against doing so. The text's phrasing "its owner shall also be made to die," even though it does not refer literally to capital punishment, nonetheless reveals how seriously we respond to such carelessness on the part of the owner. In the final analysis, one cannot say: "It was not me, it was my ox; it was not me, it was my car; it was not me, it was my lawyer."

When the next verse of the Torah declares that the owner must pay redemption money for his or her soul, this requirement effectively answers our earlier probe about responsibility. If my possession continues on a destructive path that could have been predicted and I did not prevent it, it is as if I myself perpetrated the destructive act.

True, I cannot be put to death for my act, since capital punishment by human court is limited to premeditated, witnessed and forewarned acts of capital crimes. But the very language of the Bible, "its owner shall also be made to die," expresses the extension of responsibility to the owner him- or herself!

Aristotle defines the essence of the human being in that we are social creatures, stating "I communicate, therefore I am." Some two thousand years later, Descartes proposed that what captures the human being's essence is our ability to reason: "I think, therefore I am." My teacher and mentor, Rabbi Joseph B. Soloveitchik, of blessed memory, expressed it differently when teaching this passage in *Bava Kama*: "I am responsible, therefore I am." Judaism would argue that the essence of our humanity lies in our ability to accept responsibility for our actions and their consequences.

We live in an age in which the social sciences and psychiatric journals have developed theories that minimize our own responsibilities in the face of a multitude of factors. A tale is told about three widowed mothers who meet in Miami Beach and boast of their sons' successes.

"My son is a doctor who makes $300,000 a year – and to whom does he send $50,000 each year? To me, his mother."

"My son is a lawyer who makes $400,000 a year – and to whom does he send $75,000 each year? To me, his mother."

But the winning punch line goes to the mother who proudly claims that her son is a businessman who makes $1 million a year and pays his psychiatrist $100 a minute for each of his sessions.

"And who do you think my son talks about for most of those expensive sessions? Me, his mother!"

We must all take responsibility for our actions, and, from that perspective, true maturity comes the moment the individual understands that one must cease blaming one's mother, one's father, one's teacher, one's environment or luck. Ultimately, we must hold ourselves, and only ourselves, responsible for our actions.

Nevertheless, our minor children and our animal and inanimate possessions are clearly extensions of ourselves. For them we must take personal responsibility. With regard to our influence over other responsible adults, however, we must at least take moral, if not legal, responsibility, especially when these adults were once our children and could justly claim that it was mostly from us that they were supposed to learn how to be mature and loving adults themselves. "I am responsible; therefore, I am."

The Land of Israel – An Integral Part of the Covenant at Sinai

And he took the Book of the Covenant, and
read it into the ears of the nation, and they said,
"Everything which the Lord has spoken, we shall
do and we shall hear [internalize]."

EXODUS 23:7

The Jewish nation here enters into its second covenant – eternal pact – with God, a covenant based not on the common family-nation gene pool of the children of Abraham and Sarah but rather on the common religious commitment of adherence to the word of God revealed at Sinai. From this perspective, an additional reason (to the one offered in the previous commentary) as to why the ratification of this covenant takes place after the lengthy exposition of the major civil and ritual legislation of our religious ordinances as outlined in the portion of *Mishpatim* rather than earlier, follows in the revelation of the Decalogue; after all, Judaism consists not of ten commands but of 613!

But what is difficult to understand is that between the exposition of the commands and the ratification of the covenant, there seems to be an interruption in the natural flow of the legal material for a sudden and inexplicable switch to a discussion of the Israelite conquest of the Land of Israel: "Behold I send my messenger before you…to bring you to the place which I have prepared…Little by little I shall banish them from before you until you will multiply and settle the land. And I shall place your borders from the Reed Sea to the Philistine Sea and from the desert to the river…They [the original inhabitants] will not live in your land lest they cause you to sin against Me by your worship of their [idolatrous] gods who will be for you a stumbling block" (Ex. 23:20–32). And only following this strange digression from the laws of *Mishpatim* do we return to the ratification of the covenant with which this portion concludes. What has the Land of Israel – which logically belongs with, and is indeed the major content of, the prior Abrahamic covenant of Israel as a family-nation-state – to do with the covenant of Israel as a religion? After all, religions – unlike nations – are generally not limited to specific locations or countries!

In order to understand our text in the Bible as well as the Israeli-Jewish phenomenon in history, it is necessary to probe more deeply the two major experiences of our covenants, the biblical accounts as well as their ritual expressions. God's first covenant with Abraham guarantees the eternal continuity of future progeny and land patrimony – the two most important constituents of a nation-state. This Covenant of the Pieces came as a result of Abraham's request for a divine guarantee that his descendants would inherit the Land of Israel. It outlines the extent of the divinely guaranteed borders of our land, and emphasizes the blood (of the slaughter and division of the calf, goat and ram) and divine fire which accompanied the pact (Gen. 15:7–20). The features of land and blood are found in the second covenant as well at the conclusion of our portion (Ex. ibid., as well as 24:5, 6). But unique to the first covenant is a deep sleep which God causes to fall upon Abraham, a great dark dread which accompanies that comatose sleep, and an ominous prophecy of persecution and enslavement which happily concludes with freedom and the settlement of Israel (Gen. 15:12–21). The second covenant emphasizes the Israelites' acceptance of the commands, features a sacrificial celebration which includes the pouring of blood on the altar as well as on the nation, and triumphantly concludes: "And they saw God, and they ate and they drank" (Ex. 24:3–11).

The contrast between these two covenantal experiences leads my teacher and mentor, Rabbi Joseph B. Soloveitchik, of blessed memory, to interpret the first as our national covenant of fate and the second as our religious covenant of destiny (see Soloveitchik, "Kol Dodi Dofek," "The Voice of My Beloved Knocks" in *Ha-yaḥid ve-ha-yaḥad*). An individual is not asked whether they wish to be born into a specific family or nation-state; "accident" of birth is a matter of fate, and the fate of the Jewish nation has been to suffer far more than its to-be-expected share of persecution, exile and suffering. Indeed, the Jews packed into cattle cars and sent to concentration death camps were not given the choice of exiting from the Jewish nationality. To be Jewish was their fate, and they were often forced to shed blood as a consequence.

Perhaps this is why the ritual act of circumcision is called "the covenant of the foreskin" (*Brit Mila*), whose divine command comes twenty-five verses after the Covenant of the Pieces (Gen. 17:9–14). An eight-day-old Jewish male infant is not given the choice as to whether or not he wishes some blood shed in his very organ of propagation; the ritual of circumcision expresses the Jewish fate built into the covenant of our Israeli nationality.

Not so the religious faith of the commandments of revelation; each Jew must choose whether they wish to abide by the laws or not: to keep the Sabbath or reject the Sabbath, to honor his or her parents or disregard them. The bedraggled ex-slaves who stood before Sinai and cried out "We shall do and we shall hear" were making the Jewish vision their national mission, were defining themselves as a "kingdom of priest-teachers and a holy nation," were turning their fate into destiny. The covenant of fate is imposed; the covenant of faith is chosen. To be born into a particular family-nation is our fate; to choose an ideal and ideology as our life's mission is our destiny. The infant about to be circumcised is an object upon whom a ritual is to be imposed; the bar/bat mitzva and bride/groom who have chosen a life dedicated to the ideals of Torah are subjects actualizing their deepest desires.

There are, however, special circumcisions, and even certain "actors" in every circumcision, who express chosen destiny and not merely imposed fate. In September 1970, when I was in Riga, Latvia on a special mission for the Lubavitcher Rebbe, of blessed memory, I was awakened at 2:30 A.M. with a strange, frightening but marvelous request: two brothers, one just eight days old and the other a week before his bar mitzva, were about to be circumcised. Since the Soviet Communist government which ruled at the time made participants in such a "primitive" religious ritual suffer dire consequences, the two "operations" were to take place in the dead of night at the Rombula cemetery outside Riga. The ritual ceremony had been timed to coincide with my presence in Riga since the Jewish doctor who had agreed to risk his license and perhaps his life was ignorant of Jewish law.

Words cannot describe the feelings of eeriness, queasiness, admiration and privilege which all converged in the depths of my being while intoning the circumcision blessings that dark, freezing night in the cemetery. But the most poignant moment of all was yet to come. After both circumcisions, I intoned the familiar words: "Just as [*ke-shem*] this child has entered the covenant, so may he enter Torah, the nuptial canopy and a life of good deeds." Suddenly, from the depths of silence which one can only sense in a cemetery, the father of these two boys emitted a strangled cry in Yiddish: "*Nein*, not *ke-shem*, not 'just like', I don't want his bar mitzva, his wedding, his Jewish good deeds to be like this, in hiding, in a cemetery. I want them to be in the open, with pride, in our Jewish homeland, in Israel."

Thank God, the two children I helped circumcise three decades ago celebrated their weddings in Israel. Clearly the adult actors in the circumcision ceremony – especially the young man just before barmitzva – were expressing not only Jewish fate, but primarily Jewish destiny. To a lesser extent, this is true of every parent who chooses to have his/her child circumcised. And I believe this is also true with regard to the Land of Israel.

Yes, on the one hand, every nation, and therefore any national covenant, is dependent upon a specific homeland, into which one is born and about which one generally has little choice. This is not the case, however, with regard to the Jews and the Jewish homeland, Israel. Because we have been exiled to so many lands for so many years, our return to Israel had to depend upon our choice to return to Israel, our willingness to fight for Israel, our understanding that only Israel is our promised land and ultimate home. Moreover, Israel provides us with the only possible framework for creating a society based upon Torah law; the prophetic challenge of a Jewish state is that it become a model of justice and compassion, ethics and integrity, family purity and concern for human welfare which will inspire the world towards ethical monotheism. Thus the destiny of the nation of Israel can only be fully realized in the Land of Israel dedicated to the Torah of Israel. The Land of Israel is an integral part of our destiny as the people of Sinai; we may have returned to it as a result of the merit of our strength, but we shall actualize it only as a result of the strength of our merit.

Israel's Side of the Covenant

> *And Moses took the blood and sprinkled it on*
> *the nation, declaring "Behold the blood of the*
> *covenant which God has established with you on*
> *the basis of all these words."*
>
> EXODUS 24:8

Unique among all the peoples of the world is the Jewish people – a nation and a religion at the same time. Biblically speaking, God entered into two separate covenants with the Israelites: the first was with Abraham, the first patriarch and founder of our family-nation. And the second was with all of the Israelites, presumably at Mount Sinai.

The logical moment for the establishment of this covenant was at Sinai, when 600,000 Israelites heard the divine voice presenting the fundamental laws of fealty to God, observance of the Sabbath, and the morality which demanded that we not murder or steal or commit adultery. Thus, it is strange that the covenant is not presented or ratified in the preceding Torah portion of the revelation of the Decalogue but is rather to be found at the conclusion of this Torah portion, after a whole series of civil laws and a description of the conquest of the Land of Israel:

> And Moses took the blood and sprinkled it on the nation, declaring "Behold the blood of the covenant which God has established with you on the basis of all these words."
>
> Exodus 24:8

This covenant doesn't even come immediately after the civil laws of our Torah reading. It somehow waits until after the description of the conquest of Israel. Why the long delay? Why not establish the covenant at the time when the Israelites were at the zenith of their religious experience, the revelation at Sinai?

I believe that the religious covenant was waiting for a single magic word to be uttered by the Israelites, before which the Almighty was not willing to establish an eternal agreement with them. That magic word is a verb which is very familiar to every Jew, "*Shema*" – hear, listen, eternalize. In the preceding Torah portion of *Yitro*, God says to the Israelites, "You have seen what I have done to Egypt…but now if you will hear, truly hear my voice and observe my covenant you will be for me a unique treasure among all nations…" (Ex. 19:4, 5). The Jews have seen, *ra'ah*, but apparently they have not yet heard. Only if they hear will God establish His covenant with them.

The Torah portion continues, testifies to the divine descent on Mount Sinai, and lists the ten divine words or commandments. Words are generally heard but apparently the Israelites have not yet heard them. In fact, the very verse following the commandments reads: "And the entire nation *saw* the sounds and the torches and the sound of the ram's horn…and the nation saw and trembled and stood from afar" (Ex. 20:15). They only see – they only see even the words and the sounds. Apparently God is disappointed. "And the Lord said to Moses, so shall you say to the children of Israel: You have seen that from the heavens I have spoken to you. Do not make together with me gods of silver and gods of gold…" (Ex. 20:19, 20). Since they only see and they have not yet heard, they must receive an even stronger message about not descending into idolatry. After all, suggests the divine, if you do not hear, you can even combine belief in God with belief in idols.

It is only after the laws catalogued in the portion of *Mishpatim* and God's promise to send his messenger before the Israelites to help them conquer the Promised Land that we finally find the magic word: "And he [Moses] took the book of the covenant and read it into the ears of the nation and they said, 'Everything which the Lord has spoken we shall do and we shall hear [*nishma*]'" (Ex. 24:7). Then the Almighty is ready to have Moses sprinkle the blood over the nation and establish God's covenant with Israel.

What does this Hebrew verb "*Shema*" really mean? Why is it so important? We all know the clarion call of the Jewish faith: *Shema Yisrael Hashem Elohenu Hashem Eḥad*, usually translated as "Hear O Israel the Lord our God the Lord is One." There is a fascinating difference of opinion within the Talmud (*Berakhot* 15b) as to how to explain this verse. One sage insists it means that we must express each word of the "*Shema*" prayer out loud so that our ears hear what our mouths are uttering. This explanation would certainly suggest that the meaning of *Shema* is to hear audibly with your ears. A second sage insists that the one who recites the Shema must recite it in a language that he or she understands. Apparently for him the verb *Shema* means to hear in the sense of to understand, to listen not merely audibly but also intellectually. We must listen with our minds in addition to hearing with our ears.

The third view insists that neither hearing with one's ears nor listening with one's mind is sufficient; the words of this clarion call are a commandment that we accept the yoke of the heavenly kingship, that we commit ourselves body and soul to obeying the will of the divine. I would submit that this position defines *Shema* as internalization, the ability to make the words transform our very personalities and change the essence of our beings. Indeed, Rabbi Samson Rafael Hirsch interprets the word "*Shema*" as coming from the two letter noun *ma* which means intestines; the words of God must get into our innards, into our very *kishkes*, until they remake us into different people.

God is ready to enter into a covenant, but he will only do so if we understand the life-changing ramifications of his words. Most people listen superficially and do not expect to internalize what they hear. This is not enough to merit a divine covenant. A story is told that Rabbi Yisrael Salanter, the nineteenth-century founder of the Ethicist (*Mussar*) movement, once found himself stranded in Kovno for the Sabbath. Everyone wished to invite him, but when he discovered that the local baker had no young mouths to feed at home and so he wouldn't be taking away anyone's portion of food, the great rabbi accepted the baker's invitation. The baker was an observant Jew but hardly a great Torah scholar or even a man of great intelligence. He entered his house with the revered luminary, and immediately bellowed: "*Yidineh*, wife, why are the *hallot* not covered? How many times must I remind you?" The woman, immediately recognizing her distinguished guest, had tears in her eyes as she secured the hallah cover which had already been prepared. The baker, full of self-pride after having expressed his "religiosity," then invited Rabbi Yisrael to sanctify the wine. "One moment," said the sage, "can you tell me why we cover the *hallot*?" "Of course, revered Rabbi," responded the baker, "every child knows the answer. When there are many different foods on the table, the first blessing is always made over the bread, after which no other blessing need be made. On Friday night, however, the first blessing has to be made over the wine. Therefore, so as not to shame the hallah who expects the blessing over her, we must cover her over until after the sanctification of the wine." Rabbi Yisrael looked at the baker incredulously. "Why do your ears not hear what your mouth is saying? Do you think that our Jewish tradition does not understand that a piece of dough has no feelings and would never become embarrassed? Understand that our laws are trying to sensitize us to the feelings of human beings, of our friends, of our neighbors and especially of our wives."

Only when the Jews were ready to internalize the biblical teachings into the innermost recesses of their beings, into their very *kishkes*, was God ready to establish His covenant with them.

Teruma

The Construction of the Sanctuary and the Shabbat: The Pursuit of a Living or a Life?

> *And let them make Me a Sanctuary that I may dwell among them.*
>
> EXODUS 25:8

What does it mean for God to dwell among the people? Does this not sound anthropomorphic, as if God were in human form dwelling on our street? And would the concept of a dwelling place for the divine not have been more appropriately expressed with a verse saying: "And let them make Me a Sanctuary that I may dwell in it"? Moreover, what is the strange textual link between the Sanctuary and Shabbat? This portion and the following one, *Tetzaveh*, deal with the Sanctuary. The third portion of the sequence, *Ki Tissa*, suddenly features a ringing declaration to keep Shabbat (Ex. 31:14), apropos of nothing. What is the relationship between the Sanctuary and Shabbat?

According to the Talmud,* the aspect of Shabbat that is intimately linked to the construction of the Sanctuary is the fundamental definition of precisely which activities are prohibited on Shabbat. Similarly, in the portion of *Ki Tissa*, in the midst of God saying the following to Moses about Bezalel the great architect of the Sanctuary,

> ...whom I have filled with the spirit of God in wisdom and in understanding and in knowledge and in all manner of workmanship.
>
> Exodus 31:3

The Torah suddenly moves from the Sanctuary to Shabbat:

> But verily you shall keep My Sabbath, for it is a sign between Me and you throughout your generations, that you may know that I am the Lord who sanctifies you...
>
> Exodus 31:14

Aside from the general declaration forbidding creative activity (*melakha*) on Shabbat (Ex. 20:10), the Written Torah is virtually silent on specifically what is included under the rubric of creative activity. By virtue of the fact that an additional Shabbat injunction appears precisely within the context of constructing the Sanctuary, the sages derived the definition of creative activity or "work" from the different categories of labor involved in the construction of the Sanctuary. They taught that whatever was involved in the construction of the Sanctuary is forbidden on Shabbat.

From a traditional perspective, one might therefore explain the linkage by saying that the Sanctuary expresses sanctity of space and Shabbat expresses sanctity of time. Sanctity of time is on a higher level than sanctity of space, so the Sanctuary cannot be built on Shabbat and all the activities necessary for the building of the Sanctuary became the paradigm for prohibited Shabbat activity.

But let us look more deeply into the activities forbidden on

---

* See *Shabbat* 49b.

Shabbat and I believe we shall discover an even more profound linkage between the Sanctuary and Shabbat. The Mishna (*Shabbat* 7:2) lists thirty-nine forbidden creative activities, beginning with seeding and plowing – basic agricultural activities. On the surface, there seems to be little relationship between these activities and the building of the Sanctuary. Rashi suggests that the initial group is related to the planting of herbs whose dyes were used for the Sanctuary curtains. However, if this is the case, then the eleventh listed category, baking, poses a difficult problem. According to Rashi's interpretation, it is cooking rather than baking that should have been included; after all, extracting the different ingredients needed to dye the linens required the cooking or the boiling of the herbs – not baking.

The Talmud* explains that baking replaced cooking because the author of the Mishna, R. Yehuda HaNasi, wanted to list the processes involved in the manufacture of bread; hence the Mishna lists baking rather than cooking. This talmudic response may very well be used to shed a fascinating light on all of the thirty-nine activities. If the first group of forbidden activities in the Mishna is to be looked upon from the perspective of bread manufacture, then the next grouping of prohibited activities centers around clothing manufacture, the third around leather manufacture and the fourth around building construction.

From this perspective, R. Yehuda HaNasi, the compiler of the Mishna, is adding another dimension to the prohibited Sabbath activities: Not only are they the activities involved in constructing the Sanctuary, but they are also the activities involved in producing food, clothing and shelter. He is informing us that although the human pursuit of food (bread, the "staff of life"), clothing and shelter (leather may be used for garments, shoes and tents) is legitimate and even mandatory for physical survival and certainly appropriate for the weekdays. Even animals require food and some form of protective clothing from the elements and shelter! The Shabbat, however, is to be dedicated to God. The Shabbat is to be sanctified for the soul and the mind. The Shabbat is the means to the end for which God created human beings above animals: to catapult

---

* See *Shabbat* 74b.

us into more exalted and spiritual realms of involvement. Shabbat is the key to essence and not mere existence!

The story is told that the famed Hassidic Rebbe Levi Yitzhak of Berditchev once saw a Jew running very quickly. "I am running to make my living," explained the harried businessman. "But perhaps in the process you are losing your life," remonstrated the rebbe.

Indeed, the biblical explanation of the divine gift of desert manna teaches us that

> ...not by bread alone does the human being live but by that which comes forth from God's mouth does the human being live.
>
> Deuteronomy 8:3

Targum Onkelos (in the more precise readings of the text) translates the passage thus:

> Not by bread alone is the human being meant to *exist* [*kayam*], but by that which comes forth from God's mouth is the human being meant to *live* [*hayei*].
>
> Onkelos on Deuteronomy 8:3

"Existence" (*kiyum*) refers to the physical necessities of food, clothing and shelter, while "life" (*hayim*) is the purpose of human creation, the fellowship with God which teaches us to emulate His traits of compassion, graciousness, tolerance and truth, the hallmarks of His essence. The Sabbath is given as a day in which we can free ourselves from the "rat-race" pursuit of a living, and dedicate ourselves to the more human pursuit of a life in the context of sacred time, "time off" which is really "time in," time dedicated to family, to Torah, and to God.

The building of the Sanctuary is the preparation, the means, just as the six days of the week are days of preparation, the means. The Sanctuary and the Sabbath are the goal, the purpose. To slightly change the apt phrase of Rabbi Abraham Joshua Heschel, the Sabbath is our Sanctuary in time, and the Sanctuary is our Sabbath in space. The days of the week are not yet holy time, whereas the Sabbath is a foretaste of the world

The Primary Purpose of the Sanctuary

> *According to the way I show you the pattern of the Sanctuary and the pattern of its vessels, so shall you make them.*
>
> EXODUS 25:9

What is the real purpose of the Sanctuary – the forerunner of the Holy Temple – and its significance to Judaism and the Jewish people? Our question is a crucial one, especially when we take note of the fact that the last five of the eleven Torah portions of the book of Exodus deal with the details and precise architectural plans of the Sanctuary and its accoutrements. Moreover, for the desert generation, the Sanctuary was literally erected at the center of the formation of the tribes, symbolizing its place as the center of the Jewish people. Indeed, the Western Wall of the Temple, and even the Temple Mount itself, continue to inspire and excite Jews from all over the world as the foremost religious shrine of Israel reborn. Hence our understanding of the message of the Sanctuary will go a long way in helping us to understand the message of Judaism itself.

Nahmanides, noting that the commandment to build the Sanctuary directly follows the revelation at Sinai (the portion of *Mishpatim* is a continuation of the Ten Commandments, according to the Midrash), maintains that the very function of the Sanctuary was to continue the revelation, to build a central temple from which the divine voice would continue to emanate and direct the Israelites. Therefore, the very first aspect of the Sanctuary that the Bible describes is the ark, (*aron*), repository of the sacred tablets of stone, over which is the *kapporet* with its two cherubs. The Torah testifies in the name of God:

> And I shall meet with you there, and I shall tell you from above the *kapporet*, from between the two cherubs, which is on top of the ark of testimony, everything which I will command you [to communicate] to the children of Israel.
>
> Exodus 25:22

Moses even reiterates this notion of an ongoing revelation when he reviews the historical event at Sinai in his farewell speech to the Israelites:

> God spoke these words to your entire assemblage from on the mountain amidst the fire, the cloud and the fog, a great voice which never ceases.
>
> Deuteronomy 5:19 and Onkelos ad loc.

This is likewise emphasized in our classical blessing over the Torah:

> Blessed are You...Who has chosen us from all the nations and has given [past tense] us His Torah. Blessed are You O Lord who gives [present tense] the Torah.
>
> Siddur, Morning Service

The place where the revelation continued was originally between the cherubs above the ark of the Sanctuary; it therefore is quite logical that throughout the Second Temple – in the absence of the sacred tablets and the gift of prophecy – the Great Sanhedrin, sage interpreters of God's word for every generation, sat within the Holy Temple in the office of the "hewn stone" or the "decisions" (the Hebrew word *"gazit"* means to cut or decide, to chisel a stone or to decisively cut through a problem). It is after all the function of the Oral Torah to keep God's word alive and relevant in every time and in every situation. Apparently Nahmanides would insist that the main purpose of the Sanctuary was to teach and inspire Israel and humanity with the eternal word of the divine. From this perspective, after the destruction of the Second Temple, it is the synagogues and the study houses – our central institutions of Torah reading, learning and interpretation – which are the legitimate heirs to the Sanctuary.

The mystical and Hassidic interpretations see in the Sanctuary another purpose altogether: the building of a home in which the Almighty and Israel (and ultimately, all of humanity) will dwell together. The revelation at Sinai symbolizes the betrothal-engagement between God and Israel, with the marriage contract being the tablets of stone, the biblical laws. The commandment to erect a Sanctuary enjoins us to build the nuptial house in which the Almighty "bridegroom" unites with His bride – Israel.

Hence, the accoutrements of the Sanctuary are an ark-closet (repository for the tablets), a menora-candelabrum and a table for the shewbread – the usual furnishings of a home – as well as an altar. Everyone knows that it is impossible to establish a family without every member being willing to sacrifice for another: each spouse for his or her partner, parents for children, and even children for the family unit. And if the Almighty created a world – albeit an incomplete, imperfect one – in which humanity can dwell, we Jews must create a more perfect Sanctuary so that God will feel more comfortable with us and be enabled to dwell in our midst here on earth.

From this perspective, the heir to the destroyed Holy Temples is the Jewish home, wherever it may be. It is because Judaism sees the home as the "mother of all religious institutions" that home-centered family ritual celebrations bear a striking parallel to the religious ritual of the Jerusalem Temple even to this day. The most obvious example of this is that mystical and magical evening known as the Passover *seder*, modeled upon the Pascal meal in Jerusalem during Temple times, when every parent becomes a teacher whose primary task is to convey – through songs, stories, explication of biblical passages and special foods – the most seminal experience in Jewish history: the Exodus from our Egyptian servitude.

And every Shabbat and festival meal is a mini-Passover *seder*. Even before the Friday sun begins to set, the mother of the family kindles the Shabbat lights, reminiscent of the priests' first task each day: to light the menora. The blessing over the Kiddush wine reminds us of the wine libations accompanying most sacrifices, and the carefully braided *ḥallot*, loaves of bread, symbolize the twelve loaves of shewbread which were changed in the Temple every Friday just before dusk. Parents bless their children with the same priestly benediction with which the High Priest blessed the congregation in the Temple, and the ritual washing of the hands before partaking of the *ḥalla* parallels the hand ablutions of the priests before engaging in Temple service. The salt in which we dip the *ḥalla* before reciting the blessing over bread is based upon the biblical decree, "You shall place salt on all of your sacrifices" (Lev. 2:13), since salt, which is an external preservative, is symbolic of the indestructibility of God's covenant with Israel. The songs that are sung and the Torah that is taught during a Friday night meal will hopefully further serve to transport the family participants to the singing of the Levites and the teachings of the priests in the Holy Temple. Such a Shabbat meal links the generations, making everyone feel part of the eternal people participating in an eternal conversation with the divine.

I believe that both views, the Sanctuary as continuing revelation, and the Sanctuary as the nuptial home between God and Israel, together express the fundamental significance of our Holy Temple.

Face to Face with The Cherubs

And you shall make two cherubs of gold; of beaten work shall you make them, at two ends of the ark cover.

EXODUS 25:16

Among the most famous ornaments of the Sanctuary are the two cherubs, golden figures, each with the face of a child and wings extended heavenwards, which adorned the ends of the ark cover and protected the holy tablets of testimony. There were cherubs in the desert Sanctuary built by Moses, and there were cherubs in the Holy Temple built by King Solomon one thousand years later. However, in the Sanctuary the cherubs are described as facing each other, while in the Holy Temple they are described as facing the wall of the Temple, inward, away from each other (11 Chronicles 3:7).

R. Yohanan, a talmudic sage, explains:

In one case [our portion of *Teruma* with the cherubs facing each other] Israel is doing the will of God, and in the other case [facing the wall of the Temple] Israel is not doing the will of God.

Bava Batra 99a

Rashbam explains in his talmudic interpretation that in effect, the very same ornamental piece of sculpture in the form of two cherubs was present in both sacred places, the Sanctuary as well as the Holy Temple. A miracle, or divine intervention, was involved in the direction in which the cherubs faced. Whenever the Israelites acted in accordance with the Divine Will, the cherubs would face each other, and whenever the Israelites did not act in accordance with the Divine Will, the cherubs would face the Temple wall. The behavior of the nation of Israel literally animated the sculptured cherubs. Unfortunately it was during the reign of King Solomon that the Israelites began to backslide.

The Netziv has difficulty with the notion that the change in direction was determined by the behavior of the Israelites. After all, King Solomon is described as having produced cherubs for the Temple which were specifically made facing the wall, differing from the cherubs which had been produced by Moses and Bezalel.

Hence, the famed *rosh yeshiva* of Volozhin suggests that the talmudic phrase "when Israel is doing the will of God" refers to the historical period of the desert Sanctuary and "when Israel is not doing the will of God" refers to the historical period of Solomon's Temple.

This period or era description, insists the Netziv, harks back to the famous Talmudic debate between R. Yishmael and R. Shimon bar Yochai regarding the role of Torah study in our lives. In Deuteronomy the following verse appears:

> If you will listen, yes listen to my commandments…I will give you rain for your land at the right season, the autumn rains and the spring rains, that you may gather in your grain.
>
> Deuteronomy 11:14

The sages ask, why do we need the words "…so that you may gather in your grain?" Does the Bible have to state the obvious?

R. Yishmael teaches that the verse in question comes to limit the command of God to Joshua:

> This book of Torah shall not depart out of your mouth. You shall meditate therein by day and by night.
>
> Joshua 1:8

Since one could logically conclude that the Almighty is commanding us to devote all our time to Torah and no time at all to a worldly occupation, the seemingly superfluous phrase in Deuteronomy becomes crucially important; it is underscoring the importance of a person "gathering their grain," engaging in agriculture (or any worldly occupation) at the same time as studying Torah.

R. Shimon bar Yochai disagrees vehemently.

> If a person is to plough in the ploughing season, sow in the sowing season, reap in the reaping season, thresh in the threshing season... what is to become of Torah? The fact is that when Israel does the will of God, the work of Israel will be done by others... and when Israel does not do the will of God, then they will have to break their own backs, as it says, "so that you gather in your grain."
>
> Berakhot 35a

The Netziv, in an ingenious fashion and very much in accord with Lithuanian yeshiva ideology, links this dispute with the direction of the cherubs. We must remember that the desert generation had their nutritional needs taken care of by the manna and their shelter needs taken care of by the *sukkot* (divine tents of glory). They lived a kind of primordial *kollel* existence, free to devote themselves completely to the study of Torah. They lived a life of "doing the will of God" as understood by R. Shimon bar Yochai, and therefore the cherubs of Moses' desert sanctuary faced each other.

The period of the Holy Temple was one in which the Israelites had already entered the Land of Israel and were deeply involved in the agricultural pursuits of extracting subsistence, and vital natural resources, from the land. They worked very hard, and even if they remained devoutly committed to God and to Torah, they were in the R. Shimon bar Yochai category of "not doing the will of God." Hence, the cherubs of King Solomon's Temple faced the wall.

The Netziv was the great talmudic scholar who headed the yeshiva of Volozhin. To him, the study of Torah was life and life was the study of Torah. It is no wonder that he would interpret "doing the will of God" as exclusive involvement in the study of Torah.

I would like to suggest a third interpretation of the talmudic explanation of the cherubs' direction. After all, the great Netziv notwithstanding, it was the Divine Will that the Israelites leave the cocoon of the desert and enter history and the world by tackling the real problems of settling a land, replete with devastating wars, back-breaking labor and sociopolitical decision making. Torah study is meant to give direction to our personal and material lives, but not to substitute for them. (Indeed, the normative law within the Talmud itself (*Berakhot* 35a) – as decided by both Rava and Abaye – is in accordance with R. Yishmael and not R. Shimon bar Yochai).

Hence, I would interpret the talmudic statement as indeed contrasting the desert period with the First Temple period, but with an added nuance. The cherubs' facing each other was not a result of Israel's doing the will of God; it is rather the definition, a pointing of the way, as to how to best accomplish the will of God. We truly accomplish God's will not when our sights are centered on the Temple walls, no matter how sacred they may be, but rather when our sights are centered on other people, whom we must help, support and uplift.

The cherubs protected the Torah, the tablets of testimony within the holy ark. They were of human form with wings, their faces reflecting childlike innocence and purity. Undoubtedly, our children are the protectors and preservers of Torah. For them to do so, warns R. Yohanan, it is not enough that they face the Temple Sanctuary, they must first and foremost face each other. They must be sensitive to the needs and welfare of every other individual. Only in facing each other, even more than in facing the Temple, do they accomplish God's will!*

---

* For an expanded interpretation of these ideas, see the next two chapters.

The figures who protect the Torah throughout the generations are not merely the children, who study. They are also the rabbis, scholars, and educators; the Torah leaders and Torah decisors of every generation. The symbol of cherubs teaches us that it is not sufficient that these important Torah personalities face the Temple. They must face the people. They must feel the angst and hear the cries of their fellow Jews, in order that the Torah which they teach be sensitive and relevant, and truly express a tree of life "whose paths are paths of sweetness and whose every road is peace" (Proverbs 3:17).

Moreover, the Torah scholars must face each other as well! Facing each other means recognizing each other's authority, knowledge and honest motivation to protect the Torah, even when one must respectfully disagree with the other's opinion All too often Torah scholars, winged cherubs soaring towards the heights of divine understanding, lack the breadth of vision and perspective to look at each other with respect. They erect linguistic, cultural, psychological or political barriers. They succumb to Ashkenazi or Sephardi prejudices, yield to Hassidic or Lithuanian stereotypes. R. Yohanan warns that scholars, even those whose steady gaze is never averted from the Holy Temple and the sacred texts, may not be fully doing the will of heaven if they do not look at each other!

Political leaders in Israel are also in the category of the cherubs, charged with protecting the holy ark and the tablets of testimony within it. King Solomon was aware of this challenge. He was almost obsessed with creating a magnificent edifice, a holy temple to God. His gaze was set on the Temple, but in the process he neglected to look with sensitivity upon the masses of Jews. His heavy taxation laid the groundwork for the split between the ten tribes of Israel and the two tribes of Judea, even though the revolution did not take effect until his son Rehoboam's reign. His cherubs may have faced the wall of the Temple, but they did not face each other. This is a warning to every Jewish leader of the beginning of the end.

The cherubs protect the Torah, but only when they face each other in sensitivity, love and respect.

When Angels of Destruction are also Cherubs

> *And I will meet you there, and I will speak with you from above the ark cover from between the two cherubim...*

EXODUS 25:22

How are we to understand the notion of God speaking specifically from between the two cherubs? Most basically, what is the physical appearance of the cherubs? Only if we can picture what they look like can we begin to suggest what it is that they symbolize.

Rashi's commentary, which paraphrases a talmudic statement (*Sukka* 5b), is enlightening. "The image of each was in the form of a child's face" (Rashi on Ex. 25:19). A child's face, replete with an innocent beauty, an untroubled brow, an inquisitive eye, a beautiful smile, a ready laugh, all meld into a body graced with two wings soaring heavenwards. The picture which this image provides is one of purity seeking spirituality.

This is not the first time that we have met cherubs in the Torah. The first time they are mentioned suggests, at least superficially, a brutal contradiction to the symbolism we have just presented.

In the opening sections of the Torah, we read how Adam and Eve are expelled from the Garden of Eden.

> So He drove out the human being; and He placed at the east of the Garden of Eden the cherubs, with the revolving flaming sword to guard the path to the Tree of Life.
>
> Genesis 3:24

The context of banishment and flaming sword seems to be a far cry from the scene of the cherubs in the Sanctuary. Rashi here minces no words about these sword-toting cherubs. "Angels of destruction," he calls them.

Now the true symbolism of the cherubim becomes even more confusing. What message are they trying to convey, serene spirituality or deadly destructiveness?

One interpretation which might be suggested is based upon "the child's face" feature of the cherub. A child is indeed parent to the adult. A child has almost infinite potential, either for spiritual innocence and purity or for destruction and cruelty. Fundamentally, it depends where we place the child. If he stands in the Sanctuary, atop the ark which contains the tablets of the law, then he will express purity, idealism and spirituality. If, however, he is placed outside the Garden of Eden and is given a fiery sword to hold, then he will convey desolation and doom.

Tragically, our generation is witness to the truth of this interpretation. The well-known author and critic Michael Medved once wrote that the average American watches twenty-six hours of television a week! Now that violent and salacious TV programs have replaced school and parents as primary educators, how many children are being educated with the fiery sword, rather than with the tablets of testimony? Is it any wonder that violence so characterizes Western culture?

I would like to offer another interpretation. Remember that both cherub accounts in the Torah include the cherub as being an angel with the face of a child as well as protector or guardian: in this Torah portion, guarding the tablets of testimony, and in Eden, guarding the Tree of Life. The idea of children as guardians of the Torah immediately resonates with well-known midrashim and talmudic adages. Every young elementary school student of Torah has been told that when God decided to give the Torah to the children of Israel, He first wanted them to supply a guarantor, a surety that the Torah would not simply disappear over the course of time. The Almighty required a protector for His investment, as it were.

Moses initially offered the patriarchs as a surety, then the prophets, and finally the leaders of each generation. Each was rejected in turn by the Almighty because they were too few in number. Finally Moses offers the children as a surety, and this time God accepts.

This concept of children as the only real protection and guarantee for the eternity of Torah resonates from the talmudic comment that the cherubs had the faces of children. The cover of the ark, the very protective coat of the tablets of testimony, of the Torah of the divine, is graced by the figures of children-cherubs. Torah is authentically guarded and protected when it is studied and observed by the children, continued from generation to generation. Our sages taught that the world continues to exist only by merit of the breath of innocent children studying Torah.*

There is yet another way of interpreting this symbol. Remember that in the Sanctuary, God speaks to Israel from between the cherubs (Ex. 25:22). These protectors may well be the great sages of Torah, the luminaries who dedicate themselves to the law and its commentaries in every generation. It is these dedicated individuals who protect the Torah by interpreting it meaningfully for each age and epoch, by enacting decrees and additional practices which enable the Torah to be relevant and crucial to the exigencies and cultural temper of every ear and environment. A truly great sage, even in grand old age, often retains a countenance of childlike innocence and purity. The facial countenance is often not a terrain of canals and furrows, but is rather smooth and alive with light and brightness. Such was the face of the legendary Rabbi Moshe Feinstein, the last sage in America who was considered to be the great decisor, the *gadol ha-dor*, of an entire generation. Rabbi Moshe Feinstein was a phenomenon of intellectual breadth, a master of Torah and all of its interpretations. Yet he always gave the impression, through his twinkling eyes and unfurrowed brow, of childlike inquisitiveness, innocence and purity.

---

* This idea specifically will be expanded, with a story, in the next essay.

There is yet one more dimension. Unfortunately, our Torah cannot always merely be protected from within against assimilation, against the deterioration of learning and weakening of commitment. Tragically, we also have enemies from without, who will stop at nothing to destroy us. This has been especially true since the establishment of our Jewish state, where we have been forced to fight five wars and live through debilitating intifadas in the past five decades in order to survive. When our enemies face us with guns, tanks, chariots and missiles, the necessary means of defense is to fight back in kind. For the first time in almost two thousand years, we now have the right and the merit to protect ourselves physically against our would-be destroyers.

In our generation, many yeshiva deans together with the Israel Defense Force promote *yeshivot hesder* and *makhonim* (institutes) where committed students of Torah combine sacred books with brandishing swords, protecting their future not only by studying Bible, Talmud, and codes, but also by fighting back, by striking out against the enemy with Uzis and M-16s, by driving tanks and capturing hills.

Let us revisit the first place in the Torah which mentions the cherubs.

> He [God] placed at the east of the Garden of Eden, the cherubs, with the revolving flaming sword to guard the path to the Tree of Life.
>
> Gen. 3:24

Perhaps the cherubs guarding the Tree of Life and the cherubs guarding the holy ark are much more closely allied than we previously thought, with the distinction depending not so much on predilection and location as much as on necessity and occasion. After all, the Tree of Life is a metaphor for Torah, and this is the very object also guarded by the cherubs of the Sanctuary. The Tree of Life is midrashically identified with the menora of the Sanctuary – a veritable tree with seven branches! Rashi calls the cherubs of Eden angels of destruction – still utilizing the term angels, which suggests special messengers of the divine.

If they are blessed to live in times of peace, our children will be privileged to study Torah and guard the holy ark. If they live in a generation where it is necessary to defend the Tree of Life, Torah and the menora – State of Israel – with arms, then our children must take the revolving swords into their hands and guarantee our future. Virtually all of our yeshiva's Israeli students in Israel serve in the IDF and it is customary for yeshiva deans to visit the students at their army bases. I recall one such visit, at the conclusion of a late-night Talmud lecture, as I looked out at the soldiers sitting in their army uniforms and with their weapons, yet delving deeply into a talmudic question of carrying on Shabbat. I saw, in front of me, not hardened soldiers, but sensitive students of Torah, committed to the eternity of Israel and the vision of Zion.

I saw in front of me the cherubs, protecting the tablets of testimony and the eternal Tree of Life of Eden. They are needed to protect our future with the fiery sword – but without in any way sacrificing their childlike purity and idealism. May the time soon come when the cherubs of the fiery sword become full-time cherubs of the Sanctuary, when all of our whole-hearted and idealistic youngsters will have the luxury of spending all of their time in proximity to the holy ark of the tablets of testimony.

The Protectors and Interpreters of our Torah for all Seasons

> And the cherubs will be stretching out their wings
> on high, spreading over the kapporet, as they face
> one another; towards the kapporet they shall be
> facing.
>
> EXODUS 25:20

Concerning the construction of the ark and the cherubs, two technical textual questions are raised by the Midrash and many biblical commentaries. First of all, throughout this Torah portion, the various parts of the Sanctuary are commanded to be built by Moses: "You [second person singular, *ve-asita*] shall make." The one glaring exception is the holy ark, "And they shall make an ark out of *shittim* wood...," which is written in the third-person plural (*ve-asu*) referring to the entire nation of Israel (Ex. 25:10). Why the grammatical distinction? Second, there appears to be a superfluous repetition in the biblical text. In the first instance, the Bible records:

And you shall place in the ark the testimony which I shall give you.

Exodus 25:16

And then, after the command of the construction of the cherubs and only five verses after the verse just cited, we find once again:

And into the ark shall you place the testimony which I shall give you.

Exodus 25:21

Why repeat the instruction to place the tablets of testimony into the holy ark?

The Siftei Hakhamim draws our attention to a detailed grammatical difference which may contain the beginning of the answer. The form of the verb used the first time is past tense (*natata*), albeit changed to the future in meaning by the prefix *vav* but nevertheless a past-tense form: literally, "and you have placed the tablets" (Ex. 25:16). The form used the second time is pure future tense (*titein*), literally, "you shall place the tablets" (Ex. 25:21). Explains the Siftei Hakhamim, the second verse is alluding to the second tablets which will be placed in the holy ark after the first tablets will be broken by Moses when he sees the Israelite worship of the golden calf. Rabbi Mordechai Elon, the great Bible teacher of Jerusalem, takes this idea one step further, suggesting that this second verse refers to the second Torah, the Oral Torah (*Torah she-be-al peh*), and it is precisely this Oral Torah which is magnificently symbolized by the cherubs.

In order to buttress this interpretation, allow me to remind you of another apparent difference of opinion, concerning the gender of the cherubs, which certainly impacts on the particular symbolism they are meant to convey. The talmudic sages cite an ancient tradition that the cherubs were in the form of two winged children, one male and the other female, locked in an embrace. The imagery of this tradition is one of familial purity, innocent love, physical and emotional attachment devoid of erotic lust and defilement (*Yoma* 54). But Rashi and Ibn Ezra (Ex. ad loc.) seem to have another tradition: while they accept the representation of winged children, they do not include the male-female aspect of the description. For Rashi there are two faces of young children, and for Ibn Ezra there are two male youths (*ne'arim*). Here the symbolism is not at all familial or sexual in nature, it is rather the protection and continuity of Torah through the commitment of succeeding generations, human angels taking responsibility for the eternal Torah.

The idea is even more profound. The Talmud tells how Moses, when he was privileged to scale the heavens in order to receive the Torah from God, sees the Almighty fashioning crowns adorning the various Hebrew letters. When he asks about the significance of these calligraphic details, God reveals that in the future the great sage R. Akiva will deduce "mounds of laws" from these small crowns. Moses asks to see this great sage in action, and God transports him in time to the academy of the illustrious R. Akiva. However, to Moses' confused and embarrassed chagrin, he doesn't understand R. Akiva's teaching. And then a disciple asks R. Akiva the origin of the rule he has deduced, and he responds, "It is a law from Moses at Sinai." Moses is then satisfied and comforted (*Menaḥot* 39a).

I believe that the point of this story is to stress the fact that the seeds of all future Torah interpretation lie within the Torah itself. And the Oral Torah is the development of those seeds into the magnificent fruit which will provide the necessary spiritual sustenance and divine nourishment for every generation. Indeed, "every spiritual truth and religio-legal decision which a devoted student will ultimately expound in a novel fashion was originally given at Sinai"* – if not directly at least in potential. Hence Rabbenu Yaakov Ba'al Haturim explains that the individual called to the Torah recites one blessing over the Written Torah and a second blessing over the Oral Torah, the force of the Oral Torah being expressed in the words, "and an eternal Torah has He planted in our midst." It is the task of the Torah scholars of every generation – symbolized by the two winged youths, reminiscent of a dedicated *havruta* (Torah study partnership) or by the wholehearted and naïve Torah leaders who retain a youthful and even childlike simplicity – to nurture the seeds of the Written Torah into a dynamic and ever-increasing fount of

---

* See Yerushalmi, *Megilla*, 4:1

Torah nourishment for every period and its perplexities, every era and its exigencies.

Now our original questions can all be answered. The holy ark which houses the sacred Torah must be constructed by the entire nation of Israel, indeed, by the most committed Israelites of every future generation. The Torah is protected by those who study it, interpret it and expound its message for all subsequent times. The cherubs symbolize the human partners in the expansion of Torah, largely to be found in the Oral Law, largely developed by the great Torah interpreters of each generation, individuals who soar heavenwards by virtue of their ability to extract from the divine seeds the fruit necessary for every place and every time. The Torah was given by God, but must be studied, practiced, developed and expanded by the "cherubs," the committed religious leaders who reach up to the very heavens in order to make the Torah meaningful and accessible to every Jew in every place and every time.

* * *

My Unforgettable Meeting with a "Cherub"

I was very fortunate in that Rabbi Joseph B. Soloveitchik, my teacher and mentor, introduced me to Rabbi Moshe Feinstein, the great halakhic decisor (*posek*) of the last generation, suggesting that I place before him the very difficult questions I encountered as the rabbi of a synagogue mainly comprised of *baalei teshuva* (penitents). Hence, I had the pleasure of spending many a Friday morning at the modest Lower East Side apartment of Rav Moshe, where I always received a warm smile, tea and cake (which he would often serve himself, to my extreme embarrassment) and an unforgettable lesson in Torah scholarship. Once, I came to him with a difficult issue involving a *kohen* and divorcee, who wished to marry. He taught me which questions to ask. I subsequently discovered that an act of the *kohen's* mother had rendered him invalid for the priesthood, and on a subsequent visit to the Lower East Side, secured Rav Moshe's blessing for the wedding to take place.

The couple had come to me just before my *aliya* to Israel. By the time the various issues had been sorted out, my own move had been effectuated and the bride's father had recovered from a serious heart attack, two years had passed from the time I received Rav Moshe's permission to the time of the actual wedding – which took place in Israel. After I performed the ceremony and the marriage documents were processed, an ominous question came to me from the office of the Chief Rabbi: Had I – a newly practicing rabbi in Israel – made the mistake of marrying a *kohen* to a divorcee?

Since I received the query a day before I was scheduled to be in New York, I felt my best response would be a letter from Rav Moshe. Unfortunately, the great sage was extremely ill, in Roosevelt Hospital, forbidden to receive visitors. The Friday afternoon before my return flight to Israel, his grandson, Rav Mordechai – the keeper of the gate – secured permission from the doctor to allow me a few minutes. Rav Moshe, encased as he was by the white hospital linens, looked even shorter than I remembered him, his eyes – when they weren't wincing with pain – clear and bright, his brow completely smooth and without a wrinkle; he truly had the wholehearted, even naïve, visage of a cherub.

He smiled as I entered, inquired about each family member, and asked that I say a prayer for his health at the Kotel, "which is closer to God." I began to remind him of the case of the *kohen* and the divorcee that I had brought him more than two years before. Not only did he remember the details, he even remembered the names of the prospective bride and groom. He asked his grandson for something to write on, penned a few lines confirming the permissibility of the marriage, and warmly blessed me with success in Israel. I left the hospital room in tears, deeply moved by the meeting. Only someone who truly carries the Jewish people in his heart and in his mind could have remembered so well a halakhic issue which was one of many hundreds that he had received in the interim; for him it was apparently not only a "case" but it was two individuals in distress. He may have been confined to a hospital bed, but he had wings soaring heavenward. God had granted me the privilege of meeting one of the cherubs through whom he speaks!

The Menora and the Ark: the Holiness of Marriage and Family

> *And you shall make a menora of pure gold; of*
> *beaten work the menora shall be made: its base,*
> *its branches, its cups, knobs and flowers should all*
> *be of one beaten piece.*
>
> EXODUS 25:31

What is the most crucial institution or vehicle for the proper transmission of our Jewish faith and traditions? Is it the synagogue, the study hall, the Jewish community center, the charitable organizations like UJA – or none of the above? Let us study together the details of two of the major accoutrements of the desert Sanctuary – the menora and the holy ark, two sacred objects which are to be found in synagogues even today – and perhaps we will discover the answer to our question.

The menora is not only one of the most decorative and universally displayed objects of traditional Jewish art, it is also the official seal of the modern State of Israel. The Sanctuary menora, as described in this

Torah portion, had the shape of a golden tree whose trunk extended into six branches, three on each side, replete with stems and flowers (Ex. 25:31–40). It was a tree which shed light.

The ark was the repository for the tablets of stone, which contained the Ten Commandments. A golden cover (*kapporet* or *parokhet*) was placed over and above the ark, from which two cherubs were hammered out on either side. The cherubs were formed to be looking at each other, and the Almighty communicated with Moses from between the two cherubs (Ex. 25:10–30). Rashi cites the Talmud: "They had the form of the face of a young child" (*Sukka* 5b).

The Talmud describes the special qualities of these cherubs, as well as the manner in which our gentile captors viewed these particular images:

> Rav Katina said, "When the Israelites would ascend to Jerusalem during the three pilgrim festivals, the [Temple custodians] would show them the cherubs, who were embracing each other. They would say to the pilgrims, "See how your love before the Almighty should be as the love of a man for a woman." Said Resh Lakish, "When the destruction [of the Temple] came about, the gentiles entered [the sacred shrine] and said: 'These Jews, whose blessing is a blessing and whose curse is a curse, are involved in such a sculpture?' They derided the Israelites, citing the verse 'All who [formerly] respected her, came to mock her, because they saw her nakedness.' And what was her nakedness? The cherubs, embracing each other!"
>
> *Yoma* 54a

What is the symbolism which lies behind these sacred objects and how are we to understand their significance? Why feature sculptures like the cherubs in embrace, which allowed the Romans to revile Israel as worshiping their God through pornography?

We have seen that the menora is a golden tree, symbolically reminiscent of the Tree of Life in the Garden of Eden. You will remember that the first couple was banished from the primordial garden of perfection, and humanity was prevented from eating of the tree of eternal life, because Adam and Eve had sinned by partaking of the fruit of knowledge of good and evil. Our major commentator Rashi suggests that the forbidden fruit injected within the human personality what Sigmund Freud would call the libido, substituting lust for love, illicit passion for sexual purity. That is original sin. The ultimate goal of Torah – also referred to as a Tree of Life in the biblical book of Proverbs as well as in our liturgy – is to refashion our imperfect world into the Garden of Eden, to enable a perfected humanity to finally eat the fruit of the tree of eternal life. From the perspective of Rashi's interpretation, this ultimate feat can only be achieved when sexual purity will be restored, when familial love rather than extra-marital lust will be normative human behavior. Then we will have righted the wrong, done penance for the sin which caused our existential exile in the first place.

Apparently, therefore, the Roman conquerors missed the whole point of the cherub symbolism. Our sages insist that "they had the form of the faces of young children." A young child symbolizes purity, innocence, whole-heartedness. The physical embrace of such male and female winged beings – with the pure faces of children – expresses love without lust, sexual unity which enhances family rather than sexual depravity which destroys family.*

Undoubtedly, the family, which has such powerful potential for creative supportiveness and spiritual continuity, can tragically degenerate into crippling destructiveness and pathological dysfunction. I heard it said in the name of the great Hassidic sage Rabbi Aharon Karliner that it is difficult to see the compassion (*ḥesed*) with which God created the world, unless you take into account the fact that Adam and Eve were born without parents. Nevertheless, our religious tradition holds great stock in the importance and ultimate potential of family as the matrix from which a perfected society will one day emerge – and therefore Sabbath, festival, life-cycle and family purity ritual laws and customs all aim to protect, strengthen and deepen the most positive family ties and relationships.

---

* This is in accord with the talmudic statement in *Yoma*, that the cherubs were a male and a female; Rashi and Ibn Ezra seem to feel that they were two male youths (see previous chapter).

The nation of Israel was created from the family of Abraham and Sarah; the festival celebrating Torah revelation (Shavuot) emerges from the festival of family celebration (Passover – a lamb for each family). After all, from the second day of Passover we begin to count forty-nine days to Shavuot. A dysfunctional family – Adam and Eve blaming each other for their own weaknesses – produces the first murder (Cain and Abel); unified families – when the hearts of the parents turn to the children, and the hearts of the children to the parents – will herald national and world redemption. Family depravation banished humanity from Eden; family redeemed will return us to Eden and the Tree of Life. The sacred objects of the desert Sanctuary teach us that the most important vehicle for the transmission of our tradition is the institution of family. This is the message of the menora and the holy ark cover, the golden tree and the cherubs. Only by nurturing family purity and unity will we succeed in protecting Torah and properly utilizing it to perfect all of society. And that is the highest meaning of the blessing intoned at every marriage: "Blessed art Thou, O Lord our God, who sanctifies His nation Israel through the nuptial canopy and sacred engagement [*kiddushin*]."

Tetzaveh

When Absence Proves Love

> *And you shall command the children of Israel...*
> *And you shall bring forth your brother Aaron and*
> *his sons together with him... And you shall speak*
> *to all of the wise-hearted.*
>
> EXODUS 27:20–28:3

Often what you really have is that which you give away, what you most profoundly say is what you leave unsaid when you wisely decide not to respond, and the most commanding presence is felt most keenly when that presence is not around. An example of the third phenomenon is to be found in the Torah reading of *Tetzaveh*, the only portion since the opening of the book of Exodus wherein Moses' name does not appear even once! Why not?

The midrashic answer suggests that Moses initiated his own absence. When the Israelites sinned by worshiping the golden calf less than six weeks after the divine revelation at Sinai, God's anger reaches the breaking point (as it were) and he makes Moses the following offer:

> And now leave Me alone as my anger shall burn and I will destroy
> them, and I shall make of you a great nation.
>
> Exodus 32:10

God suggests that He wipe Israel, no longer worthy of His benevolence,
from the pages of history by starting a new nation, a new branch, from
the loins of Moses himself.

Others in his shoes might have taken up God's offer, but Moses
refuses to increase his own glory at the expense of the nation. The climax of his brilliant argument is an emotional ultimatum: God must
forgive the people.

> …If not [says Moses], blot me, I pray you, out of Your book which
> You have written.
>
> Exodus 32:32

God responds to Moses' pleas. But Moses' expression of identification
with the people, Moses' selfless willingness for himself to be obliterated
as long as his nation prevails, is eternalized by the fact that in one portion
of the Torah, *Tetzaveh*, the master prophet's name is "missing in action."

But on an even deeper level, is there a further significance to
the fact that the "blotting out" of Moses' name occurs specifically in
Tetzaveh?

Even a quick glance reveals that our portion is almost entirely
devoted to the priesthood. Chapters 28 and 29 deal extensively with all
the garments that the priests are commanded to wear, particularly the
High Priest, as well as the sacrifices that shall be brought to "sanctify
the priests." In fact, *Tetzaveh* is often called *parashat ha-kohanim*, the
portion of the priests.

Without a temple, the priest's public role is severely limited. One
area, though, where his presence is still felt (particularly here in Israel
and among Sephardim even in the Diaspora) is the daily priestly blessing during the repetition of the morning Amida: at the conclusion of
the blessing for peace, the priests, attended to by Levites, stand before
the congregation and invoke the biblical blessing: "May God bless you

and keep you …" (Num. 6:24). Before intoning these words, they recite the following blessing:

> Blessed are You Lord, our God, king of the universe, who has sanctified us with the holiness of Aaron, and has commanded us to bless His people with love.
>
> from the siddur

The final words in the blessing – "with love" – raise certain questions, since *kohanim*, or descendants of the High Priest Aaron, are fairly typical people. Some are as sweet as cherry ices in July, and some are as cold as Alaskan ice cubes, but most change in accordance with their mood upon awakening – how can we measure the love-quotient felt by Mr. Cohen when he ascends the *bimah* for the blessing? How can we legislate the emotion of love which the priests are apparently expected to feel?

The first answer lies in the very nature of the priesthood, in how the Bible legislated the priestly class's means of livelihood. It's often said that if you ask a typical entrepreneur, "How's business?" if he says, "Great," it means that he is doing well and his competitor is facing bankruptcy; if he says, "good," that means it's a good market for everyone, he's doing well and so is his competitor; and if he says, "Terrible," then that means he's facing bankruptcy but his competition is earning a lot of money. Gore Vidal was once quoted by Hilma Wolitzer in the *New York Times* for his poignantly honest observation: "Whenever a friend succeeds a little, something in me dies."

Enter the *kohen*. If there is one person who disagrees with Mr. Vidal, it would have to be a member of the priestly class who served in the Temple, received no portion of land to till or business to develop, and who made his living by tithes given him by the Israelites: $\frac{1}{40}$, $\frac{1}{50}$, $\frac{1}{60}$ of their produce depending upon the generosity of the individual donor. And since the tithe was a percentage of the crop, the better the farmer makes out, the happier the *kohen* ends up. To modify the Vidal quote, a *kohen* would declare: "Whenever a farmer succeeds a little [and certainly a lot], something in me lives." Hence by the very nature of the economic structure set up by the Bible, the *kohen*-priest could truly give the blessing of prosperity and well-being to the congregation of Israel "with love."

And it was because the *kohanim* were freed from professional and agricultural pursuits that they were able to devote themselves entirely to God, the Holy Temple, and the religio-moral needs of the nation. Their single-minded commitment to the holy and the divine was symbolized by the words engraved upon the highly visible gold plate (*tzitz*) worn around the forehead of the High Priest: "Holy unto God" (Ex. 28:36). Indeed, so important was it deemed that the religious and moral message not be compromised by political sectarian considerations that the Bible legislates a total separation between the religious and legislative spheres. The tribe of Judah was entrusted with sovereign, legislative leadership: "The specter shall not depart from Judah..." (Gen. 49:10), whereas the tribe of Levi was entrusted with religio-moral leadership: "They shall teach Jacob your law, and Israel your Torah..." (Deut. 33:10). No member of the priestly class could control the bank or become a cabinet minister. Thus the *kohen*, and the religio-moral voice which he represents, emerges in a totally independent position, above the economic interests of special-interest groups and beyond the intrigues of palace politics.

From this perspective we can offer a second interpretation of the words "with love" which conclude the introduction to the priestly benediction: "Love" does not describe the emotions of the *kohen*, but rather defines the content of the blessing. The most important blessing that can be bestowed upon the nation is that we live together in harmony and love. And only a priestly class separated from petty self-interest and competitions, truly devoted to God, can hope to inspire such love and harmony!

Now we can understand why Moses' name is absent particularly from this portion of *Tetzaveh*. If the *kohanim* are to symbolize selfless commitment to God and to the nation, they cannot possibly have a better example than Moses, who was willing to have his name removed from the Torah for the sake of the future of his people! If any act in the Torah can be singled out for demonstrating pure love, with no strings attached, it is when Moses refuses God's offer to start a new nation from his loins; Moses would rather that he remain anonymous but let the people of Israel live. Indeed, the essence of Moses' greatness emerges most clearly from the portion of his absence and anonymity.*

---

* For a variation of this theme of Moses' absence in the *parasha* dealing with *kohanim*, see the following chapter.

Each Person a Priest, the Entire World a Sanctuary

> *And you shall bring forth your brother Aaron*
> *and his sons together with him from among the*
> *children of Israel, to serve as priests before Me...*
>
> EXODUS 28:1

In the portion of Tezaveh, Moses' name is not mentioned even once, while Aaron's name appears over thirty times. This is the week of Aaron, the song of praise of the priesthood. But the truth is that it is the week of all Israel as well, not just those who claim Aaron as ancestor. After all, the entire nation of Israel was created to be a nation of priests, dedicated to God. At the revelation at Sinai, the entire nation was charged with the ideal of being a holy nation and a kingdom of priests (Ex. 19:6). To be sure, during the Sanctuary and Temple periods, there was a separate priestly class of the descendants of Aaron which maintained the unique obligations of this special family, of which we retain a remnant even today, when the descendants of Aaron rise to bless the congregation during the repetition of the Amida and when the *kohanim* are called first to the Torah. However, our eventual vision calls for a universal priesthood, when every Jew will dedicate their life to divine service.

We eternalize and emphasize the universal ideal of the priesthood in the most prosaic way possible: how we wake up in the morning. Before anything else, we fill a large cup or vessel with water. With the left hand we pour some water over the right hand, and with the right hand, some water over the left hand, for three cycles. Placing our hands directly under the faucet would save time, but this act, recalling the priestly ablutions in the Temple, is to be performed *be-ko'ah gavra* (from one's own vitality), and with the use of a special vessel. The blessing we make, *netilat yadaim*, literally means the "lifting of the hands":

> Blessed art Thou O Lord our God, king of the universe, who has sanctified us with His commandments and commanded us to uplift our hands [in divine service].
>
> Siddur, Morning Service

This is the way the priests began their day of service to the divine in the Holy Temple, and this is the way every Jew begins their day of service to the divine in the world at large.

This ideal of "every person a *kohen*" continues into the daily prayers. Our prayers begin with two separate blessings that emphasize our relationship to Torah, the heart of every Jew's existence. Commentators explain that the first blessing is for the Written Law and the second for the Oral Law. Following the blessing, every individual reads two passages, one from the Torah and one from the Talmud. After all, after making a blessing over a fruit, one must eat some fruit, and so after making a blessing over Torah, one must study a passage of Torah. It is fascinating that out of the entire written Torah the passage chosen by the Men of the Great Assembly (who are generally considered the original compilers of the liturgy) is the priestly benediction, the very words intoned by the *kohanim* when they bless the congregation with peace.

On Shabbat, the ritual of blessing one's children is performed each Friday evening, when the parent, placing both hands on each child, recites the priestly blessing. Once again every parent becomes a priest and priestess.

During Passover and Yom Kippur, the custom is for married adults to wear a special white robe, the *kittel*, like the sacred garb of the priests in the Temple. During the Temple periods, we all actually became priests on the festival of Passover, as the head of each family sacrificed the paschal lamb in Jerusalem. Even today at every *seder* this priestly role is extended by the fact that we wash our hands before eating the vegetables that are to be dipped in the salt water. This act is intended to evoke the priestly custom of eating in special purity by washing before eating any vegetables touched by water. On Yom Kippur, one of the most dramatic parts of the synagogue service occurs when we fall prostrate during the Musaf Amida, and repeat the exact words which the priests chanted in the Temple.

Since the destruction of the Temple, the synagogue, with replicas of Temple furnishings such as the ark, the table, the menora, and the eternal lamp, functions as a mini-sanctuary devoted to prayer. Over the years what has evolved is that all Jews, not only priests and Levites, possess a feeling of equal opportunity inside the sanctuary in miniature.

Walk into a synagogue on a regular Shabbat, and the person leading the prayers may be the local butcher. Another individual, a pharmacist by trade, opens the ark. A third person, an architect, calls the people up to the Torah by name, and the person who actually chants the week's Torah portion may be a teenager. Many synagogues do not even have official rabbis. Other religions have a clear demarcation between the laity and the ministry, while for us all such distinctions are blurred. We are all part of the service. We are a nation of priests. Ask a non-Jewish visitor who enters the synagogue when every adult male is bedecked in the prayer shawl, swaying, eyes closed, to distinguish between the laymen and the clergy. He or she will not be able to because we all look like priests.

We have already seen how every home is to be a mini-sanctuary (page 208, on *Teruma*), how the lighting of the candles by the woman of the house at the advent of Shabbat and festivals evokes the kindling of the Temple menora; the passing of the sweet smelling spices at havdala recalls the priestly offering of the Temple incense; the dispensing of the *ḥalla* loaves reminding us of the Temple shewbread, and the table replete with food, song and prayer bringing us back to the Temple sacrificial meals led by the *kohen*-priests. Our tradition desperately wants us to express our truest calling, that we are to be a nation of priests and priestesses, dedicated to God and the humanity He created.

This dramatic idea expresses yet another message. If every person is a priest, then we must view the entire world as a sanctuary, a sacred cosmos in which the God of love may be truly comfortable dwelling within our midst. And if every Jew is a *kohen*-priest, and the priestly calling is that of a Torah teacher – "teach your statutes to Jacob, Your Torah to Israel" (Deut. 33:10) – then every Jew must teach the gentile world the seven Noahide laws of morality, the vision of a God of love, justice and compassion who desires world peace. When every individual Jew realizes his or her true calling, the world will indeed be redeemed and humanity will not learn war any more...

What's in a Garment?

> *And you shall make holy garments for Aaron your brother, for honor and for splendor... And they shall make the* ephod *out of gold, blue, purple and scarlet... And you shall make the breastplate of artistic work... And they shall be on Aaron and his sons whenever they enter into the Tent of Meeting...*
>
> EXODUS 28:2–43

In the portion of *Teruma* more than forty verses are devoted to the making of the priestly garments, and in the portion of *Tetzaveh*, another thirty verses are devoted to these same garments. Granted that priests should look different from the rest of the nation, but why isn't a white garment sufficient, something simple and functional? And why must priestly garments be so elaborately constructed, with gold beaten into threads, embroidered sashes, blues, purples and scarlet skillfully and intricately woven?

Moreover, not only do we find a wealth of details surrounding the details of each of the priestly garments, but from a certain perspective the garments seem to be the most fundamental aspect of priestly sanctity! The Torah goes so far as to caution that the priestly vestments must be worn by

> ... Aaron and his sons whenever they enter the Tent of Meeting or offer sacrifice on the altar... otherwise they will have committed a sin and they will die...
>
> Exodus 28:43

And the Talmud teaches that

> while their [priestly] garments are upon them, the priesthood is upon them; if their garments are not upon them, the priesthood is not upon them.
>
> *Zevaḥim* 7b

In other words, the garments seem to make the priest, an interesting variation on the famous sartorial advertisement: "Clothes make the man." Is this not an undue emphasis on external dress?

Over the centuries many commentators have addressed themselves to the question of the priestly garb. In the Talmud (*Arakhin* 16a), R. Annani bar Sasson asks why the biblical portion of the priestly garments is next to that of the sacrifices. The answer given is that just as the sacrifices atone for sins, so do these garments atone for sins; the tunic for murder, the breeches for illicit sexual acts, the waist sash for one's innermost thoughts, the *ephod* for idol worship, the robe for slander, the turban for haughtiness.

Nahmanides sees the priestly garments as regal robes in their own right. This garb need not be seen beyond its inherent beauty; the special clothing is one of the means by which we exalt the priest into the domain of the majestic. Our *kohanim* are our religious royalty, the majestic monarchs who preside over the Holy Temple precinct.

In the *Sefer Haḥinukh* on the 613 commandments, first published in 1523, the author acknowledges that from a psychological perspective, a person's inner being is affected by their outer garments. Thought follows action, and since a priest must have special thoughts when he performs the service, he must attempt to transform himself. Such a process of transformation begins with the act of getting dressed in special garb. To be sure, external change of costume does not necessarily create a change in inner motivation and thought, but it can, and often succeeds, in beginning the process. This is also why we are required to wear special garments on the Shabbat and on festivals. Special garments occasion special moods.

The Netziv in his Torah commentary follows the principle of the *Sefer Haḥinukh* except that he switches the focus from the priest to the Israelites coming upon the glory of the priests in their ceremonial garb. Israelites enter the Temple precinct seeking inspiration and atonement. They want to be transported spiritually into the domain of the divine, into a world of repentance and atonement. The unique majesty and glory of the priestly garb, combined with the magnificence of the Holy Temple itself, will hopefully begin to uplift the Israelites and help them to feel that they have entered the kingship of God.

These explanations certainly illuminate the complex and varied role of the priestly garments. But I would suggest that if we look at the first time a garment is mentioned in the Torah, we discover that there is more to clothes than meets the hand or even the eye.

When Adam and Eve are exiled from the Garden of Eden, the text tells us that

> the Lord God made for Adam and his wife, garments of skin, and clothed them.
>
> Gen. 2:21

God drives them out of the Garden of Eden, and because of the extreme nature of the punishment of exile, we tend to overlook how unique it is that God Himself made these garments and Himself clothed the first couple.

After all, God had commanded humanity to conquer the world, "replenish the earth, subdue it and assume dominion" (Gen. 1:28). The world is pictured as a tabula rasa for the human to discover, unravel, invent, define – an imperfect cosmos which God created for the human to do and make, to repair and perfect. And indeed people discover fire and bronze, wheels and windmills, electricity and atoms, apparently everything – except for the clothes on their back. And these they carry with them when they are banished. Why should the creation of the garments be relegated to God Himself? What can the Torah be teaching us?

Garments lie at the very root of what makes us human. Just as the Almighty created humans in His image, He also fashioned garments for the human being. Remember that, externally, only one thing distinguishes a human being from an animal, and that is that humans wear clothing, while animals do not!

It was the mocking seduction of the serpent which led to the banishment of Adam and Eve. Condemned to eat dust, the serpent remains naked. God fashions garments for human beings in order to teach them to rise above animals and above their animal natures. Naked animals follow their bare instincts; human beings must cover over and transform their naked essence in order to ennoble and sanctify themselves to become more like the divine who formed them. And since only human beings are capable of self-improvement and development, our very bodies contain a fundamental holiness which the animal world – not created in God's image – lacks. But humans must work on their naked essence, must refine and ennoble, purify and sanctify the raw essence which is nakedness. This is the magnificent idea of circumcision, this is the essence of a system of 613 commandments, and this is the symbol of clothing.

If we glance at the more visible symbols of Jewish life, we see how sanctity is associated with a covering. Inside the synagogue, the Torah scroll is covered with its special garb; this is also the case regarding the table from which the Torah is read, and the ark in which the scroll stands. There is even a strict biblical prohibition that the Levite family of Kehat not look upon the uncovered holy objects of the Tabernacle, lest they die (Deut. 4:20). Everything holy needs a covering, and it all began with the human body.

Departing from the Garden of Eden, Adam and Eve are taught the necessity of improving themselves, of sanctifying human nature, of covering their nakedness. Once they know this, they can go out and conquer the world, transforming themselves and the world around them in the process. But if they forget that the body is holy, then the world transforms them, and they live disastrously closer to their animalistic nature. Since the priests function in the Sanctuary of the divine, devoting all of their activities towards bridging the chasm between heaven and earth, it stands to reason that they must wear unique clothing to remind them and the rest of the Israelites of their unique function of maintaining the Sanctuary so that God may truly dwell in every Israelite.

An inner holiness existed in the human being created in God's image, but with the fall from the Garden of Eden, this holiness became endangered. From the Jewish point of view, clothes do not make the person; clothes do, however, distinguish the human being, reminding us of the inherent sanctity of the human body, of the necessity of separating human from beast and, at least in function in Temple times, separating religious leaders from ordinary laymen.

Urim Ve-tummim: The Magic of Democracy

> *And Aaron shall bear the names of the Children*
> *of Israel in the breastplate of judgment upon his*
> *heart when he goes in unto the holy place, for a*
> *memorial before God continually. And you shall*
> *put in the breastplate of judgement the urim*
> *ve-tummim, and they shall be upon Aaron's heart*
> *when he comes before God...*
>
> EXODUS 28:29–30

Of all the holy objects in the *Mishkan* (Tabernacle), the *urim ve-tummim* is certainly the most mysterious and other-worldly. All the other Sanctuary accouterments have more familiar parallels. An ark remains a protective covering, a table remains a base on which food is placed, a menora burns oil and gives light and special garments are part of any individual's wardrobe. But the *urim ve-tummim* was apparently unique and was worn at special times by the High Priest. It seemed biblically endowed with magical powers of decision making.

The Torah describes the intricacies of the breastplate in exquisite detail, but in regard to the *urim ve-tummim* the text remains silent. Ibn Ezra, as cited by Nahmanides, calls it the work of "a craftsman done in silver and gold," and suggests that the designs were similar to the techniques of the stargazers and astrologers. From other passages in his biblical commentaries, it is clear that Ibn Ezra believed in the accuracy of astrology, which was considered a legitimate science by many wise men of the ancient world. Since the *urim ve-tummim* was the instrument of telling the future, the Israelites depended on its message when pondering whether or not to wage a voluntary war. Ibn Ezra may be suggesting the necessity of relying on the best knowledge of the science of the day.

Nahmanides disagrees sharply with Ibn Ezra, denigrating his position with the ultimate put-down "he did not say anything." This may be either because Nahmanides opposed astrology as a valid means of arriving at the truth and/or because he believed that the *urim ve-tummim* revealed divine wisdom. Nahmanides identifies the *urim ve-tummim* with the holy letters of God. These were the letters of the names of the twelve tribes inscribed in the stones of the breastplate, and individual letters would glow like a battery-charged light in response to a question presented by the High Priest. *Urim* itself means lights, and the divine response came in the form of the specific letters that were lit up. But since letters can be arranged or interpreted in any number of ways, the *tummim* of the *urim ve-tummim*, that is, the purity (pure soul of wisdom) of the High Priest himself, should provide the proper letter placement for the right answer.

In order to visualize the process, the Vilna Gaon gives as an example the incident whereby the childless Hannah (future mother of the great judge Samuel) entered the Sanctuary. Eli, the High Priest, thinks that she is drunk, a rather strong conclusion emanating from the rather innocuous sight of a distraught woman in prayer whose lips are moving while no sound seems to be emerging. The Vilna Gaon suggests that Eli came to this assessment by enquiring of the *urim ve-tummim* to explain the woman's plight. The letters *shin, kof, raish* and *heh,* on the breastplate immediately lit up, letters which Eli put together as *shikorah,* which means a drunken woman. The truth, however, was to have read the word *ke-Sarah* (like Sarah), intimating that Hannah, like Sarah for so many years, was childless, and/or *k'sherah,* she is kosher and pure.

Apparently, Eli's inner soul, or *tummim*, was not properly activated, so he "misread" the situation in accordance with the former possibility.

Maimonides sees the *urim ve-tummim* as a divine gift awarded to a High Priest who worked for it. It is on the level of *ru'ah ha-kodesh*, (Divine Spirit), which ranks higher than a *bat kol* (heavenly voice) but does not reach the level of actual prophecy. From this perspective, it may legitimately be interpreted to mean that the power level of the *urim ve-tummim* was dependent upon the spiritual level of the particular High Priest and his ability to receive the divine message.

Rashi offers a third interpretation. According to this master commentary, the *urim ve-tummim* was the writing of the ineffable Name, which the High Priest placed inside the folds of the breastplate, by means of which light (*urim*) was shed upon the words and the words were rendered perfect (Rashi on Ex. 28:30) – perfectly true and prophetic.

On the surface, Rashi's explanation seems very close to Nahmanides. Both seem to be addressing the illuminating glow of the letters, the divinely charged battery, so to speak. But Rashi specifically mentions the ineffable divine name, and adds that this name of God was placed inside the folds of the breastplate, the very place where the twelve tribes were spelled out. I would like to suggest that Rashi may be hinting at another way of determining answers to difficult questions, different from astrology and different from the divine spirit.

Twelve stones inscribed with the names of the twelve tribes, the children of Israel, were placed on the breastplate of judgment, worn by the High Priest. When it was possible to do so, the Israelites sought God's divine knowledge from the prophets or the High Priest or the Sanhedrin (High Court). But when these institutions no longer exist, the only authority left for ultimate decision-making is the people themselves. We see this from the fact, according to Rashi, that the holiest letters in existence, the Divine Name of God, was placed within the folds of the breastplate, suggesting an intimate linkage between the people and God. And this not merely a convenient symbolic interpretation of the *urim ve-tummim*, it is rooted in our halakhic tradition.

According to Maimonides,* in the absence of a Sanhedrin or a

---

*   Kritot, end of Chapter 1.

prophet, the people, by *vox populi*, choose the king. Furthermore, the people can choose the greatest Torah scholar of the generation, and thereby re-establish *smikha*, the original ordination that emanated from God and was given to Moses, and in this way resuscitate the institution of the Sanhedrin.*

Let us mention two more far-ranging concepts in terms of how the people of Israel are seen, one from the mystical and one from the daily realities of normative communal life. First, the holy *Zohar*, the mystical text of the Jewish people, looks upon *knesset Yisrael* (the historical nation Israel, *malkhut*) and the Divine Presence (the holy *Shekhinah*) as being identical, a concept that should jolt us from our predictable natures if we could only understand its significance. Second, from the eleventh to the sixteenth centuries, the constituencies of various Jewish communities were given the power to decide on *takanot kahal* (Enactments of the Community), and once the majority agreed, these enactments became law for as long as the communities endured. After all, does not the Talmud teach us that the nation of Israel, if they are not prophets, they are at least the children of prophets (*Pesaḥim* 66a).

The significance of the ineffable Name being so intimately linked to the people and the twelve tribes means that not only does God speak to us, He speaks through us. We, the Jewish people, are the *urim ve-tummim* of God and of humanity. This means that not only does God appear in history, but the history of the Jewish people has a divine dimension. This means that a democratic decision by the majority of the Jewish people has religious as well as political significance.

The will of the Jewish people is ipso facto the will of God. The *urim ve-tummim*, God's ineffable name between the folds of the breastplate wherein were written the twelve tribes of Israel, symbolizes the importance of consulting the nation when the leader (High Priest) must make fateful decisions. Perhaps the *urim ve-tummim*, at least in accord with Rashi, reminds us that democracy, in the sense of *vox populi*, was the accepted method of decision-making from earliest history.

---

* Maimonides' interpretation of the first mishna of *Sanhedrin*, and of the mishna in *Bekhorot* 29b.

Outer Garb Makes the Priest, Inner Fire Makes the Prophet

> *And you shall dress Aaron, your brother, together with his sons; and you shall annoint them and consecrate them and sanctify them, that they may serve me as priests.*
>
> EXODUS 28:41

What makes a Jewish religious leader? The Bible delineates two great religious leaders, two complementary functionaries, the priest and the prophet, typologically expressed by Aaron the first High Priest and Moses the master prophet. Many Jewish writers and philosophers have endeavored to distinguish between these roles of leadership, perhaps the most well-known being in a masterful essay by Ahad Ha'am, where he sees the prophet as being the person who receives the divine word in its absolute and unadulterated form. It is then the task of the priest to mediate the message of God so that it is palatable and acceptable to the multitudes.

I would argue that any meaningful distinction between these two leadership functions must take into account the specific biblical laws relating to each of them; such a study may well be helpful in defining proper religious leadership for our own times.

The first distinction which must be noted is that the priest, strangely enough, merits his priesthood by his having been born to a father who was a priest, by dint of ancestry rather than aptitude.

Moreover, the *kohen* wore special garb, the ordinary *kohen* four unique garments and the High Priest eight unique garments as exquisitely described in this Torah portion. A *kohen* who entered the Temple precinct without proper garb was rendered invalid to perform the service; "his sanctity was the sanctity of the garments" (*Zevahim* 7a).

On the other hand, the prophet need have no prior prophetic lineage; indeed, Moses' personal tragedy lay in the reality that his children were not graced with his mantle of leadership. Nor did the prophet wear any unique garment; he emerged charismatically, and his message was conveyed without external trappings of pomp and circumstance.

Yisrael Eldad, in his masterful work *Hegionot Bamikra*, cogently argues that these differences between priest and prophet reflect the different aspects of leadership each must project. Religion purports to link the individual to eternity, to enable people to transcend themselves by participating in rituals which existed before they were born and will continue after they die. When one recites the Friday evening Kiddush (sanctification over the wine) with the same words and the same Kiddush goblet used by one's great-grandfather (as I am privileged to do) and expects to bequeath both the goblet and the liturgy to their great-grandchild, they participate in eternity. When a person stands at their parents' gravesite reciting the Kaddish prayer, they hear the echoes of eternity and touch mortality graced by immortality. Critical to this sense of transcendent continuity is an eternal structure, a form which is transmitted from generation to generation.

It is the *kohen* who is responsible for maintaining and transmitting this external structure, the outer form, whole and intact from parent to child, from country of exile to country of exile. Hence his sanctity is likewise – and of necessity – transmitted from father to son, and his sanctity is the exterior sanctity of garb.

However, structure without significance, form without fire, continuity without content, soon disintegrates into dead symbolism. To this end, the prophet is the priest's partner. The charismatic prophet, aglow with the relevance of God in the here and now, breathes divine fire into the external form, evokes crucial significance from the contours of the structure, and gives ethical content to the rituals of continuity. The sanctity of the prophets has nothing to do with their lineage, and everything to do with their persona, nothing to do with their external form clothed in a special way and everything to do with the fire pent up in their very bones.

Jewish leadership must dialectically express each of the two verities of priest and prophet together, true to Jewish tradition but sensitive to the exigencies of the hour, committed to the form of Jewish law but aware of the necessity of bringing God's justice and compassion to the situation at hand. The spirit of Moses and Aaron together is crucial for an authentic Jewish religious experience. Each one of us can become a *kohen*, passing down the tradition from generation to generation. Unfortunately, not everyone can become a prophet, consumed by the passionate fire of the divine and graced with the ability of making God and His message live in every generation and enter the consciousness of every Jew. And despite the difference in approach and mentality which characterizes them, despite the natural tension which divides between them – priest wary of prophetic innovation, prophet impatient with priestly involvement in legalities – the priest must pave the way for the prophet, and the prophet must be sensitive to the detailed demands of the priest. Only with reverence for our past can we forge a meaningful future; the ancient activity must express renewed meaning if the new is to become truly sanctified.

* * *

What is important is not who your father or grandfather is (or was), but who you are and who your grandchildren will be.

I was almost thirteen and my parents had just purchased my bar mitzva suit on the Lower East Side (Levy's Clothing, 8 Elizabeth Street). My father was proud and happy, and suggested that we mark the momentous occasion with a knish from Yonah Shimmel's knishery. As soon as we entered the store, I began scanning the wall for a kashrut certification. "Speak to the owner," suggested the harried salesman. Turning in to a side office, my father and I stood before a large desk at which was seated a middle-aged gentleman, with a wide girth and a bald pate. "*Yingale* (little boy), a kashrut certificate you want? Look at this picture of my father, Yonah Shimmel, the founder of our company. Do you still have the nerve to request a kashrut sign?" He pointed to a picture of a venerable looking man, replete with beard and forelocks, a high black hat, and a black frock-coat. Proud of my soon-to-be bar mitzva status, I replied with zest: "If you were hanging in the picture and your father was sitting at your desk, perhaps I wouldn't request the certificate; but since your father is hanging on the wall and you are seated in front of me, I can't buy a knish without a kashrut sign…"

*   *   *

The Search for Continuity

It was the early 1970s, and the Presidents' Conference sponsored a special dinner for Golda Meir. As the president of the Center for Russian Jewry, I was seated only a few seats away from the prime minister of Israel. The speeches were interminable, and everyone – including the prime minister – seemed relieved at finally receiving the main course. Just as Mrs. Meir was biting into her first piece of chicken, a delegation from the Reconstructionist Society for the Advancement of Judaism walked up to her and made an informal and unscheduled presentation of Rabbi Mordecai Kaplan's haggada, which highlighted our emergence from the Holocaust and entry into the Jewish State rather than our emergence from Egypt and entry into the desert. The prime minister took the book, scanned it quickly, and (surprisingly, even rudely – but the delegation had also rudely interrupted her dinner) gave it back. "But

Madame Prime Minister, you aren't known to be religious," responded
the spokesperson of the delegation. "No, I'm not religious. But I do
make a *seder* for my family. And I want my granddaughter to recite the
very same words as did my grandmother. I want everyone around the
seder table to participate in eternity."

The High Priest Anointed for War: Greatness and Limitations

> *Seven days shall the sons of the priest robe themselves upon entering the Tent of Meeting to minister in the holy place.*
>
> EXODUS 29:30

The image of High Priest is a universal one, evoking a reverent, uniquely-garbed patriarchal figure presiding over the most ceremonial rituals of the Holy Temple. What is generally not so well known, however, is that side by side with the Temple-centered High Priest there existed a second High Priest whose sphere of influence was the front lines of battle. He was called the *meshuaḥ milḥama*, or the "one annointed for war." His major concern was not the sacrificial offerings and meals, the shewbread and festival pomp-and-ceremony, expiation of sin and gifts of repentance; he was rather occupied with elements of war and the spirit of the fighters, the morale on the front lines of battle and the courage of the soldiers, who was to serve and who was to be exempted, the brave and the bereaved, the fearless and the frightened.

The differences between these two parallel High Priests found expression in a very unique law. The position of the Temple High Priest was hereditary, the crown of priesthood moving from Aaron to Elazar and down the genealogical line from father to son. But when it came to the Priest Anointed for War, heredity was not a factor. On the contrary, here was one priestly position that could not be bequeathed.

Intuitively, we understand that the Torah must distinguish between Temple leadership and battleground inspiration. Nevertheless, even the West Point military academy in modern times gives special preference to certain select families which have provided it with students for many generations.

In his commentary *Torah Temimah*, Rabbi Baruch Epstein raises this issue, after first directing us to the talmudic passage which discusses the differences of genealogy:

> One might think that the Priest who was anointed for War may inherit his position as does the son of the High Priest. However, the Torah states "Seven days shall the sons of the priest robe themselves upon entering the Tent of Meeting to minister in the holy place" (Ex. 29:30) – only the one who may enter the Tent of Meeting [the High Priest] bequeaths his position to his sons, and he who may not enter the Tent of Meeting [such as the Priest Anointed for War] cannot pass on his position to his son.
>
> *Yoma* 73a

"Why not?" asks Rabbi Epstein. And he explains that the Priest Anointed for War required unique qualities of inspirational ability and psychological expertise; he had to imbue the soldiers with courage and at the same time weed out those who were so frightened of battle that their fears could become contagious and endanger the lives of others.

The Torah itself – in Deuteronomy – presents us with the job requirements of the Priest Anointed for War:

> And it shall be when you draw near unto the battle, the priest

shall approach and speak to the people and say to them, Hear O Israel, you are about to wage battle against your enemies. Let not your hearts faint. Don't be afraid and do not tremble. Don't be terrified because of them, for the Lord your God is He that goes with you to fight for you against your enemies and to save you.

Deuteronomy 20:2–4

A person who could genuinely inspire the nation had to be possessed of a tremendous measure of faith and fearlessness himself. He couldn't be a priest giving lip service over a radio station thousands of miles from the front. Clearly, the psychological and emotional strengths as well as the bravery evidenced by going into the thick of battle, required character traits that were not necessarily passed down from father to son.

Just because a father is willing to endanger his life, does this mean that his son will necessarily do the same?

Torah Temima goes on to cite the Jerusalem Talmud (*Ta'anit* 4:5) which informs us that the Priest Anointed for War also needed the ability to "discern between different musical sounds." This may be a reference to the skill of listening to the people as they described their fears and weaknesses. Some had to be comforted and convinced; others had to be sent home so as not to lower the morale of their comrades. The Priest Anointed for War had not only to exhort but also to listen; he had not only to hear the words but also had to discern the music behind the words. He had to be a master preacher, actor, teacher and psychologist; a person of rare charisma and sensitivity. The corpus of Temple rituals, the "dos and don'ts" of the sacrificial and liturgical prescriptions, could be transmitted from parent to child, from generation to generation. But inspirational and psychological expertise is not open to transmission from father to son! Any country whose chiefs of staff and defense ministers are chosen because of family connections will soon find that it has no future generation to carry on its traditions. I believe there is also a second reason for the distinction between High Priest and Priest Anointed for War. Implicit in the concept of rule-by-heredity is the desire for continuity. The royalty of England, a Hassidic court, and the Jewish priesthood all express a desire to keep their institution alive, from generation to generation to generation. And there is no better guarantee for continuity than the creation of a dynasty, the legacy passed down intact from parent to child. A system where the mantle of leadership moves in this manner has the best chance of achieving the closest thing to eternity. To the extent that the rituals of the Holy Temple had to be preserved in their exact form, the best way to do so was to keep it in the family. Each individual priest – and certainly the High Priest himself – had something important at stake in the preservation and the continuity of their share of family knowledge. Therefore it wasn't necessary to bequeath the high priesthood to a charismatic outsider; just being the next in line was sufficient insurance for the future.

The phenomenal renaissance of the Hassidic movement in modern times, despite the fact that 80% of the pre-World War II Hassidic leadership was destroyed in the Holocaust, can only be explained by the fact that it was a dynastic movement. After the war, the scholarship or piety of a rebbe-candidate took a back seat to how closely related he was to the last rebbe who was killed by the Nazis. A grandson, even a nephew, could serve as the focal point of rejuvenation for a particular Hassidic line. Belz crowned a nine-year-old as their rebbe, affectionately known as the *yanukah* (lit. "nursing child") and today it stands as one of the most influential groups on the Hassidic landscape. Yet the *Mussar* yeshivot, which did not nurture the notion of familial continuity, never emerged from the ashes of Auschwitz. There were 180 Nevardok schools of *Mussar* before World War II. Today, that particular brand of *Mussar* is virtually extinct.

When it comes to the priesthood, the same principle is at work. We want everything to be exactly as God commanded it, and the best way to make sure that the tradition survives in its exact form is to invest it with the special requirements of a parent to child dimension. This is why the High Priest's job was hereditary, even if the son couldn't exactly fill the father's shoes in terms of his personal qualities of intellect and spirit. The important element is the continuity of the position; once we introduce the notion of the "best man for the job," then the intrigues and political battles begin, sometimes producing a successful leader, and sometimes a total disaster.

I once heard it said in the name of Rabbi Abraham Yitzhak Hakohen Kook that it is precisely because continuity is the purpose of genealogical transmission that the Priest Anointed for War is not a hereditary post. We want the Holy Temple and the sacrificial-liturgical ritual to be eternal; we certainly hope and pray that war is only a temporary and transitory necessity on our path to national and universal peace. Indeed, the Mishna teaches that implements of war are considered to be a burden and not an ornament, and we are therefore forbidden to take them up on the Sabbath unless faced with a life-threatening situation.

> The sages rule that weapons are a disgrace, as Isaiah says (Is. 2:4): "They shall beat their swords into ploughshares ... humanity shall not learn war."
>
> *Mishna Shabbat* 6:4

What message would we be broadcasting if we made the Priest Anointed for War an eternal position? An eternity of war? Obviously such a message goes against the heart of Judaism. On the contrary, we only wish to continually preserve the High Priest of the Holy Temple, which is an institution dedicated to loving and pursuing peace, a building whose very stones are forbidden to be hewn by the sword.

Ki Tissa

To Count or Not to Count

> *When you take the sum of the children of Israel after their number, each one shall be counted by giving an atonement offering for his life. In this manner, they will not be stricken by the plague when they are counted. Everyone included in the census must include a half-shekel.*
>
> EXODUS 30:12–13

To count or not to count is not the question, but rather how to count! And whom you cannot count! At first glance, one of the more curious laws in the Torah is the prohibition to count Jews. The Talmud records:

> R. Elazar said, "Whoever counts an Israelite, transgresses a [single] prohibition, as it is written, 'And the number of the children are as the sand of the sea which cannot be measured'" (Hosea 2:1). R. Nahman bar Isaac says, "He transgresses two prohibitions, as the verse concludes, 'and cannot be counted.'"
>
> *Yoma* 22b

Given this, how are we to understand the opening of the portion of *Ki Tissa*, where God commands Moses to count the Israelites?

Count, but not by counting heads, but rather by counting the half-shekel coins which every Israelite was commanded to bring. But isn't this actually a subterfuge, a kind of legal fiction? Moreover, what is the significance of a half-shekel? If you're using coins, would a whole shekel not better represent the "whole" person?

Furthermore, how are we to understand the word "*tissa*?" The Hebrew root implies "lifting up." Rashi, citing Targum Onkelos, informs us that it means to obtain, or to receive, which is how most translations treat the word: "When you take sum of the children of Israel...." The Midrash (*Pesikta Rabati 11*) picks up on the idea of "lifting" but goes one step further; more than to lift, *Ki Tissa* is about uplifting, not just to raise but to exalt. And in this count of counts, we are exalting not only Israel, but also the God of Israel. "In whatever manner you can uplift this nation, uplift. For it says, *ki tissa et rosh bnai Yisrael* [When you lift up the head of the children of Israel]. And there is no head of the Jewish people except for God."

How are we exalting God by counting half-shekels?

Perhaps a fascinating talmudic discussion between the two religio-political parties of the Second Commonwealth, the Pharisees and the Sadducees, will help us understand the importance of a census in the first place. Everyone agrees that we are forbidden to mourn during the first week of the month of Nisan because this marks the original establishment of the *tamid*, the daily sacrifice, in the Temple, but they disagree as to how the daily sacrifice should be funded. The Sadducees, who represented the aristocracy, believed that specific donors could, of their own free will, defray the cost of the daily offering, while the Pharisees insisted that the universal half-shekel payments be used for these offerings (*Menaḥot* 65a). Apparently the Pharisees, forerunners of Rabbinic Judaism, which gave us the Talmud, wanted the daily offering to remain a national enterprise, a gift to God from every single Jew. And the only way to guarantee its "democratic" spirit would be to insist on equal contributions, where the Rothschilds and Tevyes had equal input:

The rich shall not give more and the poor shall not give less than one half-shekel when giving an offering before the Lord, to atone for your souls.

Exodus 30:15

This idea is implicitly discussed and further illuminated in the Jerusalem Talmud, where we find the sages debating the reason for the Torah's choice of the half-shekel in this portion. R. Yehuda explains that "since they sinned at half-day [the celebration of the golden calf began at midday] they had to give a half-shekel." R. Pinhas, in the name of R. Levi, attributes it to the selling of Joseph. "Since the brothers sold the first son of Rachel, Joseph, for twenty silver pieces – and with Benjamin being too young and Joseph not being a recipient, each of the ten brothers received one-half shekel" (*Shekalim*, 2:3).

I would like to suggest that both of these opinions are two sides of the same coin: both idolatry and sibling rivalry reflect a world in which the value of national unity and togetherness is of paltry significance.

Idolatry results from feeling impotent in a world controlled by external and irrational forces which we humans can at best "bribe," but can never work with in partnership. And the sale of Joseph, the expulsion of one brother from a family, expressed the view that one segment of a nation has the right to destroy, banish, or delegitimize other segments of the nation with whom they ideologically disagree and over whom they can exercise political or physical control.

The half-shekel census for the daily Temple sacrifice is a specific remedy for national feelings of internal fractiousness and ultimate impotence. The very taking of a census affirms national pride and self-confidence; it asserts the importance of every individual member as contributing to the whole.

And why a half-shekel? Simply stated, we are being taught that every Jew is incomplete without every other Jew. Every Jew must be brought closer, not pushed away. The whole is comprised of the sum of its parts, and every part is unassailably precious.

A story is told about two Hassidic masters who had spent their youth studying together in a yeshiva and sharing every imaginable adventure and crisis. Upon going their separate ways, they exchanged photos by which to remember each other. But one of the young men took the photo of himself and tore it in half, and then he tore the photo of his friend in half as well. It's not enough, he explained, to remember the other; it is far more important to always remember that without the other, each of us is only half a person, an incomplete specimen.

But, if the half-shekel contribution is such a laudatory act, a symbol of Jewish national strength and unity, why should the Torah consider it a sin to count Jews? Indeed, the very pride of the nation seems to be in the counting!

To answer this question, and to deepen our entire attitude towards the census, we must interpret the midrashic image in the name of R. Meir:

> God removed a coin of fire from under his throne of glory and He showed it to Moses, saying, 'This is what they shall give.'
>
> *Tanḥuma, Ki Tissa, 9*

How are we to understand this coin of fire? Did not Moses know what a half-shekel coin looked like? Fire symbolizes the spirit of God which resides within the nation of Israel, the *Shekhinah* who dwells in the midst of each individual of the nation. Israel was forged and formed by the divine voice at Sinai and is best described as a burning bush* which is never consumed by the inspiring sparks and flames of fervor that emerge from its depth; much the opposite, it is that very fire of the divine which provides the fuel for Israel's eternity.

From this perspective, the whole is not merely comprised of each of its parts; the whole is greater than the sum of its parts. The whole is not only the Jewish nation; it is also the God who resides in our nation, the very God who is uplifted together with His people when each of them is counted – and when it is thereby understood that every Jew counts! And the whole is not merely the Jewish nation today. It is also the Jewish nation of yesterday and tomorrow. It is not only *klal Yisrael*, the entire nation; it is also *knesset Yisrael*, historic and eternal Israel. Yes, the nation as a united whole is significant – but that is only part of the

---

* The biblical word used for the burning bush is *sneh* which has similar letters to the word *Sinai*.

story. The children of the patriarchs and matriarchs and the parents of the Messiah must always include their forbears as well as their progeny in a total assessment of where we stand and what we stand for.

And this "eternal" aspect of our existence is really the reason why we do not count Jews. We don't count because we can't count. Since the Jewish people are an eternal people, all those Jews who have lived before us, and all those Jews who haven't even been born yet, are part of our nation, part of *knesset Yisrael*. In the words of Rabbi Joseph B. Soloveitchik, the daily sacrifice is not an offering of partnership (*korban shutfut*), but rather an offering of historic community (*korban tzibbur*). And if Israel includes within it the metaphysical idea of a historic nation, how can we ever count eternity?

Sweet and Not So Savory Spices: The Jewish Melting Pot

> *And God spoke unto Moses: Take unto you sweet spices, stacte [nataf], onycha [shelet] and galbanum [helbena], these sweet spices with pure frankincense [levona], all of an equal weight.*
>
> EXODUS 30:34

Ne of the most unique aspects of the Sanctuary, continued in the Holy Temples, was the sweet-smelling spices of the incense burned on a special altar and whose inspiring fragrance permeated the House of God. In the portion of *Ki Tissa* the Torah lists the different spices, and their names – in Hebrew or English – are strange to our modern ears. But stranger still is the Rabbinic commentary that one of those spices – specifically *helbena* – is hardly sweet smelling. On the contrary, as Rashi writes, *helbena* "...is a malodorous spice which is known [to us as] *gelbanah* [galbanum]. Scripture enumerates it among the spices of the incense to teach us that we shouldn't look upon the inclusion of

Jewish transgressors in our fasts and prayers as something insignificant in our eyes; indeed, they [the transgressors of Israel] must also be included amongst us" (Rashi, ad loc.).

Rashi is conveying a most significant Rabbinic insight. The community of Israel – in Hebrew a *tzibur* – must consist of all types of Jews: righteous (the letter *tzadi* for *tzaddikim*), intermediate (the letter *bet* for *benonim*), and wicked (the letter *reish* for *resha'im*), just as the incense of the Sanctuary included spices of unappetizing fragrance. Perhaps because we must learn to take responsibility for every member of the "family" no matter what their behavior, perhaps because what appears to us as wicked may in reality be more genuine spirituality, perhaps because no evil is without its redeeming feature or perhaps merely in order to remind us not to be judgmental towards other human beings, the message of the incense could not be clearer: no Jew, even the most egregious sinner, dare be dismissed with mockery and derision from the sacred congregation of Israel. Every Jew must be allowed to contribute, and only when every Jew is included does the sweet fragrance properly emerge.

We have already seen how the Torah portion of *Ki Tissa* contains another striking example of the significance of every single Jew in Israel in the aftermath of the great sin in the desert. We read that soon after the revelation at Sinai, Moses' prolonged communion with the divine frightened the people into worshiping a golden calf. Our sages teach:

> And God said to Moses, "Go down" (Ex. 32:7). Interprets R. Elazar: God was commanding Moses to descend from his elevated position. The only reason I gave you greatness is because of Israel, and now that Israel has sinned, what do I need you for?'
>
> *Berakhot* 32a

God is reminding Moses that God's covenant with Abraham was with every single Jew. No Jew dare be discounted; every Jew must be loved, taught, and at least given the opportunity to come closer to God and our traditions. Even the Jew who is serving idols must be spoken to, ministered to!

A month or so after this portion is read, the *seder* itself becomes a living demonstration of the necessity to include rather than to exclude any Jew. Take note of the proverbial four children: the wise child, the wicked child, the simple child and the child who knows not what to ask. It is instructive that the wicked child is not defined by the compiler of the haggada as one who eats non-kosher food or desecrates the Sabbath; the wicked child is rather the one who says "Of what value is this work for you?" Wickedness is defined as excluding oneself from the general Jewish community. And even if a person excludes herself – and is therefore called wicked – we dare not exclude her. Our *seder* table must always be welcoming enough to include everyone, no matter who.

Indeed, towards the end of the *seder* we are instructed to open the door for Elijah the prophet, forerunner of the Messiah. In the past I've commented that opening the door for Elijah seems superfluous given Elijah's uncanny ability to visit every single *seder* in the world; anyone capable of accomplishing such a remarkable feat certainly would not be stopped by a closed door. One answer that I've proposed is that the opening of the door is not really for Elijah; it is rather a symbolic gesture of opening the door to the fifth child, the child who has moved so far from the Jewish people that he isn't even at the *seder*! We must go out to find him – even if he is at a neighborhood disco or a Far East ashram – and invite him to come back in. And why is Elijah associated with this gesture toward the fifth child? The closing verse of the last prophet included in the canon, Malakhi, declares: "Behold I will send Elijah, the prophet, before the coming of the great and awesome day of God, and he shall turn the hearts of the fathers to the children, and the hearts of the children to their fathers..." (Malakhi 3:23). No one, not the "wicked" child, and not even the "invisible" child, is to be excluded from the *seder*, the commemoration of our first redemption. Parents and children must all join together in a loving and accepting reunion.

There is a fascinating halakhic ramification of our desire to include rather than to exclude. The Talmud (*Eruvin* 69b) suggests that a public desecrater of the Sabbath is comparable to an idolater, whose wine cannot be drunk and who cannot be counted for a statutory quorum (*minyan*) for prayer. Does this mean that a Jew who does not observe the Sabbath laws and rituals forfeits his rights to belong to a proper Jewish congregation? One of the towering Torah giants of nineteenth-century Germany, Rabbi David Zvi Hoffman, raises this very question in his collection of responsa, *Mellamed Leho'il* (Responsum 29), where he resoundingly rules that the talmudic comparison no longer applies. He explains that during talmudic times, when the overwhelming majority of the Jewish people was observant, and when a Jew was defined in terms of their Torah observance, any Jew who publicly desecrated the Sabbath was effectively testifying to their exclusion from the Jewish people. Therefore, in talmudic times, a public Sabbath desecrator became the equivalent of an idolater; in effect, the perpetrator of such a public crime was excluding himself from the congregation of Israel and such a person was thereby relinquishing any rights to Jewish privileges. However, explains Rabbi Hoffman, when – sadly enough – the overwhelming majority of Jews are not observant (and today this is even truer than it was in nineteenth-century Germany), a Jew who publicly desecrates the Sabbath is not at all making a statement of exclusion from the peoplehood of Israel. On the contrary, the very fact that such a desecrater attends a synagogue (if only a few times a year) and is willing to partake in the service indicates a definite feeling of belonging and a will to belong to the historic community of Israel. Therefore, Rabbi Hoffman concludes, a Sabbath desecrater must not only be included in a *minyan*, but must be encouraged to become more involved.

* * *

A Curious Postscript

On a recent plane trip from New York to Israel, I felt myself awakened by a rather startling question. Someone wanted to see my *tzitzit* (ritual fringes). Still half asleep, I opened my shirt, showing the aggressive questioner what he wanted. I thought that perhaps he needed to borrow them. "Good," he said, "in that case please join us for a *minyan* for morning prayers." Somewhat confused, I asked him what my wearing or not wearing *tzitzit* had to do with my joining the *minyan*. "You know," he said, "you can't pray with just any Jew. But chances are that a Jew who wears *tzitzit* also observes the Sabbath."

I was quite taken aback, to say the least. I reminded the zealot that the source for the requirement of ten people for a *minyan* was derived from God's statement to Moses, "How long must I suffer this evil congregation...?" (Num. 14:27). And the evil congregation to which God is referring is the ten out of twelve scouts who didn't want to conquer the Land of Israel. Since the word "*eda*" (congregation) refers to ten scouts, we know that ten comprise a *minyan*. Now these ten scouts are considered to have committed one of the most grievous sins of the Bible by their refusal to leave the desert and inhabit Israel. If such individuals are the very source for a congregational quorum, how could someone be excluded if he doesn't wear the ritual fringes?

I did not choose to pray with such a hand-picked group; I chose rather to pray with those who had been rejected by the *tzitzit* checking *minyan* gatherer, confident that they would be far more acceptable to the God of compassion and unconditional love to whom we pray!

The Highest Sanctity, the Human Soul

> God told Moses to speak to the Israelites and
> to say unto them, "But my Sabbaths shall you
> observe, for it is a sign between me and you
> throughout your generations, that you may know
> that I am the Lord who sanctifies you."
>
> EXODUS 31:13

What is the repetition of the command to observe Shabbat
doing in the midst of the description of the Tabernacle in the portion
of *Ki Tissa*?* For the last six biblical chapters – ever since the start of
Teruma – we've been dealing with the elaborate and complex details
of the construction and sacred appurtenances of the Tabernacle. Then,
seemingly apropos of nothing, the Torah suddenly switches topics: "But
my Sabbaths shall you observe." What is the connection?

One reason may be the overwhelming amount of exacting labor

---

* This question has been previously dealt with from another perspective. See
Teruma, pp. 209-213.

that the Tabernacle's construction required, as described in the preceding portions. Undoubtedly, it was important to finish the task as soon as possible, providing a sanctuary which would connect the Israelites to their parent in heaven. We are also aware of how builders of massive and important construction projects will exert all human effort to finish a project, even going full steam ahead seven days a week if necessary. Shabbat may be holy, but so is the Tabernacle. What about working on Shabbat to get the Tabernacle built as soon as possible, thereby allowing the divine service to actually begin? Is it not possible to justify such activity? After all, it is all for the sake of God, for the enhancement of the holy! According to Rashi, the verses dealing with Shabbat in this portion specifically come to forestall such an analysis. Commenting on the verses quoted above, Rashi writes:

> Even though you may be anxious and alert to do the work promptly, Shabbat must not be pushed aside for its account.
>
> Rashi on Exodus 31:13

Rashi points out that the word *"akh"* (but) comes to serve as a limitation, to exclude something. "The terms *"rak"* and *"akh"* are always limitations, to exclude [*lema'et*] Shabbat from the construction of the Tabernacle" (Ex. 31:13, Rashi ad loc.). Hence the Torah is emphasizing that despite the best of intentions, no work on the Tabernacle can take place on Shabbat!

Nahmanides disagrees sharply with Rashi's usage of the exegetical laws of limitations. Indeed, according to biblical rules of hermeneutics, the result should be the exact opposite of what Rashi claims: not excluding the Tabernacle from work on Shabbat, but rather excluding the usual prohibitions from Shabbat, and allowing the Tabernacle to be constructed even on Shabbat. Ordinarily, if I speak of an all-inclusive concept, the exception will tell me that a specific circumstance falls outside the purview of the usual application of that system. For example, the Torah commands that on Yom Kippur everyone fast. There is an exclusion or limitation pertaining to Yom Kippur regarding people who are seriously ill; the usual prohibitions of eating and drinking on that day do not apply to them. Similarly, if the *akh* is a Shabbat exclusion or limitation referring to the Tabernacle, it should mean that the construction of the Tabernacle is excluded from the usual Shabbat prohibitions, and hence it ought to be permitted to construct the Tabernacle on Shabbat. To be sure, Nahmanides agrees with Rashi's halakhic conclusion that work on the Tabernacle does not abrogate Shabbat. He merely disagrees about the way Rashi derives that halakha. Nahmanides simply includes the Tabernacle in all of the usual Shabbat prohibitions, and refuses to see it as any form of exception to the general Shabbat rules. He must therefore use the word "*akh*" to teach something else – to refer to another situation (other than the construction of the Sanctuary) which is indeed excluded from the usual Shabbat prohibitions. For Nahmanides, this is the commandment of saving a human life – *piku'ah nefesh. Akh* comes to tell us that we must waive all Shabbat prohibitions in order to save a human life, that the preservation of life is excluded from the ordinary applications of Shabbat observance.

Although Rashi and Nahmanides interpret the function of the word "*akh*" differently, Rashi excluding Shabbat from the work of the Tabernacle, and Nahmanides excluding Shabbat when it poses a danger to human life, I would like to suggest that if we combine both of these interpretations, we arrive at a fundamental and majestic truth about Judaism. In looking at Shabbat in relation to the Tabernacle, Rashi's *akh* reminds us that although the holiest and most exalted physical endeavor in this world may be the building of the Tabernacle, nevertheless *akh et shabtotai tishmoru* – You must still observe my Sabbaths; Shabbat day is holier than the Tabernacle. Quite simply, the sanctity of time is greater than the sanctity of space. One of the reasons for this is that a sanctuary in time (to use Rabbi Abraham Joshua Heschel's beautiful metaphor for Shabbat) can never be destroyed by human weapons, whereas our sanctuary in space (the Holy Temple) has tragically been destroyed twice. Perhaps that is the deepest reason why Jews have managed to live without their Temple, but we could never have survived as a people without Shabbat.

Nahmanides goes one step further. He knows that Shabbat is holier than the Tabernacle, but he stresses a sanctity greater than both a sanctuary in space and a sanctuary in time, namely, the sanctity of the human being, the sanctity of human life created in the divine image. This highest sanctity of all is even alluded to in our verse, which begins with "But my Sabbaths shall you observe [*akh et shabtotai tishmoru*]" and ends with "For it is a sign between Me and you throughout your generations, that you may know that I am the Lord who sanctifies you" (Ex. 31:13). How will we know this? On one level, when we observe Shabbat rest, it is as a testimony to the divine creation of the universe. But on a deeper level, when we set aside our Shabbat rest in order to preserve a human life, we truly understand the exalted nature of the human being – precisely because humans were created in the image of the divine. On Shabbat I can transgress all the laws in order to save a single human being. In effect, God is saying that the holiest of all his creations, more than any building or any day, is the human being! This fundamental teaching, that in the pyramid of the sacred we advance upwards from sanctity of space to sanctity of time to sanctity of human being, is a principle we tend to overlook in the midst of all our other holy pursuits. Even the most punctiliously observant often seem oblivious to the sacred character of every single individual, Jew or gentile. And the truth is that in the final analysis, it is the human being who either endows or removes sanctity from space as well as from time!

In the area of space, this truth is self-evident. Human beings create or desecrate a home, an office, a synagogue, a Temple – depending on what they do within them. This is even true of ritual objects, which are material articles in space. It is even true of a Torah scroll: The Talmud tells us (*Shabbat* 116a) that a Torah scroll written by a heretic (with improper intent) is to be burnt.

This is the case, even if that particular scroll appears on the surface to have letter-perfect script and the highest quality parchment. And I would submit that the same principle obtains to the sanctity of time.

Two great Hassidic rebbes, the Voorker and the Kotzker, were once discussing holiness. The Voorker compared the commandment of living in a sukka (booth) with that of taking the "four species" during the Sukkot festival. According to him, the sukka was the more sacred command because, while the command of the four species enables one to hold or encompass holiness, in the sukka it is holiness which holds or encompasses the individual. The Kotzker responded that from this perspective, Shabbat remains the holiest of all commandments. After all, a person can always walk out of the sukka, but he or she can never walk out of the Shabbat! But I respectfully disagree; after all, does not an individual walk out of the Shabbat, if they leave the Shabbat table to go to a cinema, or opt not to have a Shabbat meal with candlelight, Kiddush and *zemirot*, or interrupt the Shabbat meal with angry words or slanderous gossip!? Hence, the highest sanctity of all must still be the human being, who even has this ability to determine the sanctity of time.

Each and every Shabbat we must confront this profound truth of our tradition, that the human being stands at the apex of the sacred. Shabbat teaches – as those of us who have seen medical emergency volunteers with walkie-talkies leaving Shabbat prayers to get into an ambulance and respond to an emergency can testify – that saving a life on Shabbat is not a violation of the law, but is indeed the highest fulfillment of the Shabbat laws and the Torah ideal.

When the Means Becomes Confused With the Ends

> *It is an everlasting sign between Me and the*
> *children of Israel; for in six days the Lord made*
> *the heavens and the earth, and on the seventh day*
> *He ceased from work and He rested.*
>
> EXODUS 31:17

Astructural outline of the last five portions of the book of Exodus shows that this section begins with the Sanctuary and its various parts (*Teruma* and *Tetzaveh*, goes on to the Shabbat command (beginning of *Ki Tissa*), continues with the account of the golden calf episode (the bulk of *Ki Tissa*), again mentions the Shabbat command (beginning of *Vayak-hel*), and finally returns to the details of the Sanctuary construction (the bulk of *Vayak-hel* and *Pekudei*). Thus we have Sanctuary, Shabbat, golden calf, Shabbat, Sanctuary, with the Sanctuary comprising close to four entire portions at the beginning and at the conclusion,

Shabbat only comprising several verses in each instance, and the central golden calf episode comprising three-quarters of a portion.

Even if we say that there is no set chronological order to the Torah, there must, after all, be a sound logical and psychological order to the book of divine wisdom! So how can we understand the Sanctuary description being interrupted by the golden calf episode, which is in turn surrounded before and after with Shabbat commands?

In order for us to understand the inner logic behind this seeming disorder, we must first understand the sin of the golden calf. Is it really possible to imagine that only forty-one days after the great epiphany at Sinai, the Israelites could sink to the abysmal depths of idolatry? How could Aaron, Moses' elder brother and High Priest of Israel, have ever agreed to make a molten calf for the people to worship?

Nahmanides explains that the Israelites were not initially seeking a God substitute; they were rather seeking a Moses substitute. They panicked when the great leader who had communicated to them God's concern and God's laws did not descend from the mountain on the day they had expected him to, and in their desolation and desperation they reverted back to the symbols they remembered from Egypt. There the molten calf served as the seat, or the mediator, upon which the divine idol rested.

> And the nation gathered around Aaron and they said to him, "Arise and make for us gods [*Elohim*, leaders] who will go before us, since that Moses, the personality who took us up from the land of Egypt...we do not know what happened to him."
>
> Exodus 32:1

After Aaron produces the molten calf, he declares:

> "There shall be a festival for the Lord [*YHVH*] tomorrow."
>
> Ibid. 5

The nation was apparently seeking a flesh-and-blood, material representative, or representation, who would bring them closer to the divine, a Moses substitute rather than a God substitute (Nahmanides ad loc.).

Tragically, the experiment failed. The calf, which was supposed to be merely the means towards the end of divine worship, was transformed into the ideal itself, the very objective of the nation's service. "And they brought burnt offerings and they drew near peace offerings [to the calf!] and the nation sat to eat and to drink and they rose to make sport" (Ex. 32:6). The means had become the end; the calf, instead of directing the Israelites to the invisible God of the universe, became itself the god of hedonistic orgies and materialistic pleasures. The mediator became the message!

The Almighty understood from this tragic debacle that the Israelites were not on the lofty spiritual level that could enable them to appreciate a purely immaterial God of the spirit. They needed some physical intermediary which they could touch and feel in order to inspire them to reach loftier heights. After the sin, God commanded the building of a Sanctuary, a magnificent edifice which could inspire divine worship. "And let them make Me a Sanctuary [as a means to the end] that I may dwell among them [the only genuine end, having the divine spirit resting within each and every Jew]. The Sanctuary could become the "kosher" calf, the continuation of Moses throughout the generations.

Therefore, immediately following the commandments of the Decalogue and *Mishpatim*, the Israelites are commanded to construct the Sanctuary, the vehicle by means of which God's inspiring words would continue to enter Jewish hearts, minds and consciousness. But the danger always existed that the means would become transformed and perverted into the end, that the Sanctuary would be seen as the purpose and not just the process. After all, human beings major in mistaking the means for the ends, in turning the process into the purpose. Do we not all too often devote ourselves exclusively to our jobs to the exclusion of our families, forsaking the very individuals whom we claimed were the reason behind the purpose for all of our hard toil?

As a result of this danger, the Torah concludes the laws of the Sanctuary with the admonition: "But my Sabbaths shall you observe." Whatever is involved in the construction of the Sanctuary may not be done on Shabbat. Shabbat is holier than the Sanctuary; the Shabbat is the purpose of the Sanctuary! After all, the purpose of the Sanctuary is to inspire us to want to meet the divine, whereas Shabbat is that very meeting itself; Shabbat is dedicated to the Lord Himself. The Sanctuary is the means, Shabbat is the end. We dare not confuse the two.

And what does it mean to become introduced to God, to enter into a meeting with the divine? "Just as He is compassionate, so must you be compassionate; just as He gives freely [unconditionally], so must you give freely; just as He is full of loving-kindness, so must you be full of loving-kindness" (Maimonides, Laws of Knowledge, 1:10). This is the end; all else is means!

And so the Bible follows the command to erect the Sanctuary with the more important command to observe Shabbat. The oasis in time is more significant, and ultimately supersedes, the oasis in space. The God of compassion and loving-kindness is more important than the Temple of gold and silver, than the priestly institution of honor and glory, pomp and circumstance. In order to underscore the warning, the Bible then documents the golden calf debacle whose tragedy lay in substituting means for ends. The Torah again stresses the true end goal of Shabbat, and can finally conclude by returning to the Sanctuary only after the crucial lesson of the hierarchy of religious values has properly been taught and conveyed.

The Sanctuary must lead to the Sabbath, a meeting with the divine which suffuses the individual with divine values and traits. The confusion of the golden calf must never be allowed to be repeated. Religion may be inspired by temples of gold and silver, but true religion can only be found where its adherents are individuals expressing the divine attributes of compassion, loving-kindness and truth. Humans must become the sanctuaries within whom the divine dwells!*

Permit me to offer yet one more layer of interpretation. When Moses and Israel sang their great song of thanksgiving at the splitting of the Reed Sea, they declared: "This is my God, and I shall build a house [sanctuary] for Him" (Ex. 15:2) (according to Targum, the Hebrew word

---

* For a similar treatment, see my commentary on *Teruma*, pp. 215-218. However, here I suggest that the Sanctuary is mainly a means to the Sabbath, whereas there I suggest that the Sanctuary and the Sabbath are each ends. In my previous treatment, I was interpreting the Sabbath and the Sanctuary from an eschatological perspective.

"*naveh*" is taken to mean house). Rabbi Samson Rafael Hirsch expands this interpretation to read: "This is my God, and I shall be a house for Him." In other words, I shall make myself, my thoughts, feelings and actions into a vehicle for the expression of His essence and His will.

Perhaps this is really what the verse means: "And let them make Me a Sanctuary that I may dwell among them" – that they may become My sanctuaries, My house, that their bodies may express My wishes, and their mouths speak My words. A sanctuary must be the vehicle that inspires the individual Israelites to become God-like living expressions of the true and compassionate God. The Sanctuary is the means; the Sabbath is the end. Food, clothing and shelter is the means; being in fellowship with God is the end. Building a house for God is the means; being a house for God is the end.

Reb Yisrael and Am Yisrael:
When Death Takes a Holiday

> *And God said to Moses, "Go down, for your*
> *people, whom you have taken out of the land of*
> *Egypt, have been corrupt."*
>
> EXODUS 32:7

The biblical reading of *Ki Tissa* recounts the tragic episode of the Jews turning to idolatry barely forty days after the revelation at Sinai, the possibility of which could never have entered the mind of Moses; if it had, he never would have left them alone. He told them he would return in forty days; they expected him on the fortieth day and he prepared to rejoin them only on the forty-first day. They panicked, and began to ecstatically worship the Egyptian idol of a golden calf. Moses went atop Mount Sinai, ascending to the very supernal realm of heaven in order to continue to receive God's law. And then God suddenly says to Moses:

> ...Go down, for your people...have been corrupt...they have made a molten calf, and have worshiped it...
>
> Exodus 32:7–8

Commenting on this verse, R. Eliezer interprets:

> God said to Moses: "Get down from your greatness. The only reason I gave you greatness is because of Israel, and now that Israel has sinned, what do I need you for?"
>
> *Berakhot* 32a

Picture the situation of the most perfect, spiritual ivory-tower *kollel* in history: God is the master teacher, as it were, and Moses the disciple. Nevertheless, the Almighty insists that Moses leave his sacred sanctuary and go down to the people! After all, God did not make a covenant with individual Jews, no matter now elite or noteworthy they may be; He made a covenant with an entire nation!

This special quality of the Jewish nation is confirmed in a nearby talmudic passage which records two curious happenings in the academy of the same R. Eliezer whose interpretation has God remind Moses of his primary responsibility to the continuation of Israel. One of R. Eliezer's students was serving as prayer leader for the congregation. When he was excessive in the amount of time he spent praying, the other students complained to R. Eliezer. R. Eliezer answered, "Does he then pray longer than did Moses, who prayed for forty days and nights?"

The text goes on to describe how on another occasion the student who served as the prayer leader rushed through the prayers. When the others complained to R. Eliezer this time as well, the teacher replied:

> Does he pray more quickly than did Moses [when Moses prayed for his sister Miriam], as it is written, "Heal her now, O God, I pray thee?!"
>
> *Berakhot* 34a

Why does the Talmud record this incident? Is it simply to show us that the academy of R. Eliezer was very much like the academies and congregations in our own day, at least with respect to one thing: Some prayer leaders take too much time and some take too little time, and the congregation is never satisfied, always complaining. Clearly, the point of the contrast is to teach us the great range of prayer, from forty days and forty nights of beseeching to a mere few words: "Heal her now, O God, I pray thee." (Num. 12:13). And, on a deeper level, R. Eliezer teaches his students precisely when lengthy devotions are appropriate and when quick prayers are appropriate. His basis is the teacher of us all, Moshe Rabbenu. When it comes to a prayer on behalf of the nation, Moses prays for forty days and forty nights. Indeed, R. Avihu, in a most daring commentary, interprets God's words to Moses in this very context – "Let me alone and I will destroy them" (Ex. 12:13) – that Moses refused to let God alone! Moses took advantage of the window God opened for him and he

> grabbed onto God like someone who grabs his friend by his garment, and says before him: "I won't leave You alone until you forgive the Jewish people."
>
> *Berakhot* 32b

What gives Moses the right to act so aggressively with God? It is because the Jewish nation has a claim on God. After all, God entered into a covenant with the nation and guaranteed the nation eternity; indeed, it is the Jewish nation whose mission it is to teach ethical monotheism to the world and bring about redemption. God guaranteed Jewish survival – and that the nations of the world would eventually be blessed through Israel – at Abraham's initial election as well as in the Covenant of the Pieces. But God makes no such guarantee to any individual Jew, even if the individual is the righteous Miriam, sister of Moses. In praying for an individual, one dare not persist too much.

From this perspective, we may begin to understand a very difficult point of Jewish law. If a close loved one for whom we are obligated to mourn – a child, a parent, a sibling, a spouse – is buried just a few minutes before the onset of a festival, close family members are expected to enter the festival – sit down to a *seder* celebration, for example – with only joy in their hearts, devoid of the smallest scintilla of sadness (at least according to Maimonides). "The public joy of the festival must overwhelm the personal sadness of the mourner," teach our sages in Tractate Moed Katan.

Many who have gone through such a tragic experience feel a double sense of loss: not only the loss of a beloved family member, but also the loss of the mourning process, which is so therapeutically cathartic. And how can they be expected to celebrate a festival if their hearts are in a state of shock? How can we understand a legal system which, while apparently recognizing the emotional needs of individuals during this most vulnerable period of their lives, nevertheless, in this instance, strips them of this time-honored way of dealing with their loss in the fellowship of close family and friends and by sharing memories about the deceased.

Why does halakha, which always seems to be so sensitive to human emotional needs – as evidenced by the laws of mourning – seem in this case to be so unfeeling? I believe that the biblical interpretations we have analyzed until this point provide the key to understanding.

When an individual stands before an open grave of a loved one, the mystery of death raises fundamental questions as to the meaning and worthwhileness of the entire enterprise called life. What does it all mean, why endure the struggle and the pain? After all is said and done, the angel of death eventually overcomes everyone – the strongest, the bravest, the richest, the most powerful – and makes a tragic mockery of the person who was and is no more.

To this mystery of death there are two responses. The first is the fundamental Jewish belief in the eternity of the soul, of the human being having been created in the image of God. The human body is the external home for the spark of the Almighty on High, which is the inner essence of the human being, transcends our physical being, and lives eternally in the dimension of the divine.

The second response lies in the eternity of the Jewish people. Yes, time, death conquers everyone, each individual Reb Yisrael, but death will never conquer *Am Yisrael*, the Jewish nation. And insofar as an individual links their destiny to the Jewish nation, leaves behind children, students – beneficiaries who have learned from their commitment to the historic lifestyle, literature and values of the nation – that individual lives eternally. Insofar as an individual Jew is a link in the eternal and glorious chain of historic Jewish being, they continue to live in those links which preceded them as well as in those links which follow – who exist in the chain in no small measure because of that individual. As our sages teach, "Father Jacob never died; as long as his children [who follow in his ways] are alive, he is alive" (*Ta'anit* 5b).

Shabbat is a day dedicated to God: "You have sanctified the seventh day to Your name," states the Friday evening Amida liturgy. The festivals, however, are days dedicated to the uniqueness and eternity of the Jewish people: "You have chosen us from all other nations … exalted us from all other tongues," states every festival Amida. The festivals override mourning because the festivals give a powerful response to death; it is in the eternity of the Jewish nation that every committed Jew who ever lived finds their personal eternity. The festival representing eternal Israel transcends the mourning for Reb Yisrael because the nation provides the truest solace for the individual loss. When one embraces eternity, individual mourning must be suspended.

This was what God taught Moses, and R. Eliezer taught all of us. A life dedicated to our nation is ultimately a life best lived and is a life that never ends. It is life immortal – as immortal as the Jewish people.

The Broken Tablets and a Whole Nation

And it happened that when he came close to the encampment and he saw the calf and the dancing that Moses became very angry; and he cast from his hands the tablets and he broke them under the mountain.

EXODUS 32:19

Engraved by God Himself, the tablets which Moses brings down from Sinai are certainly unique. But after witnessing the debasement in front of the golden calf, Moses does not hesitate to smash the holiest objects in existence. The Talmud suggests that instead of being irritated, God actually blesses him with continued strength for his actions, *"Yeyasher kohakha asher shibarta"* (*Shabbat* 87a).

The tablets' destruction needs clarification. Memories grow dim and even extraordinary visions fade, so the tablets could have served as solid proof – visible, touchable, real – of the ancient roots of this nation. The tablets were miraculous, divine. They were "...written on both sides, with the writing visible from either side" (Ex. 32:15), despite the fact that they were chiseled through and through, a phenomenon which defies comprehension. And up until now, God appeared either in dreams and visions, in burning bushes, or by miraculously suspending the laws of nature. This is the first time that written and engraved words are described as having been formed by God Himself. The Bible states, "…written by the finger of God" (Ex. 31:18) "…and the writing was the writing of God…" (Ex. 35:15), expressing the truth that not only does God act in history and communicate words to mortals, but He, Himself, with His own hands as it were, prepared for humanity the great gift of His book, the secret of how to secure humanity's future. What could be greater proof of God's beneficence? Yet Moses smashes them to smithereens. Why commit such a seemingly sacrilegious and ungrateful act?

The various biblical commentaries (and even subsequent artists) have treated this action in different ways: for one Moses acts in a fit of anger, for another in weak frustration, and for a third Moses is making a resolute teaching demonstration. Whatever may have been Moses' true motivation, the sages of the Talmud applaud his action: "God himself gave his approval to Moses' act." It is precisely this divine approval which is especially difficult to understand. After all, the tablets of Stone were the most holy objects of the world, "the work of the Lord and the writing of the Lord" (Ex. 32:16)! Does it not seem as if Moses is pouring salt on the wounds perpetrated by the Israelites dancing in idolatrous debauchery? A review of the various commentaries will not only demonstrate the complexity of Moses' daring action but may very well answer our question.

Seforno seems very much in tune with Michaelangelo's vision of Moses when he interprets the smashing of the tablets as an expression of the prophet's justifiable anger.

> When Moses saw that the Israelites were rejoicing in the desecration that they had created, he became angry, and despaired of his ability to correct this egregious sin.
>
> Seforno, on Exodus 32:19

Rashbam, who is generally known for his close adherence to the most literal meaning of the text, here takes a very different approach.

> When Moses saw the calf, all of his strength failed him. He no
> longer had any energy and so he cast the tablets far away from
> him in order that they not damage his legs as they were falling.
> This is what people do when they can no longer bear their heavy
> burden. Such is the interpretation I saw in the *Pirkei deRabbi
> Eliezer* and this is the basic understanding of the text.
>
> Rashbam, on Exodus 32:19

For Rashbam, Moses was not angry as much as he was disappointed, despairing, disillusioned. His interpretation is touchingly reminiscent of a beloved rabbinic friend of mine whose teenage son was rebelling against a life of Torah observance. The young man understood his father's pain and left the following note on his father's pillow: "Beloved father, both of us are blind. I do not see how much I have learned from you, and you do not see how much you have taught me. You think I threw the tablets brazenly in front of your face. That is not at all the case. I merely found them too heavy to bear, and so they dropped from my hands...".

Rabbi Meir Simcha of Dvinsk derives a crucial lesson from Moses' action: no object is intrinsically holy. Regardless of the beauty of the letters or how carefully scribal laws have been followed, a Torah written by a heretic must be burned because the false belief of the scribe can undo the scroll's potential holiness, rendering it null and void. Conversely, but similarly, even a Decalogue written by God Himself must be sanctified by the Israelites, who are expected to live by its precepts. When the Israelites worshiped the golden calf, in effect discarding and denigrating the words and will of God, they were emptying the tablets of their sanctity, denuding the tablets of their divinity.

By breaking the tablets, Moses wants to strikingly demonstrate that there was no longer any sanctity to the Torah if the people who are supposed to be its recipients forsake its ways...

*   *   *

A Din Torah

When still a rabbi in Manhattan, I was asked to adjudicate between a principal and a fifth-grade teacher who had been summarily dismissed.

The class was generally unruly, but was especially feisty during daily morning prayers. The young teacher was at her wit's end attempting to instill some respect in her students, at least during prayers. One morning she just "lost her cool," and threw the prayer book to the floor. The shocked students came to order, but when they reported the incident to their parents, the principal was inundated with calls from irate parents. The teacher was dismissed. When, during the hearing in my office, I asked the teacher to explain her action, she calmly replied: "I merely learned from Moshe Rabbenu." She won the case – and was reinstated!

Moses, Passionate Defender of Israel

And now, if You will, forgive their sin; and if not,
please blot me out from the book You have written.

EXODUS 32:32

Moses broke the tablets, and in the last commentary I suggested some reasons for this action. In addition, there are a number of commentaries that see the act of Moses as a passionate statement of defense on behalf of the Israelites. The holy *Zohar* suggests that the golden calf episode is like a tragic tale of love, marriage and betrayal. The revelation at Sinai expressed a sacred marriage between God and the children of Israel, an unprecedented event in mankind's history. Moses was the marital attendant, and the tablets were the *ketuba*, the marriage contract. The Talmud (*Shabbat* 88a) discusses how God lifts Mount Sinai over the nation at the time of revelation, which suggests the image of a *ḥuppa*, a nuptial canopy, hovering over the bride-nation. But even before the honeymoon is over, Moses finds the new bride committing adultery with a false god, the golden calf. His act is a supreme attempt to defend his nation, to remove their sin of adultery by destroying this marriage contract with God. After all, if there is no marriage contract, there is no adultery, by definition. Moreover, if the Israelites could stoop to idolatry so soon after the miracles of the Exodus and the revelation at Sinai, there is apparently a tragic weakness, a fatal flaw, in Moses' leadership. Part of the blame must fall on his own shoulders, if only for not having trained someone to keep the people inspired even in his absence. From this perspective, suggests the *Zohar*, Moses broke the tablets in order to share in the Israelites' guilt.

Based on this, Ibn Ezra writes:

> Moses broke the tablets which were in his hands like a contract of testimony, thereby tearing asunder the marriage contract between God and Israel.
>
> Ibn Ezra, on Exodus 32:19

Rabbi Joseph B. Soloveitchik once gave an interpretation which is similar in attitude to that of Ibn Ezra. The Mishna teaches that "there is no act of *me'ila* after another act of *me'ila* except in the case of … a sacred vessel" (*Me'ila* 5:3). "*Me'ila*" is a technical term for the usage of a holy object for one's personal benefit. If, for example, an individual takes an article of the sacred garb of the Temple priests and wears it for a family party, they commit the grave offense of *me'ila*. Generally speaking, however, once one individual has so "secularized" a holy object, if another individual then uses that object in a similarly personal way, they have not transgressed. Once an object has been removed from the realm of the sacred it loses its sacred status; it may be consequently used for one's personal benefit with impunity. Nevertheless, the Mishna teaches that a sacred vessel in the Holy Temple can never lose its sacred character, no matter what. Hence, if an individual takes a laver from the Temple and uses it for personal use, and then a second individual uses that same object for their personal use, the second individual also transgresses the sin of *me'ila*. Sacred vessels retain their sacred character eternally.

The stone tablets upon which were written the divine revelation of the Ten Commandments must be seen as sacred vessels. When Moses breaks them, he is giving a crucial message to God: These broken tablets shall still retain their sanctity! After all, they are divine vessels. And that is why the broken tablets were also placed in the holy ark of the Sanctuary alongside the new tablets which Moses later hewed on the tenth day of Tishrei (Yom Kippur). By breaking the tablets, Moses reminds God, as it were, that the Israelite nation is also a sacred vessel. After all, God has called Israel His treasure, His kingship of priests and a holy nation, the means by which the world will learn the necessary truth of ethical monotheism. If a sacred vessel can never lose its sanctity, then the Israelite nation likewise can never lose its sanctity. This is Moses' way of stating the necessity of God's forgiveness of Israel.

According to this interpretation, the smashing of the tablets is an expression of Moses' ultimate defense of his beloved nation – and the extent to which we must never lose faith in the power and eternity of our people.

I believe there is yet another reason why the tablets were broken. According to the sages, these shattered tablets were not scattered to the wind, but were accorded special importance. In fact, when Moses later brings down another set to be placed in the ark's sanctuary, the broken tablets were placed right alongside the whole ones. Why? Did Moses have a change of heart about having broken them, perhaps in a moment of unbridled anger?

In a debate going back many generations, the question is asked about which takes precedence, the nation of Israel or the Torah of Israel? King Solomon says of the Torah: "The Lord created me as the beginning of His way [*reshit darko*]" (Prov. 8:21), which would suggest that the Torah comes first, but in Jeremiah we find, "Israel is holy to the Lord, the first fruits [*reshit*] of His increase" (Jer. 2:3).

Nation or Torah? In fact, these are the two most basic ways to express one's Jewishness. Do I devote the lion's share of my time to preserving my nation by teaching Torah to the masses, doing military service in the IDF, fighting anti-Semitism and strengthening the Jewish State, or by studying Torah and strengthening the meticulousness of my observance of the commandments?

When God informs Moses of the nation's debauchery and offers, perhaps as a ploy or even a test, to start a new beginning from Moses' loins alone with the words "Leave Me alone…and I will destroy them and I shall make of you a great nation," (Ex. 32:10), Moses demurs:

"Blot me out of Your book." When he finally gets to see with his own eyes how the Jews worship the idol, and he breaks the tablets, it is as if he were returning them to God and responding to God's offer: "I will not start a new nation. I'm breaking the tablets. Better a whole Jewish nation descended from Abraham, Isaac, Jacob, Sara, Rebecca, Rachel and Leah with a broken Torah, than a broken nation and a whole Torah. The nation will eventually make the Torah whole!"

Stored next to each other in the ark, the broken and whole tablets teach us that it is sometimes necessary to break our most sacred object to preserve Israel's survival. "There are times when one must act for God – and nullify Your Torah" (Ps. 119:126). Moreover, when God gives Moses and Israel a second chance and the whole tablets are brought down again, we learn that what is whole may emerge from what is broken. The Midrash teaches that the second tablets contained the Oral Torah, the interpretations, decrees and enactments of the sages of each generation. God learned from the failure of the first tablets – without the Oral Law – and the subsequent act of idolatry only forty days after the tablets were given, that the only Torah which would last would be a Torah which empowered the nation to complete it, a Torah which also had the input of great Torah giants of every generation – a Torah which would be a partnership in its making between God and Israel. Every wise parent and educator knows that unless the child or student adopts the teaching as his or her own, it will never last as a significant aspect of their adult life.

But at the same time, we must be sensitive to the fact that there never could have been new tablets without the shattered old tablets. Did not the State of Israel emerge from the broken tablets of Auschwitz and Treblinka? Is not our most important goal to create a whole people forged from the broken fragments of our nation, the lessons learned from past mistakes, and our ability to mend that which is torn and to repair that which is broken?

Moses and Elijah – Comparison and Contrast

> And now, go and lead the people towards the
> place which I have spoken to you; behold, my
> angel shall go in front of you…
>
> EXODUS 32:34

The haftorah reading for the portion of *Ki Tissa* highlights the prophet Elijah. A comparison-contrast between the two great leaders, Moses and Elijah, would be highly instructive.

Elijah the Prophet in many ways follows the prototype of Moses. Both are zealots, Moses killing the Egyptian taskmaster and smashing the tablets, and Elijah raging against the wicked Israelite monarchy and the Jewish idolaters. Elijah was persecuted by King Ahab and Queen Jezebel who wished to kill him, and Moses was on Pharaoh's "wanted" list, the prophet's life so much in danger that he had to flee to Midian. Moses demonstrated God's power at Sinai before 600,000 Israelites, and Elijah demonstrated God's power at Mount Carmel before 600,000 Israelites.

Moses felt he had to break the commandments in order to establish them, and so he smashed the tablets of stone; Elijah felt he had to nullify the prohibition against building a "high altar" in order to demonstrate the superiority of God over Baal. Moses was critical of his people, saying, "Listen, you rebels," and Elijah was critical of his, saying, "How long will you stand in two opposite directions?" Moses split the Reed Sea, Elijah split the Jordan River. Moses suffered the indignity of Korah's rebellion without receiving the backing of his people, and Elijah hears from Queen Jezebel that "at this time tomorrow I shall have your life," knowing that only twenty-four hours after his great miracle at Mount Carmel, no one would stop the queen from carrying out her threat. Perhaps she couldn't have gotten away with it immediately after the miracle, but twenty-four hours later… people forget quickly!

Most important of all, Elijah receives the very same message from God as did Moses. Let us examine Elijah's miracle in greater depth. The Israelites have long entered the Promised Land, and the holy Temple proudly adorns Mount Moriah, but the Israelites have begun to worship the idol Baal; even the king and queen of Israel, Ahab and Jezebel, are themselves wicked idolaters. Elijah, out of deep frustration with Israel's backsliding, decides to perform a daring experiment to attempt to establish God's rule, although by doing so, he would be transgressing God's law against building an altar outside the holy Temple. He builds an altar on Mount Carmel, sets up the 450 prophets of Baal with a bullock on one side, stands himself next to a bullock on the other side, and before 600,000 Israelites at the foot of the mountain challenges the other prophets to see whose prayers would be answered! Like Moses, he decided that "there are times when one must act for God – and nullify your Torah" (Ps. 119:126).

The prophets of Baal cried out, slashed themselves with knives and swords until their blood flowed, all to no avail. Elijah prayed, "Answer me, O Lord, answer me," and a divine fire descended from heaven, consuming Elijah's bullock. Six hundred thousand Israelites cried out "The Lord He is God" (I Kings 18:39). It is the moment of Elijah's greatest triumph – but a short-lived triumph it is. Although Baal has been discredited, and many of Baal's prophets are put to death, the idols' humiliation is forgotten in very short order. Baal worship was accompanied by orgies of debauchery which great numbers of Israelites enjoyed far more than the straight morality of the Bible – and most individuals believe what they want to believe, despite the facts to the contrary. So Queen Jezebel tauntingly sends a message to Elijah: "At this time tomorrow, I shall make your soul like one of theirs [the prophets of Baal]" (1 Kings 19:2). And she hints as well that after twenty-four hours, no one would lift a finger to protect Elijah from the queen's assassins!

Queen Jezebel's threat rings true to Elijah, since the Israelites demonstrated their short memory by the very next morning. The prophet had every right to expect that the morning after his tour-de-force extravaganza at Mount Carmel, synagogues would be filled to overflowing, religious day schools would have long lines of students clamoring for entry, and adult education classes would be packed to the gills. Indeed, Elijah was probably working the entire night to find extra rooms for prayer services, extra Torah teachers for *daf yomi* (daily Talmud page) and expanded classrooms. But alas, his labor proved to be superfluous. The religious and ethical climate had changed barely at all on the morning after. Elijah is profoundly disappointed, just as Moses must have been bitterly frustrated when the Jews worshiped the golden calf only forty days after the miraculous revelation at Sinai!

What happens in the very next chapter after the great tour-de-force miracle is most instructive. Elijah is distraught at the lack of religious response the morning after. He is frightened by Jezebel's threat, so he begins to flee. He has no encore to perform. He now asks the Almighty to take his soul. God sends him back to Mount Horeb, the place of Moses' great public miracle. There the Almighty passes before him, sends a powerful, mountain-breaking and rock-shattering wind, and teaches him:

> After the wind came rushing thunder, but not in the wind is God.
> And after the rushing thunder came fire, but not in the fire is God.
> And after the fire came a still small voice.
>
> 1 Kings 19:11, 12

God is teaching Elijah that it is not in the dazzling supernatural miracles that God is to be found and human nature is changed; it is only in the still, small voice of care and concern, of constancy and continuity. The Almighty is teaching Elijah the very same message He attempted to teach Moses when he describes Himself as a God of love, compassion and tolerance: long-lasting, personality-changing inspiration is effectuated not by supernatural "stunts," but by silent sensitivity, by heartfelt outreach, by graduated, internalized, patient, repetitive, stage-by-stage, day-by-day development.

Unfortunately, neither Moses nor Elijah seems to have been able to assimilate this message. Moses breaks the tablets and strikes the rock, while Elijah brings down fire from heaven to consume Israelite generals and their men (II Kings 1). Both great prophets are not really of this world, and so are not buried naturally, with Moses' burial place unknown to this day and Elijah transported to heaven. Each are great prophets for the eternity of the generations, but each seemed to have been stymied and frustrated by the hard-headed and stiff-necked Israelites of their own generation.

There is, however, a final prophecy of hope and triumph. The prophet Malakhi's last words – with which biblical prophecy concludes – are that Elijah will herald God's great and awesome period of redemption, when

> The hearts of the parents will turn to the children and the hearts of the children to the parents.
>
> Malakhi 3:24

It was Elijah who had bitterly denounced the Israelites before God when he fled to Horeb and prayed to the Almighty to take his soul:

> I have acted with zeal, yes zeal, on behalf of the Lord. God of Hosts, since the children of Israel have forsaken Your covenant [*brit*] and destroyed Your altars [of sacrifice].
>
> I Kings 19:10

The Midrash teaches that God has bidden Elijah to be present at every circumcision ceremony and at every Passover *seder* so that he can see "with his own eyes" the commitment of Israel to the covenant, the dedication of Jewish families to the single remnant of sacrifice we have left, the *seder afikoman*. Ultimately, teaches Malakhi, the still small voice of love will reign supreme when "the hearts of the parents will turn to the children and the hearts of the children to the parents." Only then will redemption come.

Why Is Our God a Hidden God, Whose
Justice and Compassion Are Often Elusive?

> *And He said, "You will not be able to see My face,*
> *for no human can see My face and live."*
>
> EXODUS 33:20

The Torah portion of *Ki Tissa* raises the most complex and controversial theological issues with which all seekers of faith must wrestle: the definition of God, and the question of theodicy (divine justice in a world in which the righteous often appear to suffer and the wicked often appear to prosper). These challenges present themselves within the context of Moses' seemingly sacrilegious act of shattering the stone tablets of testimony, and God's command that he hew new tablets of stone to replace the shattered ones. I believe that a careful reading of our biblical text will illuminate the Torah's approach to these very significant and sensitive issues and events.

Chapter 32 of the book of Exodus opens with two contradictory scenes happening simultaneously: Moses receiving from the Almighty the sacred tablets of testimony in his hideaway with the Divine Presence, and the Israelites' worship of the golden calf in their encampment down below. God informs Moses that he must descend from his lofty heights "for your people ... have been corrupt" – combining an awful threat with a personal promise:

> Now leave Me alone [do not try to stop Me] when I unleash My wrath against them to destroy them, and I shall [begin again] by making from you a [new] great nation.
>
> Exodus 32:10

Moses offers a heartfelt prayer nonetheless, emphasizing the fact that Israel is God's nation and not Moses' nation, and invoking the divine covenant with the patriarchs as well as the potential desecration of God's name in the eyes of the Egyptians as reasons for His not destroying the Israelites. We are immediately informed that

> God refrained from doing the evil that He planned for His people.
>
> Exodus 32:14

Moses then descends from the mountain, sees the Israelites dancing in front of the golden calf, and smashes the tablets. The three thousand leaders of the idolatry are slain in punishment. Moses then turns to the Almighty with another request, now that the nation has been saved from extinction:

> And it happened on the morrow... And Moses said, "You [the Israelites] have sinned a great sin. I shall go up to the Lord. Perhaps I shall gain forgiveness for your sin."
>
> Ex. 32:30

Moses is not satisfied with having averted punishment for his nation. He wants the Israelites to be forgiven, to be purified.

> And now if You will, forgive their sin; but if You do not forgive their sin, blot me out from Your book.
>
> Exodus 32:32

In essence, Moses is asking: "Remove me from recorded history, but purify our people nonetheless." Penalize me, says Moses, but renew and forgive Israel.

God responds by explaining to Moses that people must purify themselves! Only those who sin are to be blotted out.

> Now you [Moses] go and lead the nation...I shall send before you an angel [agent of Mine]...to the land flowing with milk and honey...
>
> Exodus 33:2, 3

In effect, God is saying that He will lead behind the scenes, through leaders like Moses, through a nation ready, willing and able to redeem and be redeemed. Now the Israelites are not satisfied; they do not wish to be led by God's angel-messenger; they want God in their midst, manifest to all as the God of love and compassion, clearly directing every phenomenon and event before the eyes of everyone.

God responds:

> I dare not ascend among you, because you are a stiff-necked people, and I may very well have to destroy you on the way.
>
> Ex. 33:3, 5

God is explaining that if He becomes manifest, so must His punishment immediately become manifest, because one cannot love and foster goodness without hating and destroying evil. The nation of Israel might conclude its history and its mission almost before it begins as a people. Hence, God must work through messengers, through people, through intermediaries, with whom He establishes a partnership. In an incomplete, imperfect world, God must appear "through a glass darkly," behind the curtain, in order to allow for repentance of the wicked and the ultimate perfection of the world together with His human partners. Only then will God be manifest, His name great and sanctified.

It is within this context that God commands Moses:

> Hew for yourself two tablets of stone like the first ones...
>
> Ex. 34:1

These second tablets are not like the first ones – not in design and (according to the Midrash) not even in content.

The first tablets were the writing of God, by the finger of God; the second tablets are human writing by human finger. The Midrash teaches that these second tablets included the Oral Law, a corpus of teachings which would develop throughout the generations and which would add the interpretations and decrees of the pious scholars of Israel to the initial words of the divine.

It is as though God is explaining that just as He created an imperfect (incomplete) world, so did He decide to give Israel an incomplete Torah.

The process of redemption is apparently going to be a lengthy one, fraught with trial and error, a historical process of education which is predicated upon a partnership between God and Israel. God will not deal with us directly; for Him to do so would mean immediate reward and punishment, which would more likely result in immediate destruction following a national transgression. God will operate through intermediaries, people who will lead, and through a Torah which will give direction. There is a special relationship between God and Israel, there is an ultimate promise of redemption.

And so God reveals His name: *YHVH*, the God of historic process, of future becoming; the God of patience and forgiveness, who has the cosmic time to wait for humanity to repent and for the world to ultimately redeem itself (See Ex. 34:6, 7 and *Yoma* 69b). In the month of Sivan was the public divine revelation at Sinai, in the month of Tammuz (forty days later) the smashing of the tablets, and on Yom Kippur (eighty days later), the second tablets and the new covenant based on Israel's repentance. The people of Israel must come of age by taking responsibility for their actions and for the world; God is hidden behind the curtains of the Holy of Holies in the Sanctuary-Temple. The mask that covers Moses' face when he descends from the mountain for the second time reflects the mask that will hide the Almighty from directly guiding His people and His world. Neither Israel nor humanity are yet ready for such direct divine intervention. The new paradigm for God-in-the-World will not be direct revelation at Sinai but rather the Israelites' repentance on Yom Kippur, or – even more to the point – the masquerade of Purim, when God's name is not directly present in the Scroll of Esther ("Esther" literally means hiddenness). The Israelites must now carry their new responsibility of Oral Law and human activity on their long march towards redemption.

Vayak-hel–Pekudei

Sanctuary and Sabbath Revisited

> *And Moses assembled [vayak-hel] all of the*
> *congregation of the children of Israel and said*
> *unto them: ... Six days shall work be done, but*
> *the seventh day shall be for you, a day of complete*
> *rest for the Lord.*
>
> EXODUS 35:1–2

The portion of *Vayak-hel* opens with the command to keep the Sabbath. This raises once again that fundamental question of the very strange order of the last five portions of the book of Exodus, Sanctuary – Sabbath – golden calf – Sabbath – Sanctuary.*

Thus the Torah commands us first to create a Sanctuary, to establish a center of the sacred, which is after all the purpose and ideal of a kingdom of priests and a holy nation. But the sacred can easily be profaned – as history in modern life can testify – with holy wars, Iranian Khomeini-ism and fanatical stone-throwing and book burning. Hence,

---

* See essay *Ki Tissa* on pp. 295-299.

in the middle of the construction of the Sanctuary (the first two portions, *Teruma* and *Tetzaveh*, are dedicated to the Sanctuary) comes the travesty of the golden calf (the portion of *Ki Tissa*), which serves as an eloquent warning to subsequent generations not to pervert, or idol-ify, the holy. It then becomes perfectly logical, or rather psychological, to now return and conclude with the positive message of the Sanctuary as the Torah does in its two concluding portions of *Vayak-hel* and *Pekudei*. And the Sabbath is the beacon of light which teaches the essence of Judaism, preventing its perversion into a golden calf of idolatry.

The Sabbath is the most central pillar of our faith. It is no accident that the very first law which was given to the Israelites after the splitting of the Reed Sea – before the revelation at Sinai – was the Sabbath (Ex. 15:25; Rashi ad loc. citing *Sanhedrin* 56b), and the first law explained to a would-be convert (Jew by choice) is likewise the Sabbath (*Yevamot* 47). In all of my experience in attempting to expose Jews who have wandered far afield from their faith to the glories of their Jewish heritage, I have found that there is no more powerful introduction to returning to Judaism than the Sabbath experience.

And how does the Sabbath accomplish this? Certainly the delightful glow of the Sabbath candles, the warmth of the Kiddush wine, the familial and congenial togetherness of delectable Sabbath meals replete with angels of peace, praises to women, blessings of children, songs of holiness and words of Torah, all contribute to the creation of a special and unique day dedicated to physical relaxation, spiritual creativity and existential well-being.

But the Sabbath is more than that. It contains the essence of the Jewish ideal, the purpose for which we were chosen by God, and the mission which has the power to unite all of us in the pursuit of a common historic goal (*vayak-hel*). The "oasis in time" evokes the three most seminal moments in Jewish history, three moments of past and future that more than any others serve to define our Jewish present. A description of these moments are to be found in each of three main Amidot (standing prayers) which are recited by observant Jews every Sabbath. On Friday evening we evoke and re-experience the creation of the world ("And God completed the heavens and the earth and all their hosts…"), on Sabbath morning we evoke and re-experience the

revelation of the law at Sinai ("Moses rejoiced with the gift of his portion... the two tablets of stone he brought down in his hands"), and on
Sabbath afternoon we evoke and attempt to experience the redemption
("You are One and Your Name is One" – and the prophet Zekhariah
teaches that only ".... on that day [of Messianic redemption and universal peace] will God be One and will His name be One"). Creation,
revelation and redemption are the three pillars which form the bedrock
of the Jewish message and mission.

Creation reminds us that there is one omnipotent creator, and
the entire world consists of His limited, but still exalted, creatures. The
very creaturehood of all of humanity serves to unite all individuals in a
bond of inescapable unity. The very fact that we share the same parent
in heaven means that we are all of us siblings on earth: whites and blacks,
Israelis and Palestinians. The corollary of God the Creator is God the
Redeemer, God who will not allow any of His children to be enslaved
by any of His other children. Hence the two versions of the Decalogue
as well as the Kiddush prayer define the Sabbath as both a memorial
to creation as well as a memorial to the Exodus from Egypt. And the
Sabbath remains an eternal reminder that any expression of the sacred
which does not include sensitivity to every human being and respect
for the freedom and integrity of each of God's children can only lead to
the perversion of the golden calf idolatry.

Revelation reminds us that there can be no freedom without
structure, no respect for self without taking into account the needs of
others, no love without law. The Torah remains our God-given blueprint
for the kind of meaningful and sacred lives which lead to more perfect
families and societies. In this sense, Judaism is a revolutionary concept,
an idea and lifestyle which will not rest until human nature is perfected
and the world is redeemed. Thus the final Sabbath Amida evokes that
longed-for period when the world will be redeemed as a result of the
Torah, which has the power and the purpose to perfect the universe
under the kingship of God, in effect to revolutionize society.

But the tragedy of most revolutions is that the leaders themselves
usually lose sight of what it was that they fought for in the first place.
Indeed, all too often the beneficiaries of the revolt are guilty of greater
crimes of avarice and greed and despotism than were those against whom

they rebelled. This was true of the Maccabean revolt, the French revolution, and the Communist revolution in our own time. Equality and fraternity were the sanctuaries of Voltaire and Lenin; the blood baths of Robespierre and Stalin became their golden calf perversion.

The genius of Judaism lies in its ability to maintain the future ideal as an ever-present reality of our daily lives. In this way we can never forget what we are striving to accomplish, nor can we allow ourselves to become cynically disillusioned as to the possibility of our attaining it. Hence each workaday week of frustration and sadness is climaxed by a Sabbath – a taste of the World to Come, a glimpse into the longed-for period of peace and harmony. Each Sabbath reminds us of the pure taste of the Sanctuary, and prevents us from descending into the depths of golden-calf materialism and idolatry.

The story is told of a Hassidic rebbe who always rejoiced mightily upon sharing the Sabbath meals with his congregant-disciples. People who were bent over with burden and toil each week, whose brows were creased with anxiety and whose eyes were clouded with worry, would become almost miraculously transformed into tall and clear-eyed princes and princesses with their new-found freedom and faith at the advent of Shabbat. But alas, the picture would change during the "third meal" late on Shabbat afternoon. As the sun would begin to set, the songs would become somber and the mundane concerns would return to haunt the faces and backs of the Jews who were forced to return to reality. And the rebbe would look heavenwards and beseech: "How long, dear Father? Can you not redeem us now!?"

But at one particular Sabbath "third meal," the rebbe's eyes became animated with a strange glow. He banged on the table, crying out: "I have it, my beloved disciples. We shall force God's hand, wage a rebellion against Heaven. We will bring about the redemption – now. The plan is breathtakingly simple. We will not recite the havdala [the prayer of "separation" which concludes the Sabbath and begins the week]. If the Sabbath never ends, redemption never ends. If there is no havdala, we will never have to return to the weekday world."

The Hassidim were entranced. They danced and sang joyous tunes long past the appearance of three stars, long past the conclusion of the Sabbath in other congregations. But then their wives began looking for them; after all, the children had to be fed and bathed, clothes had to be washed, food had to be cooked. One by one each disciple embarrassedly returned to his family, leaving the rebbe as the lone revolutionary – until the rebbe's rebbetzin entered the scene, complaining that the week had to begin, for there was much necessary work to do. With tears coursing down his cheeks, the defeated rebbe made havdala. A voice then came down from heaven: "Redemption shall come, and the world will experience a never-ending Sabbath. But this cannot occur until all of Israel really wants to be redeemed, really works to be redeemed, and until every Jew internalizes the message of the Sabbath and reaches out to every human being, making each day a Sabbath, creating a new world order, an eternal period of peace and love."

Vanities and Virtues

> *He made the copper laver and its copper base out*
> *of the mirrors of the service women [armies of*
> *women] who congregated to serve at the entrance*
> *of the Tent of Meeting.*
>
> EXODUS 38:8

The Sanctuary and all of its furnishings are described in exquisite and sometimes seemingly repetitive detail, but the laver, the large basin within which the priests sanctified themselves by washing their hands and feet prior to each divine service, is an exception to this rule.

Several aspects distinguish this washbasin. First of all, virtually all the other items in the Sanctuary are given exact measurements, but here the Torah speaks in general terms. The precise dimensions of the laver and its base are not given. Are not these details important, and if not, why not?

Perhaps the answer to this question is found in the latter part of this same verse, where we are told that the laver was made of the "mirrors of the service women." According to R. Samson Rafael Hirsch's Torah commentary, the phrase *"ba-marot ha-tzovot"* (mirrors of the service women) suggests that the copper mirrors were not melted down at all, but that the laver was "...fitted together almost without any alteration at all, so that it would be recognizable that the basin consisted actually of mirrors" (Commentary to Ex. 38:8).

Even if this first question is answered, a second question comes in its wake. Of all contributions to the Sanctuary, why should the mirrors retain their unique identity? Does it not seem odd that the very accouterment found in every woman's possession, the very symbol of vanity, would find a new incarnation as a central piece inside the Sanctuary? Indeed, without first stopping at the laver to wash their hands and feet, the priests could not begin the Temple service.

How "vanities" could become such a significant aspect of our Sanctuary is the subject of a fascinating debate between two major commentaries.

Ibn Ezra writes as follows:

> It is the custom of women to beautify themselves, to look at their faces every morning in copper or glass mirrors... And there were in Israel women who served God, and decided to turn away from all the physical material blandishments of this world. They therefore gave their mirrors away to the Sanctuary as a gift offering because they no longer had the need to beautify themselves. From that time on they would arrive daily at the doorway of the Tent of Meeting to pray and to listen to the details of the commandments. That is the reason why the biblical text says they came in hordes [armies], *tzovot*, at the entrance to the Tent of Meeting; they were so numerous.
>
> Ibn Ezra, on Exodus 38:8

Ibn Ezra is here describing the first women's prayer service and study hall (*bet midrash*) at the door of the Sanctuary's Tent of Meeting, a remarkable fact in itself, especially since he maintains that it was so popular that it attracted "armies" of women. But his main point is to stress an ascetic aspect of the women's relationship to God. Since mirrors represent the physical desires of this world, once the women acquired the higher spiritual plane of involvement in prayer and study, they no longer had any use for the mirrors and gave them away to the Sanctuary.

For Rashi, however, the inclusion of the women's mirrors inside the Sanctuary is the story of a religious metamorphosis, not the rejection of the physical but rather the sanctification of the physical, and herein, it seems to me, lies the true message of the sanctuary. Rashi explains that when the daughters of Israel brought a gift offering of the actual mirrors, they were initially rejected by Moses

> because they were made for the evil instinct. But God said to Moses: "Accept them; these are more beloved to me than anything else. Through these mirrors the women established many armies in Egypt." [A play on the word *tzovot*, service women, which literally means armies, and a reference to the armies of children whom the women brought forth.] When the husbands would come home exhausted from backbreaking work, their wives would bring them food and drink. And they would take the mirrors, and would appear together with their husbands in the reflection of the mirror. Thus they would entice their husbands and they would become pregnant.
>
> Rashi, on Exodus 38:8

According to Rashi, the mirrors represent the unswerving faith of the Jewish women, their supreme confidence in a Jewish future. After all, the Israelites were being enslaved and their male babies thrown into the Nile during the Egyptian subjugation. Logic certainly dictated not having any children, refusing to bring innocent babes into a life of suffering and possible death. But there was also a tradition of the Covenant of the Pieces (Gen. 15), a promise of redemption, a charge to teach the world ethical monotheism. Consider what would have happened if the Israelite women had not found a way to entice their husbands. Jewish history would have ended almost before it began, in the very first exile of Egypt, devoid of a next generation of Jewish continuity. In effect, the transformation of these mirrors of desire into the laver of purification is the Torah's way of rewarding the women for their devotion and explaining to future generations the biblical ideal of the sanctification of the physical, the uplifting of the material. The key here is that they looked into the mirrors and saw themselves and their husbands. They looked into the mirrors and saw armies of a Jewish future. Had they seen only themselves, and not their husbands and their progeny, their place in Jewish history would hardly have been as exalted.

Which of these interpretations is easier to accept? Perhaps the following talmudic passage can clarify matters. We read in *Nazir* an account of Shimon the Just, High Priest and one of the last Men of the Great Assembly:

> All of my life I never ate from a Nazirite's sacrificial offering, except once, when I saw a Nazirite coming towards me from the south. He was beautiful of eyes, goodly of appearance, with magnificent curly hair. I said to him, "My son, why have you decided to destroy such beautiful hair?" [because ultimately a Nazirite gives his hair as a sacrifice upon the altar]. He said to me, "I was a shepherd … and I once went to draw water from the well and I looked at my reflection in the water. An evil instinct began to overcome me [because I fell in love with myself]. And I said [to the evil instinct], empty one, do you not realize that ultimately you will just be worms and maggots? And I took an oath to become a Nazirite." And Shimon the Just said, "I stood and I kissed him on the forehead, and I said to him, 'May all Nazirites be like you.'"
>
> *Nazir* 4b

Why was this Nazirite different from all other Nazirites? Implicit in Shimon the Just's account is that all others who took this ascetic vow were in some way violating an inherent principle in the Torah by denying themselves what the Torah permits – the rationale, according to many commentaries, behind the Nazirite's sin offering. But this particular Nazirite was doing what he had to do in order to save himself from the narcissistic danger of becoming attracted to the mysterious depths of his own reflection. He was on the way to a life of egoistic self-love and self-absorption which he felt could only be put in check by his becoming a Nazirite.

How different is Rashi's brilliant description of the mirrors. The greatness of the Jewish women in Egypt is that they looked at the reflection not only of themselves but of their husbands as well. And because they saw their husbands as well as themselves, they also saw, and provided for, Israelite future and Israelite destiny. They were concerned not only for their own pleasure, but also for the material pleasure of husband and wife which is only realized to its greatest degree in the creation of children, who represent personal and national continuity and future.

An amazing talmudic text brings home this point to a striking degree:

> Rav Katina said: When the Jewish people would go up to Jerusalem during the festivals, the keepers of the Sanctuary would roll back the curtain covering the holy ark, and would reveal to the Jews who came up to Jerusalem, the cherubs, which were in the form of a male and female embracing each other. And they would say to them, to the Jews: 'See the love which God has for you, like the love of a male and female.'
>
> *Yoma* 54a

And the cherubs had the faces of small children, symbol of Jewish continuity. Love for another, expressed in the highest form by love of lover for beloved, husband for wife, is the greatest manifestation of sanctity, and it is precisely this male-female attraction which has the power to secure our Jewish eternity.

The Sanctuary is sanctified by the mirrors of the women in Egypt, who taught, by their example, how to turn the most physical human drive into the highest act of divine service. In a very real sense, the Sanctuary itself, replete with intricately detailed expert craftsmanship, exquisite and expensive ornamentation, and gold and silver filigreed ritual objects, was similarly an attempt to take the very basic human passion for gold and beauty, which so perverted the Israelites at the incident of the golden calf, and utilize this very materialistic drive to inspire them to divine service. "And let them make among Me a Sanctuary that I may dwell within them."

The Importance of Function

> And Moses erected the sanctuary, and he fastened
> its sockets, and he placed its boards, and he
> inserted its bars, and he installed its pillars.
>
> EXODUS 40:18

We have often queried the significance of the five Torah portions which conclude the book of Exodus, and especially the repetitions which we find in the detailed descriptions of the accoutrements of the Sanctuary. Even if we concede the very profound theological message of *Ki Tissa* and the unique prescription of the priestly garments in *Tetzaveh*, we are still left with the initial delineation of the furnishings of the Sanctuary in *Teruma* and the seeming repetitions thereof in *Vayakhel-Pekudei*. Why not a general statement to the effect that "And Moses did as he was instructed in the construction of the Sanctuary"!?

Rabbi Elhanan Samet, in his groundbreaking study of the portions of the Bible from a structural-narrative perspective, explains as follows: The commandment to make the various furnishings of the Sanctuary is given by God in the Torah portion of *Teruma*. The precise performance of the Israelites of every detail of the divine command is detailed in the Torah portion of *Vayak-hel*; this is perhaps to emphasize the fact that we must serve the Almighty in precisely the manner which He commands, no more and no less, in order to protect Judaism from religious fanaticism and zealotry. The actual completion, the final hammer blow of the construction of each sacred object, is presented in the Torah portion of *Pekudei*.

From an Israeli perspective, I might explain the importance of emphasizing the finish in a separate Torah portion by bringing to your attention a typical phenomenon of Israeli construction: Ninety percent of the work generally gets done efficiently and even almost miraculously, but the last ten percent requires cajoling, entreating and sometimes (even usually) never gets done at all. And it goes without saying that the last ten percent is quite critical, especially during a rainy winter season!

But in a more serious vein, let us investigate the construction of the sanctuary table (*shulḥan*) in order to understand the true reason for the order of description. The divine command to make a sanctuary table is presented in the portion of *Teruma* in eight verses (Ex. 25:23–30), beginning with "You shall make a Table of acacia wood, two handbreadths long, a hand-breadth wide, and a hand-breadth and one-half in height," and the description of the actual execution or making of the Table is detailed in the portion of *Vayak-hel* almost precisely paralleling the command in *Teruma*, in only seven verses (Ex. 37:10–16). What is missing in the execution? In the portion of *Teruma*, the last verse of the commandment regarding the construction of the Table tells us: "And you shall place upon the Table the shewbread before Me always" (Ex. 25:30); and then, towards the end of the portion of *Teruma*, we find: "And you shall situate the Table outside the curtain on the northern side of the Sanctuary" (Ex. 26:35). These two features, the function of the Table (for the shewbread), and the placement of the Table, while commanded in *Teruma*, are not included in the actual construction of the Table in the portion of *Vayak-hel*; but these two features are specifically mentioned in the portion of *Pekudei*: "And he [Moses] placed the Table in the Tent of Meeting on the side of the Sanctuary northwards just outside the curtain, and he arranged the arrangement of the bread before the Lord as the Lord had commanded Moses" (Ex. 40:22, 23).

Why do we need the separate portion of *Pekudei* to tell us that the function and placement of the sacred Table of the Sanctuary were carried out? One might suggest a logical, technical reason: The specific placement of the Table as well as its function as repository of the shewbread could only be effectuated once the entire Sanctuary had been completed. Placement is a matter of relative space, each sacred object placed in relationship to the other sacred objects, and the various Sanctuary placement and functions could not take place unless the Sanctuary had reached its final stage of construction. This final completion occurs only in *Pekudei*, and therefore it is only in this Torah portion that we find the phrase "just as the Lord commanded Moses" (Ex. 40:17–32) appearing, not only once but actually seven times.

I would like to suggest another reason for the significance of *Pekudei* as the portion of the "finish," the portion which emphasizes the placement and function of the sacred object. Each of us must see ourselves as sacred vessels, placed upon this world-Sanctuary in order to fulfill a specific task which is crucial if human society is to be perfected under the kingship of the divine. Rosh Hashana, the Jewish New Year, ushers in the introspective period known as the Ten Days of Repentance. It also is called the Day of Remembrance. One of the most stirring prayers on this Day of Remembrance begins: "You [God] remember the deeds of the historic world, and are *po-ked* all the creatures from the earliest time." The Hebrew word "*po-ked*" is usually translated as "taking notice of," a synonym for remembering. However, the late Rabbi Shraga Feivel Mendlowitz, zt"l, Dean of Yeshiva Torah Vadaas maintained that the verb comes from the noun "*tafkid*," or function, and therefore the phrase ought to be translated, "You give a specific function to every creature from the earliest time."

The most proper and penetrating question of repentance that an individual ought ask him- or herself is, "Am I in the right country, doing the right thing? In the one chance at life which God grants me, am I pursuing the proper path in the proper locality?"

The Hebrew word "*pekudei*" can also be translated as the plural "functions," for each vessel – whether a sacred physical object or a sacred human subject – completes its reason for being only when its unique function is actually performed. Only then can a vessel be considered as fully formed, can a life be assessed as having been truly lived. We can only pray that we are utilizing the unique gifts which the Almighty has imbued within us to perform the right function in the proper place; only then will the divine orchestra play its completed symphony, and only then will the perfected world-Sanctuary provide a home for God to dwell in our midst.

The Washbasin Revisited:
We Are More Than Meets the Eye

> *And he set the laver between the Tent of the Meeting and the altar, and put water there for washing. And Moses and Aaron and his sons washed their hands and their feet...*
>
> EXODUS 40:30–31

Before the priests would enter the Tent of Meeting or approach the altar, they were commanded to wash their hands and feet from the laver. Not doing so was a capital offense, as expressed in the portion of *Ki Tissa*:

> If they are not to die they must wash with the water before entering the tent of meeting...
>
> Ex. 30:20

The washing of one's hands and feet may have been the easiest of all the required rituals in the Sanctuary, but that didn't make it any less significant. On the contrary, not only was it the prerequisite for the priest's presence in the Sanctuary, but the washing of the priests has become an essential part of the halakhic life of every Jew – such as washing one's hands upon rising, or before the eating of bread.

Therefore it's interesting that the very last physical item connected to the rituals of the Sanctuary that the Torah mentions is the washstand, or laver. The portion of *Pekudei* closes the book of Exodus. *Pekudei* means "These are the accounts of…", and that's exactly what the portion does: a detailed summation of everything that God commanded and the architects constructed. After nearly half of the book of Exodus's devotion to the Sanctuary, this portion provides the closing statement. And what is the last Sanctuary "furnishing," in effect the sum-up, which is recorded in the Torah? The washstand. True, the enclosure is also mentioned, but the enclosure is not a physical item; a *hatzer* (as the Torah calls it), encloses space, defining an area between other spaces. It is certainly not part of Sanctuary ritual as we understand the washstand to be.

If it's true that the Torah wants us to pay particular attention to this washstand, then we must reread its description in the previous portion:

> He made the copper laver and its copper base out of the mirrors of the service women [armies of women] who congregated to serve at the entrance of the Tent of Meeting.
>
> Exodus 38:8

It is significant that the Torah speaks of the mirrors of the women. After all, a mirror is one of those objects which is at best taken for granted as we gaze into it and check for excesses and wrinkles, and at worst causes us slight embarrassment at our vain concern with physical appearance. Is it not strange that such "vanities" are to be considered worthy of being used by the priests to sanctify their hands with water before the start of any ceremony or offering?

When the commandment was originally given in *Ki Tissa*, the Torah did not command the women to donate their copper mirrors. Indeed, as we have previously seen, Ibn Ezra calls the women's contribution a victory of spiritual values over physical vanity. The daughters of Israel didn't need these mirrors anymore; they wanted to serve God by emphasizing good deeds over good looks, and their gifts of the mirrors were symbolic of this change.

Rashi, in questioning the *Midrash Tanḥuma*, describing how the women enticed their husbands by means of the mirrors to have sexual relations with them, wants to stress that one should not be quick to reject the physical – even sexual – aspect of our existence. If anything, Judaism ennobles sex and love within marriage, which is why *"kiddushin,"* the Hebrew for marriage, is rooted in the word for holy, *"kadosh"*! When two separate people become physically united in order to become partners with God in creating another person, they are engaging in one of the holiest acts a human being can pursue. And if a mirror can help in the process, what finer material is there for the sanctification of the priest's hands before he performs the divine service?

Moreover, from this perspective, the mirrors signal to God the women's profound faith in a Jewish future. Imagine Egypt under Pharaoh's rule, a Holocaust of 210 years' duration! Knowing that his sons would be drowned in the Nile and his daughters forced to live with Egyptian slave-masters, why on earth would any Hebrew want to bring more children into the world?

But thank God for their wives, the Almighty is teaching Moses. The women remembered the divine promises made to the biblical patriarchs and matriarchs which foretold the ultimate redemption of the people and their entry into the Promised Land. The women urged their husbands not to despair, to believe in a Jewish future! In the midst of torturous persecution, slavery and infanticide, bringing more Jewish children into the world was an act of supreme faith. And the mirrors were the instruments for the expression of that faith.

I believe yet another lesson lies in the sanctity of the mirrors. The Hebrew word for mirror, *marah*, has the very same letters as *mareh*, appearance. And seeing our appearance in a mirror does not only emphasize our physical selves. We all realize that we are more than that which the mirror reflects. After all, the mirror does not show our inner selves, our memories and aspirations, our dreams and our fears. Every time the priest would sanctify his hands and look in the mirror, he would be inspired to reflect not only on his own face, but on all the faces of all the people who would be seeking atonement in the Sanctuary. Let us ponder for a moment: Who commonly came to the Sanctuary? People in search of atonement, individuals bringing guilt and sin offerings. Hence, the danger would lie in how easy it was to forget the individual behind the person who arrived with his offering. It was too easy for the priest to make his human judgments based upon the single instance when he would see the supplicant with his sacrifice; he would tend to forget that one who commits a sin is not necessarily a sinner. A one-time lapse does not necessarily define an individual's character and personality! One of the important lessons the mirror taught is that people are not how they appear to be on the surface. Just as the priest understood that the face staring back at him in the laver is hardly the total picture – there's a lot more to us than what stares back in the glass – so too he could not possibly judge his "clients" by the reason they entered the Sanctuary.

And is this not the true message of the women's gift? After all, the women who beautified themselves for their husbands were an easy target for a cynic to ridicule their efforts as a jaded expression of inappropriate physical desire. But perhaps the message of the mirrors was the exact opposite: Don't look at me only as I appear now in the mirror; look at me also as you saw me as a bride and look at me as the mother of your future children. The present snapshot is only a small part of the story; human history, and certainly Jewish history, dare not be judged only by the picture of the moment!

Looking at people is an art, and when the prophet describes how the future Messiah will look at people, he stresses that "…he shall not judge after the sight of his eyes…" (Is. 11:3). We must learn to see within, and not only to look without.

Similarly, we find the admonition in the Ethics of the Fathers, "Judge all people favorably" (*Avot* 1:6). This phrase can also be taken to mean: "Judge the entire person, all of the person [*kol ha'adam*], her manifold activities as well as her inner self – and then you will come to a favorable assessment."

Thus we see the central role of the washstand in the structure of the Sanctuary: the faith of the Jewish women despite the fact that their husbands' spirits were broken, and the importance for the priest to look deep and hard at himself as well as others to ascertain a true and full picture. In the final analysis, our reflection in a mirror is only a small part of who we really are.

The End of Exodus and the Four Parashot

> *And he set up the courtyard around the sanctuary*
> *and the altar, and he placed the screen gate of the*
> *courtyard, and Moses completed the work.*
>
> EXODUS 40:33

Why repeat all the details of the construction of the Sanctuary after we have already heard them when they were initially commanded? For example, with regard to one of the priestly garments, the Bible commands:

> And they shall make the *ephod* of gold, of blue, and purple, scarlet
> and fine twined linen, the work of the skillful workman.
>
> Exodus 28:6

And then, telling us of the command of the execution, the same words are repeated, practically word for word:

> And he made the *ephod* of gold, blue, and purple, and scarlet,
> and fine twined linen. And they beat the gold into thin plates...
>
> Exodus 39:2

If there is a difference, it's that the first time around the Israelites are given the command, and the second time the Torah records that the command was indeed performed. Would it not have been simpler to deal with the entire execution of external building, furnishings and priestly garb with the single verse: "And the Israelites built the Sanctuary exactly as God commanded"?

In order to understand the significance of the repetition, it is important to remember that the Almighty desires an intimate relationship between Himself and the people of Israel. That is why they are commanded to build a Sanctuary in the first place: "in order that He may dwell among us." However, worshiping the golden calf – whoring after strange gods – was a betrayal of the ideals given at Sinai. In effect, the Israelites commited adultery, scarring the love and intimacy God had just bestowed upon them. Were God only a God of justice, this would be the end of the Jewish people, their sin mandating a punishment which would have meant the end of Jewish history before it really began.

But since God is also a God of compassion, He forgives. But can we legitimately expect forgiveness for as heinous a crime as idolatry? Will the Almighty take Israel back even after they have committed adultery? Herein lies the true significance of the repitition of each and every painstaking instruction regarding the Sanctuary. God places his nuptial "home" with Israel before they sin with the golden calf, and God accepts their construction of the nuptial home after they have sinned with the golden calf. The repetition is a confirmation that the intimacy between God and Israel has been restored, that the relationship between God and His bride, Israel, has returned to its original state of mutual commitment and faith. The repetition of the exact details is essentially God's gift of repentance.

It is interesting to note that during the weeks when we read the concluding portions of Exodus, the calendar is usually host to another sequence of special readings, wherein a second Torah scroll is removed from the ark for an additional reading as well as a special haftorah reading from the prophets.

The first special reading is *Shekalim*, which speaks of the obligation of every Jew to give a half-shekel to the Sanctuary. This represents an act of commitment: a pledge of a covenantal relationship between God and Israel that is four thousand years strong, demonstrated in our daily lives by the giving of our "half-shekels" to build our sanctuaries – yeshivas and synagogues, day schools and outreach centers – thus bringing God within our midst. Financial commitment is also the traditional halakhic form of betrothal (symbolized in the wedding ring).

The second special Sabbath – right before Purim – is *Shabbat Zakhor. Zakhor* means "remember": Remember to destroy the evil Amalek. Amalek is not only the power that would destroy us from without, but is also the force threatening to destroy us from within. Amalek may also be seen as the winds of assimilation and self-destruction! When the Torah at the end of the portion of *Ki Tetzeh* (Deut. 25) records how Amalek attacked the tired and the weak straggling from Egypt, those who did not fear God, this does not refer only to those who were physically weak, but also to the spiritually weak, those whose link to the chain of Israel had become inadequate and indifferent. Amalek enters when Israel ceases to fear God! This Sabbath always precedes Purim because back in Shushan there were two threats, Haman/Amalek from without and a nation deep in the amnesia of assimilation from within, seduced by the (hardly kosher) invitations to the palace of Ahashverosh, with all the non-kosher wine and shrimp one could enjoy. Israel, betrothed by the shekel to God, had now succumbed to the temptation of Amalek, substituting the temptations of gold and licentiousness for their God-groom.

Israel having been defiled by the lure of assimilation, *Para,* the next special Sabbath portion, encapsulates the process of purification. We should know that even if our impurity stems from death, the highest degree of impurity, we have the red heifer to cleanse us.

Finally the Sabbath of *HaHodesh* brings us towards a new beginning. "*Hodesh,*" the Hebrew word for month, is also bound up with "*hadash,*" new, and "*hidush,*" renewal. In effect, the moon is the messenger of change and renewal, the ability to emerge from total darkness to a state of fullness, totality, and the perfection that awaits us on the fourteenth of Nisan when Passover begins.

Thus *Shekalim, Zakhor, Para* and *HaHodesh* parallel the portions of *Teruma, Tetzaveh, Ki Tissa* and *Vayak-hel-Pekudei*. The journey begins with commitment and love, stumbles through failure and sin, but finally ends with the possibility of purification and renewal, individual and national freedom as symbolized in the festival of freedom, Passover, which always falls two weeks after the Sabbath of *HaHodesh*.

The Courage to Walk into Uncertainty

> *And the cloud covered the Tent of Meeting, and the glory of the Lord filled the Sanctuary. And Moses was unable to enter the Tent of Meeting because the cloud rested upon it...*
>
> EXODUS 40:34, 35

What is the significance of the symbol of the cloud, and its twin symbol, fire? These are the two symbols of the Divine Presence expressed by the Torah: a cloud, described here at the end of the book of Exodus as resting on the Sanctuary as well as in the book of Numbers as directing the Israelites in the desert by day (Num. 9:15–23), and fire, which directed the Israelites in the desert by night, and also confirmed the divine acceptance of a ritual sacrifice (ibid., Ex. 24:17, I Kings 18:38). These symbols together comprise the heavens: the Hebrew word "*shamayim*" is comprised of two words, "*aish*" (fire) and "*mayim*" (water), water being the substance that clouds are made of and turn into. Fire and water are also the ultimate antinomies, the eternal opposites. Since the heavens are the abode of the divine, they also express the consummate paradox which miraculously brings together in peace even those elements which seem to be constantly at war with each other, fire and water!

Furthermore, clouds express protective cover and life-giving rain, security as well as growth and development. And fire expresses warmth, which likewise nurtures life, as well as creativity, as evidenced in the myth of Prometheus: The Greeks thought that fire must have been stolen from the gods themselves, since all inventiveness stems from the proper use of fire.

The Torah conveys yet another message through these two powerful symbols of the Divine Presence. The Torah insists that as long as the cloud rested on the Tent of Meeting, Moses was forbidden from entering it – unless he was expressly summoned by God. Hence the book of Exodus concludes with Moses' inability to enter the Sanctuary (Ex. 40:35), and the book of Leviticus opens, "And God called out unto Moses and the Lord spoke to him from the Tent of Meeting" (Lev. 1:1). The Midrash goes so far as to declare that "the Holy One Blessed be He took hold of Moses and physically brought him into the cloud." The Midrash goes on to explain that the letter *aleph* at the conclusion of the word *"vayikra"* (And He called) is small to stress that as long as the cloud was in evidence, Moses would require a separate and specific summons from God before he could stand in the presence of the divine and enter the cloud.

Similarly, while it is true that fire has the ability to bring warmth, it can also devour and destroy. One benefits greatly when coming in close proximity to fire, but one can get burnt by getting too close for comfort. The great R. Eliezer declared,

> Warm yourselves by the fire of the sages, but be careful of the coals lest you be burnt.
>
> *Mishna Avot* 2:15

If this is true of Torah sages, how much more so must this be true of the Almighty Himself!

From this perspective, the symbols of cloud and fire are warning us to temper our love and desire for closeness to the divine with reverence and awe, which engender distance. "Serve the Almighty with joyous love, but let there be a degree of trembling in your exaltation."* Too much familiarity can lead to a relaxation of discipline, and ecstatic devotion of the moment can sometimes overlook a religio-legal command. Passion is a critical component of religious piety, but it must by moderated by divine law or it can run wildly into the fanaticism of jihad and suicide killings. As the Psalmist declares,

> Cloud and haze are around Him, so righteousness and just law establish His throne.
>
> Psalms 97:2

The lack of clarity expressed by a cloud and the inability to gaze directly into a flame express one of the deepest truths of the Jewish message: Religion is not so much paradise as it is paradox. God demands fealty even in the face of agonizing questions and frightening uncertainty. Egypt, with its omnipresent waters of the Nile and its unchanging social order of masters and slaves, represents certainty. The desert, on the other hand, and especially the manna-less and Moses-less and rain-starved Land of Israel, represent the unknown. God demands that we have the courage to enter into the abstruse haze, to scale the heights of the unknown, and to take the risk of uncertainty as to immediate outcome, in order to act as His partners. We must attempt to make light from darkness, order from chaos, gardens from swampland, and justice from inequity. And just as the Almighty took a risk, as it were, by creating a human being with freedom of choice, so too must we take risks by venturing into the unknown.

> I remember the loving-kindness of your youth, the love of your engagement years, when you went after Me in the desert, in a land which was not planted.
>
> Jeremiah 2:2

Perhaps only a people who believe in a God who cannot be circumscribed

---

* See Psalms 2:11 and also Psalms 100:2.

by form or defined by sculpture can have the courage to attempt an adventure whose every step has not been charted in advance; perhaps only a nation which has fealty to a God who is profoundly unknowable can enter into a cloud of the unknown. But even if the precise details of the challenge are not specified, we do have a Torah that specifies right and wrong ways to pursue our goal. And, at the very least, the end goal is certainly guaranteed,* when

> Nation will not lift up sword against nation, and humanity will not learn war anymore.
>
> Isaiah 2:4

and

> ...when knowledge of the Lord [at last!] will fill the world as the water [from the clouds] will cover the seas.
>
> Isaiah 11:9

---

* See also essay on *Vaèra*, pp. 39-43.

Biblical Commentators Cited in this Volume

Mishnaic Era

Onkelos HaGer. Disciple of Rabbi Eliezer and Rabbi Yehoshua, two of
the great rabbis from the Tannaic period. His famous translation of
the Torah into Aramaic is known simply as "The Targum."

Yonatan ben Uziel. Disciple of the Famed Tanna "Hillel." Noted biblical translator, whose Western Aramaic translations include many
midrashic tales.

11ᵗʰ Century

Sa'adia Gaon (Egypt & Babylonia, c. 1000). Head of Babylonian Academy towards the end of the Geonic period. Translated the Torah
into Arabic.

Yitzhaki, Shlomo. RASHI (France, 1040–1105). Our foremost commentator on the Torah and the Talmud.

12th Century

HaLevi, Yehuda (Spain, 1075–1141). Noted Torah scholar and poet. Author of the *Kuzari*.

Ibn Ezra, Abraham (Spain, 1089–1164). Noted poet and grammarian. Author of commentary to the Bible.

Maimonides, Moshe ben Maimon. RAMBAM (Spain & Egypt, 1135–1204). Author of *Mishneh Torah*, a comprehensive halakhic code of Jewish law; and of the famous philosophical treatise *Guide for the Perplexed*.

Shmuel ben Meir. RASHBAM (France, 1080–1158) Grandson of Rashi, one of the Ba'alei Tosafot. Author of commentary to the Torah.

13th Century

Nahmanides, Moshe ben Nachman. RAMBAN (Spain, 1194–1270). Famous biblical commentator and talmudist. His biblical commentary will often quote the commentaries of Rashi and Ibn Ezra.

14th Century

Jacob ben Asher, Ba'al Haturim (Germany & Spain, 1275 – 1340). Son of the famous Talmud commentator known as the "Rosh," the Baal Haturim composed the four volume halakhic work known as the *Tur*. He also wrote a commentary to the Torah, making extensive use of *gematria*.

Ibn Kaspi, Joseph (Provence & Spain, 1279–1340). Biblical commentator, philosopher, and grammarian.

15th Century

Abarbanel, Don Isaac (Spain & Italy, 1437–1508). Noted statesman and

minister for kings of Spain, Portugal and Italy. Author of commentaries to the Bible, the Passover Haggada and *Pirkei Avot*.
Arama, Yitzhak. (Spain, 1420–1494) Author of *Akedat Yitzhak*.

16–17th Century

Horowitz, Isaiah. Shelah HaKadosh (Prague & Israel, 1565–1630). Noted kabbalist. Author of *Shnei Luhot Habrit*.
Seforno, Ovadiah (Italy, 1470–1550). Author of commentary to the Bible.

18th Century

Attar, Haim ibn (Morocco, 1696–1743). Author of *Ohr Hahayim* commentary on the Bible.
Berditchev, Levi Yitzhak ben Meir (Poland, 1740–1810). Founder of Hassidism in Central Poland. Author of *Kedushat Levi* commentary to the Bible.
Gaon, Eliyahu ben Shlomo Zalman. GRA (Eastern Europe, 1720–1797). Noted talmudist and biblical scholar. Fierce opponent of Hassidism.
Shneur Zalman of Liadi. Ba'al HaTanya (Russia, 1745–1812). Famed scholar in both Talmud and Kabbala. Founder of Habad Hassidim. Author of the halakhic work known as *Shulhan Arukh HaRav*, and of *Likutei Amarim*, referred to as the *Tanya*.

19th Century

Berlin, Naftali Tzvi Yehuda. NETZIV (Russia, 1817–1893). Head of the famous Yeshiva of Volozhin. Author of commentary to the Torah called *Ha'amek Davar*.
Blaser, Isaac (Russia, 1837–1907). Famous halakhic scholar who served as rabbi of St. Petersburg, and thus referred to affectionately as "Reb Itzele Peterburger." Author of *Pri Yitzhak*.
Kagan, Yisrael Meir. Hafetz Haim (Poland, 1839–1933). Famous rabbinical

scholar who lived in the town of Radin, and refused to accept any official positon in the rabbinate. His most famous works are the *Hafetz Haim*, which details all the laws against slandering one's fellow Jew; and his six volume halakhic treatise called *Mishna Berura.*

Hirsch, Samson Rafael (Germany, 1808–1888). Author of six-volume commentary to the Torah, originally written in German.

Hofman, David Tzvi (Germany, 1843–1921). Dean of the Hildes heimer Rabbinical Seminary. Author of commentary to the Torah, originally written in German.

Kotzk, Menahem Mendel (Poland, 1787–1859). Noted scholar and disciple of Rabbi Simha Bunim of Pesishkha.

HaKohen, Meir Simha (Russia, 1843–1926). Rabbi of Dvinsk. Outstanding author and talmudic scholar. Author of biblical commentary *Meshekh Hakhma,* and also of a commentary to the Rambam's *Mishneh Torah* called *Ohr Sameah.*

Salanter, Israel Lipkin (Eastern Europe, 1809–1883) Founder of the *Mussar* movement.

Schneerson, Menahem Mendel. (Russia, 1789–1866). One of the great Torah scholars of his generation. Grandson of the Ba'al HaTanya, and third leader of the Habad (Lubavitch) Hassidic movement. His series of halakhic responsa is called *Tzemah Tzedek.*

20th Century

Amiel, Moshe Avigdor (Gorodna, Antwerp & Tel Aviv, 1882–1945). Served as Chief Rabbi of Antwerp, Belgium, where he authored a commentary on the weekly Torah portion, called *Hegyonot el Ami."* He later emigrated to Israel and served as Chief Rabbi of Tel Aviv, establishing a famous Yeshiva high school there named "Yeshivat HaYishuv HaHadash."

Bernstein, Isaac (London, 1931–1994). Outstanding orator and Torah scholar. Famous for his weekly Torah lessons, which were later assembled and distributed as a series of tapes.

Besdin, Moshe (New York, 1913–1982). Director of James Striar School, Yeshiva University.

Eldad, Israel (Tel Aviv, 1910–1996). Active leader of underground activities leading up to the establishment of the State of Israel. Author of *Hegyonot BaMikra*, insights and commentary to the weekly Torah portion.

Epstein, Barukh HaLevy (Russia, 1860–1942). Noted author and biblical scholar. His commentary to the Torah, *Torah Temima*, expounds on each sentence from the Bible as quoted in the Talmud, thus emphasizing the connection between the Oral Law and the Written Law.

Feinstein, Moshe (New York, 1895–1986). Foremost halakhic authority in the United Staes during the twentieth century. His series of responsa were published in seven volumes as *Igrot Moshe*.

Goren, Shlomo (Tel-Aviv, 1917–1994). Served as Chief Chaplain to the Israel Defense Forces, and later as Chief Rabbi of the State of Israel. His scholarly discourses on the weekly Torah portions were compiled after his death and published in *Torat HaMikra*.

Kook, Abraham Isaac Hakohen (Jaffa & Jerusalem, 1865–1935). Founder of the Israel Chief Rabbinate. Author of many philosophical works and a commentary to the prayer book called *Olat Re'iya*.

Leibowitz, Nehama (Jerusalem 1905–1997). Noted biblical scholar and teacher. Author of thousands of "stenciled" sheets prepared as "guides" to assist in the study of the weekly portion.

Schneerson, Menahem Mendel (New York, 1902–1994). Seventh Rebbe of Habad Hassidim. Noted Torah scholar and author of *Likutei Sichos*, insights into the weekly portion with emphasis on Rashi's commentary.

Soloveitchik, Joseph B. (Boston, 1903–1993). Master Talmud teacher, Yeshiva University. Author of numerous philosophical and halakhic works including *Halakhic Man* and *The Lonely Man of Faith*. Famed worldwide for his lectures in Talmud and biblical exegesis, and credited with being a major interpreter of Modern Orthodoxy.

Index

Index

Jerusalem Talmud

Maimonides – Mishneh Torah

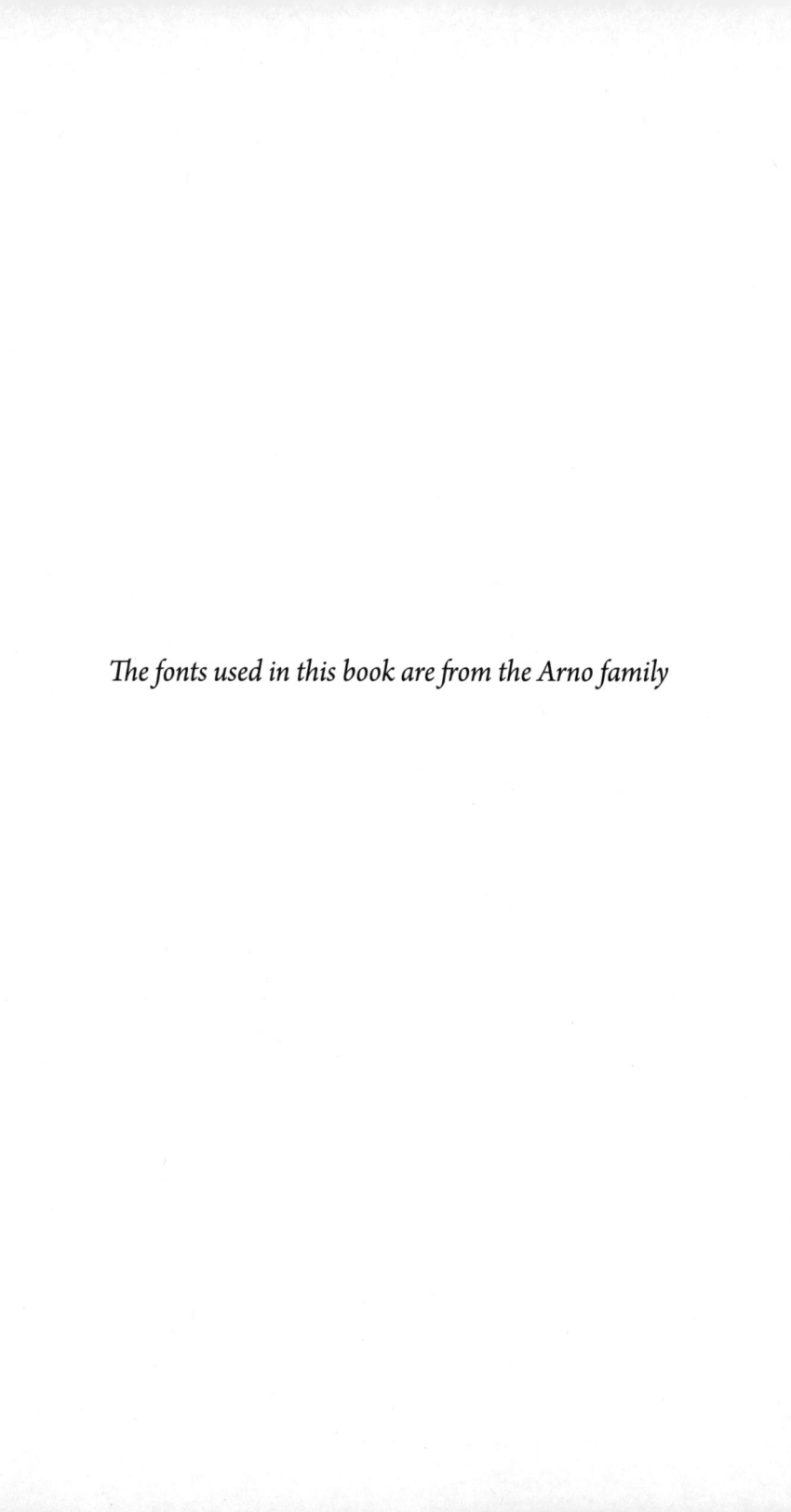

The fonts used in this book are from the Arno family

Other works by Shlomo Riskin
available from Maggid

Bereshit: Confronting Life, Love & Family

Vayikra: Sacrifice, Silence, Sanctity and Salvation

A Gift for My Grandchildren
God Messages: Just Listen

Yad L'Isha

Si'aḥ Shulḥan, a Hebrew halakhic encyclopedia

Maggid Books
Contemporary Jewish Thought
from
Koren Publishers Jerusalem